Survival Skills for the New Nurse

A DAVID T. MILLER BOOK

SURVIVAL SKILLS
FOR THE
NEW NURSE

Jane Meier Hamilton, R.N., M.S.N.

Hamilton Consulting
Blue Bell, Pennsylvania

Marcy E. Kiefer, R.N., M.S.

Lutheran General Health Care System
Park Ridge, Illinois

J. B. LIPPINCOTT COMPANY **Philadelphia**

London   Mexico City   New York
St. Louis   São Paulo   Sydney

Sponsoring Editor: Paul Hill
Manuscript Editor: Don Shenkle
Indexer: Carol Kosik
Art Director: Tracy Baldwin
Design Coordinator: Anne O'Donnell
Designer: Katharine Nichols
Production Supervisor: Kathleen P. Dunn
Production Assistant: Carol A. Florence
Compositor: Bi-Comp, Inc.
Printer/Binder: Malloy Lithographing, Inc.

6 5 4 3 2 1

Library of Congress Cataloging-in-Publication Data

Hamilton, Jane Meier.
  Survival skills for the new nurse.

  "A David T. Miller book."
  Includes bibliographies and index.
    1. Nursing—Social aspects. 2. Nurses—Psychology.
  3. Professional socialization. I. Kiefer, Marcy E.
  II. Title. [DNLM: 1. Nursing. 2. Professional
  Competence—nurses' instructions. WY 16 H218s]
  RT86.5.H35 1986   610.73   85-24052
  ISBN 0-397-54554-1

The authors and publisher have exerted every effort to ensure that drug selection and dosage set forth in this text are
in accord with current recommendations and practice at the
time of publication. However, in view of ongoing research,
changes in government regulations, and the constant flow of
information relating to drug therapy and drug reactions, the
reader is urged to check the package insert for each drug for
any change in indications and dosage and for added warnings
and precautions. This is particularly important when the
recommended agent is a new or infrequently employed drug.

To all new nurses,
who are the hope and future of our profession,
and
to all experienced nurses,
who support and encourage the development
of new nurses

Preface

As nursing students graduate and enter the profession of nursing, they face one of life's major role transitions. They leave behind the student role and assume that of practicing nurse. On the darker side of this challenging transition are many questions, insecurities, and doubts. On the brighter side, however, are the hopeful energy, idealism, and deep caring of the new nurse. Undoubtedly, each new nurse will, at some point, experience both the dark and the bright side of the transition into nursing. But which will predominate? What can be done to promote a positive transition?

Survival Skills for the New Nurse is designed to support senior nursing students and beginning nurses in making the transition into the work world. The book's chapters identify key dynamics involved in the transition from the student nurse to the practicing nurse role. Practical strategies and skills for constructively coping with the challenges and changes of this role transition are described.

Chapter 1 assesses the nature of the role transition faced by new nurses. It identifies the problems associated with this role transition and offers specific strategies for mastering them. Chapter 2 identifies the importance of recognizing one's values. It examines the benefits and liabilities of the values clarification process and suggests practical methods for clarifying values. Chapter 3 examines the concept of power and its importance for new nurses. It describes the sources of power, how to develop power, and how to exercise power as a new nurse. Chapter 4 analyzes the dynamics of work groups. It describes strategies for working more effectively with peers, with managers, and with staff members on other units. Chapter 5 explains the value of linking with a professional support system. It discusses ways to develop and use a network, a peer support group, preceptors, and mentors. Chapter 6 highlights important facts about stress. It outlines skills for managing stress in personal and professional situations. Chapter 7 differentiates assertive from nonassertive and aggressive behavior. It describes the preparatory, core, and accessory skills of acting assertively. Chapter 8 explores traditional views, which influence commitments. It examines the rewards and liabilities of being committed to a profession and to a family. It also identifies practical skills for successfully handling dual commitments.

Included at the end of each chapter are a series of exercises. The purpose of these exercises is to encourage readers to apply the content of each chapter to their own lives.

From our experiences in clinical practice, nursing education, consulting, and business, the ideas for this book were born. As we observed and talked with nursing students, clinicians, managers, and nonpracticing nurses, we grew acutely aware of the struggles new nurses experience. Being nurses ourselves, we wanted to help. Our own rewarding and painful experiences with the transition into nursing taught us skills that worked and lessons about those that didn't. We trust our ideas and experiences will be of help to new nurses.

Jane Meier Hamilton, R.N., M.S.N.

Marcy E. Kiefer, R.N., M.S.

Acknowledgments

From the start, we have been fortunate to receive tremendous support from many people. This support has helped us in countless ways and here we wish to express our thanks:

To Rob Hamilton and Karl Haviland, our husbands, for their encouragement, caring, and confidence in our abilities.

To Peggy Brookins and Joanna Werling, our typists, for their patience, tenacity, and professional skills.

To all of the nurses and other professionals who helped to shape our ideas and careers.

To Sherry Aleksich, Katharine Jeffers, Jan Summers, Pat Tydell, and Shauna Wapotish, our colleagues, who offered their insight and constructive criticism in editing this manuscript.

To David Miller, our editor at J. B. Lippincott Company, for his valuable suggestions, sensitive style, and guidance through the publishing process.

Contents

1 Roles in Transition: Making the Move from Student to Practicing Nurse

On a brisk, sunny, April morning, Donna Duncan looks out her window and sees some daffodils poking their heads up through the frozen ground. She feels energized and happy to know that at last the cold winter seems to be coming to an end. Donna herself feels like one of the daffodils. She has experienced a long cold winter in her nursing career. In spite of the fact that she has only been working for about 10 months, it has been a very difficult 10 months. Only within the past 2 weeks has she begun to sense that her own "spring thaw" is starting, that perhaps some of the conflict she felt this past year is beginning to be resolved.

In reflecting back over the past year, Donna starts at the beginning, her graduation in June. She was happy that the goal she had dreamt of and for which she had worked so hard was finally hers. Within 3 weeks of graduation, another long-sought goal was also achieved. She married Tom. Donna and Tom had been sweethearts during the 4 years of college and they were thrilled to call each other husband and wife.

They moved away from their college town to a smaller community about 60 miles away. Tom took a new job, as did Donna. In July, Tom and Donna began working at their new jobs. Both began work with great enthusiasm and energy, anticipating the challenges that lay ahead. Donna was particularly interested in testing and using all of the skills she had learned in school. Mixed with the excitement was some disappointment at not being on a pediatrics floor. However, Donna didn't let that bother her. She just looked forward to the day when she would be able to work in the specialty she loved most, pediatrics.

Donna remembers those first few weeks on the unit as a real whirlwind. There was so much to absorb. She had classes in the morning with the staff development instructor. Each afternoon she had unit orientation with her head nurse. Donna was sure she would learn a lot from the head nurse, who seemed very competent and understanding, someone Donna could look up to and respect. Donna found her new peers extremely interesting and admired their nursing expertise. She was awed at their self-assurance and skill. She hoped she could prove herself as effective as they were. During the initial weeks, every day was exciting. Donna came home at night and told Tom about fascinating patients to whom she was assigned, new staff members she met, the challenges of her professional position, and the pride she felt in earning an income. It all seemed so wonderful, better than Donna could have ever hoped for.

Just as summer turned to fall, Donna's first happy days soon faded to the chill and shock of recognizing her own, the hospital's, and her co-workers' flaws. She felt conflict rising within her when she began to realize that the way nursing was practiced on this medical-surgical floor was not what her instructors would have supported. She saw patient care given haphazardly. Nursing histories were done incompletely. Nursing care plans were done sketchily, or often left blank. And no one ever took the time to sit down and really talk with the patients.

These realizations upset her and threw her into a tremendous turmoil. Donna longed to be back in school with her friends and to have only a few patients assigned to her. She felt like a failure because the things she learned in school were being compromised by the quick pace and the continual pressure of heavy patient assignments. Donna was not able to give the kind of nursing care she knew she was capable of giving. She began to develop a sense of bitterness and betrayal. "Why didn't the instructors prepare me for this? Why didn't they put reality into the nursing curriculum? Why didn't they teach me what I needed to know to *really* be a nurse?" Donna began to feel badly about herself, her nursing care, and her professional preparation.

She also began to take work worries home with her. Nursing pressures began to interfere with her relationship with Tom. She was always tired when she went home. She developed many colds during the winter and didn't have the energy to go out partying as she had the year before. Tom began to ask her if she really belonged in nursing. He would ask her to look at herself and see what this was doing to her. Sometimes Donna would listen; at other times she would lash out angrily at him. At still other times, she would withdraw and remain quiet, worrying and wondering how she would ever resolve this conflict.

The nurses on her unit didn't seem to understand what Donna was going through. They would say, "Oh! you'll get used to it, give yourself time," or "That stuff from school is baloney. You're going to have to get with the program or else you're not going to make it, Donna." The only ones who seemed to understand any of what she was going through were two other nurses who graduated at the same time she had. Sometimes they would talk about it, commiserating about how awful nursing really is. Even the commiseration didn't seem to help for very long.

Yes, it was a difficult year, but just as the spring follows the winter, Donna realized 2 weeks ago that some of her tension was beginning to lessen. Tom noticed it also. Last week he told her that she was laughing for the first time in months. With that feedback, she has begun to look at herself and to realize that she is moving into a new phase. She is moving beyond her anger at the system—both the hospital and school. She is moving to a stage in which some solutions to the conflicts are emerging.

Over the past 10 months, Donna has learned many lessons. She has clarified her own values and priorities in nursing. The values she holds today are a combination of academic and real-world values. Neither the instructors from school nor the nurses in the hospital have all of the answers to all of the patient care problems. Donna realizes that both have something valuable to say about nursing care. Donna is beginning to feel comfortable enough to stand up for her school-bred values in some circumstances and adopt real, work-world values in other circumstances. As Donna sees the daffodils poking their heads up from the icy ground, she sees herself poking her own head out from withdrawal, anger, and isolation. She is beginning to feel more a part of the work group on her unit and is slowly starting to feel as though, if she keeps at it, she may finally feel the freshness of spring in her life.

What Is Involved in Assuming the Nursing Role?

Graduation from school and beginning work as a nurse is one of life's most challenging role transitions. You leave behind the comfortable, familiar role of the student and are called on to assume that of the practicing nurse. On the dark side of this major transition are many questions, insecurities, and frustrations. On the bright side are the hopeful energy, idealism, and deep caring that you bring to your nursing career. Undoubtedly you will, at some point, experience both the dark and bright side of the transition into nursing. But which will prevail? What can be done to encourage a positive and successful transition into professional nursing?

Perhaps the best way to start is by looking at the concept of roles and, more specifically, the role of the nurse. If you examine the expectations associated with your roles and how you feel about those expectations, you can begin to take charge of your life by beginning to control, rather than be controlled by, your roles. You have three choices in dealing with a given role. You can accept it as defined; you can choose to let go of it; or you can choose to accept some aspects of it and make changes in other aspects. In any case, a developed understanding of the roles you hold gives you greater control over yourself and offers you some guidance in assuming your nursing role.

What Is a Role?

A role is a set of expectations that are associated with a position you hold in society. You hold many different positions in society and therefore have many different roles. There are several types of roles that you hold or may hold.

The first category of roles is *acquired*. You choose or adopt these roles as you go through your life. Some examples of acquired roles are spouse, parent, nurse, and student. Another category of roles is *ascribed*. Ascribed roles are given to you without your choice. The primary ascribed role you have is your sex role. Other ascribed roles are your roles as sibling and child. In each of these ascribed roles you do not have a choice. You do not choose to be born, to be male or female or to have brothers or sisters. These contrast with acquired roles. You choose to marry or not to marry, to have a child or not to have a child. You choose a profession.

A very important fact to recognize about your roles is that they are distinct from your identity. Your identity, who you are as a unique individual person, is not shared by anyone else in the world. You carry your identity with you throughout your life in any situation you encounter. Your identity springs from within you.

In contrast to identity, roles are generalized, not unique. They are shared by many different people. There are many nurses, many wives or husbands, many first-born children, but there is only one you. Also, roles are assumed and retired at different times in your day-to-day life as well as throughout the larger span of your entire life cycle. At different points in your life, perhaps, you will be a spouse, a parent, or a nurse. But there will be other times in your life when you are not playing these roles. Finally, in contrast to your identity, which springs from within you, roles originate outside of you. They are constructs of society. Roles are designed and promulgated by society to fulfill the needs of society. Roles are composed of sets of expectations that act as guidelines for behavior. Roles describe for us what behavior is expected or desirable in relating to other people. Society has constructed roles and their sets of expectations to provide order, structure, and predictability within society. Without roles and their concomitant expectations or guidelines for behavior, coordinating so many people would be impossible.

The value of roles, then, is to structure society. The guidelines for roles that form a framework for society are very worthwhile on a *macro* level. However, on an individual or *micro* level, expectations occasionally clash with your identity. Sometimes what you value or who you are as a unique, individual person does not mesh harmoniously with what society prescribes as role-appropriate behavior. Sometimes your interests clash with the expectations of the roles you fulfill. Donna Duncan experienced this clash between her identity and her nursing role. Her personal commitment to meeting all the psychosocial and physical needs of patients clashed with the expectation that those who fulfill a nursing role must maintain a large patient assignment. As in Donna's case, when your identity clashes with any of the roles you fulfill, you experience a sense of dissonance or confusion, resulting in discomfort.

Why Do I Experience Conflict Within My Nursing Role?

As a new nurse, it is very important that you look at yourself and your identity vis-à-vis the nursing role. Your self-concept, or how you view yourself in the world, is a component of your identity. Your professional self-concept is the view you hold of yourself as a nurse. It is not uncommon for new nurses to experience a clash between their professional self-concepts and the nursing role as defined by the work setting. The roots of this all-too-familiar clash between identity and role emerge from three areas: the traditional roots of the nursing role, the divergence between school and work-world expectations, and the developmental nature of a career. These three factors contribute to the conflict you feel between yourself and your nursing role.

Table 1-1   **Sex-Role Stereotypes**

Masculine	Feminine
Aggressive	Bashful
Articulate	Caring
Assertive	Delicate
Autonomous	Devoted
Capable of leading	Does not use harsh language
Controlling	Easily deceived or cheated
Decisive	Enjoys children
Enterprising	Feeling
Individualistic	Feminine
Influential	Genial
Intense personality	Innocent
Logical thinker	Loving
Manly	Mild mannered
Physically active and strong	Peacemaker
	Sensitive to others' needs
Powerful	Soft-hearted
Risk-taker	Soft-spoken
Self-reliant	Submissive
Self-sufficient	Understanding
Stands up for beliefs	Vulnerable to flattery
Wants to win	

The traditional roots of the nursing role are analyzed and are clearly explained by Joann Ashley in her book *Hospitals, Paternalism, and the Role of the Nurse.* In her book Ms. Ashley documents the social, political, and economic factors that contributed to the development and evolution of the nursing role in the United States. By describing the development of American hospitals, nursing education, hospital administration and the medical profession, she identifies the origins of the nursing role. This complex set of factors, which developed in the late 19th and early 20th centuries set the stage for nurses to be viewed as angels of mercy, handmaidens of physicians, housekeepers for the sick—self-sacrificing, dependable, cooperative, nurturing, caring, efficient, dependent, and subservient.

Many of these nursing role expectations are intimately linked with the traditional role of women in American society. At its inception and still today, nursing is primarily a woman's profession. The early expectations of a good nurse were very closely linked to the societal expectations of a "good woman." The traditional guidelines for fulfilling the male and female roles, called *sex-role stereotypes,* are listed in Table 1-1. Although much has been done to alter the traditional female and nursing role, vestiges of the past still remain. Most nurses, men and women, find the traditional sex roles and nursing roles limiting. Many people and societal forces are actively promoting changes in traditional sexual and professional roles. But change is difficult and slow. One reason new nurses experience a clash between their identity and the nursing role comes from society's slowness in moving toward less traditional nursing and sex roles. Individual growth sometimes progresses more rapidly than societal, institutional, or professional growth. Times like this are uncomfortable for individuals.

A second reason new nurses experience a clash between their professional identity and their nursing role is that there is a divergence between the values promulgated in nursing schools and those experienced in the work world. The work of Marlene Kramer documents this clash. Her books *Reality Shock* and *Path to Biculturalism* document key factors that play a part in socialization to the nursing role. Kramer illustrates how both the process and the content of socialization in nursing education differ from the process and content of socialization in the working world. She defines schools and employers of new nurses as two different subcultures with disparate values, beliefs, and sets of expected behaviors. Kramer documents how role expectations shift after a student leaves school and assumes the role of practicing nurse. Faced with the clash between old student role expectations and new work-world expectations, Kramer states that the new nurse experiences reality shock.

According to Kramer, reality shock is the startling discovery, as well as the reaction to this discovery, that school-bred values conflict with work-world values. Reality shock, as Kramer describes it, is composed of several different phases: honeymoon, shock or rejection, recovery, and resolution. These phases are described in Table 1-2. In the case of Donna Duncan, described at the opening of this chapter, Donna clearly experienced the honeymoon phase early in her employment and moved into shock shortly thereafter. Her tendency to focus on the past; her feelings of withdrawal, anger, resentment, and confusion; and her outrage at the hospital system were clear signs of being in the shock phase. Toward the end of the case, when Donna began to feel the return of a sense of humor and a lessening of tension, she demonstrated behavior that is associated with entry into the recovery phase of reality shock.

How Donna or any other nurse, confronted with reality shock, ultimately resolves the situation has a great impact on the future of her or his nursing career. Kramer describes a variety of strategies for resolving reality shock. She identifies job hoppers, rutters, organization women, lateral arabesquers, burned-outs, quitters, and bicultural troublemakers. In her model, Kramer sees all of these strategies except bicultural troublemaking as maladaptive responses to reality shock. The bicultural troublemakers are those who maintain the school-bred values that are functional in the work setting and surrender those that are dysfunctional in the workworld. In resolving reality shock, work-world bicultural troublemakers assume the work-bred values that are functional for the system in which they work. Bicultural troublemakers are capable and comfortable enough to challenge those work-bred values which are in conflict with their own professional values. It takes time to progress through the phases of reality shock and reach the point of resolution. When encountering reality shock, many new nurses experience painful clashes between their professional self-concept and the role expectations of nursing.

The third major reason that your identity and nursing role clash relates to the developmental nature of your career. As defined by Healey, a career is a sequence of positions that you occupy as you proceed through your work life. These major positions include work-related roles such as those of student, employee, and pensioner, together with complementary civic and familial

Table 1-2   **Kramer's Phases of Reality Shock**

1. Honeymoon
   Exhilarated and challenged by nursing
   Happy and excited about work
   Idealistic, seeing nursing through rose-colored glasses
   Receiving support and positive feedback
2. Shock or rejection
   Disillusioned with nursing
   Preoccupied with or longing for the past; rejecting the
       idealism of school
   Bitter or feeling betrayed
   Rejecting standards of co-workers
   Morally outraged, angry, depressed, or withdrawn
   Excessively fatigued or ill
3. Recovery
   Regaining a sense of humor
   Less tense and more relaxed
   Regaining perspective and objectivity
   Better able to understand actions and reactions of others
   Better able to meet work demands
4. Resolution
   Job hoppers—resolve conflict by frequently changing
       jobs in search of the ideal job
   Rutters—resolve conflict by limiting job involvement
       and professional commitment
   Organization women—resolve conflict by surrendering
       school-bred values and by adopting dominant work-
       world values
   Lateral arabesquers—resolve conflict by moving into a
       safe, more idealistically structured environment in
       which school-bred values prevail
   Burned-outs—resolve conflict by chronic complaining
       and by turning the conflict inward
   Quitters—resolve the conflict by leaving nursing
   Bicultural troublemakers—resolve conflict by realisti-
       cally assessing work-world demands and by respond-
       ing to those demands with behaviors based on func-
       tional school-bred and work-world values they have
       chosen themselves

roles. How your career develops depends on what you choose to pursue in your work life. This development is an expression, as well as a shaper, of your identity.

Your career is developing on the basis of what you have done in the past, what you are doing now, and what you want to do in the future. Your nursing career has been developing for a long time. In the "preoccupational phase," that is, during your childhood and adolescence, you worked to develop habits, attitudes, behavior, skills, and a self-image that characterized you as a unique person. Through your experiences you learned of the meaning and value of work. You recognized the need to choose a career and you began to explore possible types of life work that are consistent with your personal characteristics, abilities, and interests. During the preoccupational phase of your career, you explored various nursing programs and chose one. You pursued a program of study, developing the necessary knowledge base, sets of skills, attitudes, and thought processes required for the practice of nursing.

Upon graduation, you completed that "student phase" and entered a new "occupational phase" of your career. During the occupational phase, it is important for you to develop full competence in practicing nursing. In addition, it is important for you to consolidate and improve your professional self-concept as well as your status within the profession of nursing.

As your nursing career has evolved and changed in the past, it will continue to grow and develop in the years ahead. You will certainly experience changes in your capabilities, interests, priorities, awareness, and professional values. These shifts are normal in the life cycle of any career, just as developmental changes are a normal part of the life cycle of every human being. At various points in your career you will most probably experience shifts in the amount of personal energy and time you commit to your career. No one can guarantee what your career path will be or what turns it will take in the future. What you can certainly expect is that your involvement with nursing and health care will be a lifelong process and that you will experience changes throughout that time. Do not expect constant comfort, self-confidence or clarity as your nursing career takes shape. Rather, expect that you will have periods of great professional satisfaction and challenge, alternating with periods of dissatisfaction, confusion, and distress. The fluctuation between professional satisfaction and discontent is a sign of a dynamic involvement with your nursing career and reflects professional growth. As in any developmental process, transition and change from one level or phase of development to another are always accompanied by discomfort, crisis, and questions. As a new nurse, you are experiencing one of the major transitions in your nursing career. The questions, fears, discomfort, and distress are all signs that you are engaged in a growth process.

Growth is occurring internally, in terms of what you expect of yourself as a nurse. Growth is also occurring externally within the profession of nursing and within the health care environment at large. Economic, educational, legal, regulatory, technical, and competitive forces are revolutionizing the health care system and the expectations of nurses within the system. As these internal and external forces create powerful changes, it is imperative that you take charge of your nursing career, acting assertively rather than reacting passively to the demands for change.

How Can I Assertively Manage the Problems Associated with Role Changes?

The process of assertively managing the role changes that you as a new nurse experience involves a two-step process. The first step is *assessment;* the second is *action.* Both steps complement each other and the action flows directly from your assessment, much as the intervention phase of the nursing process flows from your assessment of patients.

In assessing the role changes that you experience as a new nurse, look at the specific situations you find uncomfortable, challenging, or new. List these problems on a piece of paper. Role problems fall into any of three categories: role conflict, role overload, or role discontinuity. Use the following information to assess the nature of the role problems you are facing.

Role Conflict Assessment

The first type of role problem you can encounter is called *role conflict*. Role conflict occurs when you feel you are being pulled in two different directions by the roles in your life. Role conflict exists when you are (1) fulfilling two or more roles with incompatible expectations or (2) trying to fulfill incompatible expectations within one role. The essential problem that you or any other new nurse faces in role conflict is knowing the role expectations but being unable to fulfill them all.

The first type of role conflict, as experienced when two roles clash, is illustrated when a staff nurse wakes up to find that her or his child has a temperature of 102°F and that the child cannot go to the day-care center with a fever. The expectations associated with the role of staff nurse demand that the nurse arrive for work on time and work the assigned shift. The role of parent demands that you care for your sick child. The staff nurse cannot both arrive for work on time and work the scheduled eight hours, as well as stay home and take care of the sick child. The two roles, parent and nurse, are in conflict.

The second kind of role conflict, as experienced when expectations clash within one role, can be understood by examining how expectations within the single role of nurse are often incompatible. Recall Donna Duncan's situation in which she was expected to care for a large number of patients efficiently. This expectation clashed with Donna's expectation that she be an empathetic good listener and focus on the psychosocial as well as physical needs of her patients. Both efficiency and empathy are role expectations of nurses. At times, however, it was not possible for Donna to meet both of those expectations. If you put yourself into this situation and imagine you are Donna, you can feel the frustration that is characteristic of role conflict.

Role Overload Assessment

The second role problem frequently encountered by new nurses is called *role overload*. When experiencing role overload, you feel overwhelmed because you have too many role expectations to fulfill in a limited amount of time. Characteristically, role overload finds you feeling pressured by external time demands. These pressures can arise from either (1) holding too many roles simultaneously or (2) having inadequate time to fulfill the expectations associated with your role.

Some familiar illustrations of role overload are working on a unit that is understaffed. In addition, you might experience role overload by simply being involved in many different relationships and activities. For example, if you hold a full-time job and are responsible for maintaining a home and relationships with your children, parents, church or community, you might be familiar with the fatigue and frustration associated with role overload.

Role Discontinuity Assessment

The third role problem you will certainly encounter as a new nurse is called *role discontinuity*. The essential problems of role discontinuity are ambivalence about surrendering the safety of a familiar role, confusion regarding how to fulfill the new role expectations, and doubts about how satisfying the new role will be. As the name implies, role discontinuity arises when (1) a new role replaces an old role or (2) new expectations replace old expectations within one role. Essentially, role discontinuity occurs when you are faced with role change, and usually this is an uncomfortable experience.

Your life as a new nurse is replete with illustrations of role discontinuity. The practicing nurse role has replaced that of student. The expectations of a staff nurse are different from those of a student nurse. Do you remember the days when you had only two patients? Within the profession of nursing, the traditional nurse role is continually being revised and updated. In addition, traditional male/female roles within our society are undergoing change. You may also be experiencing role discontinuity in other roles in your life. Perhaps you are moving from being single to married or from married to divorced. Perhaps you are moving from being childless to a parent or from being a son or daughter to one who has lost a parent. You may also be moving from being a citizen of one town or community to membership in another. If any of these situations are present in your life, you will probably recognize the doubts, confusion, and ambivalence that are characteristic of role discontinuity.

As you encounter role conflict, role overload, or role discontinuity, expect these problems to have an impact on your life. Whether these role changes are perceived positively or negatively, as a challenge or a crisis, depends on how you view them and on how you choose to respond to them. They affect all aspects of your personal life—your self-concept, emotions, physical well-being, mental outlook, and the sense of meaning in your life. These role changes also affect your professional life—your performance, self-confidence, commitment, energy level, and creativity.

Finally, these role changes influence your interpersonal relationships, both in your private life and in the work setting. There is an interaction between your personal and professional life; one cannot be strictly separated from the other. Role problems in one area of your life have an impact on your performance and feelings in all the other areas.

Beware of the potentiating effects of role problems. Just as certain medications intensify the effects of some drugs, simultaneous role problems intensify your experience of these challenges and changes. Experienced together, otherwise simple role problems become difficult, or unpleasant to handle. In addition, role changes that might otherwise be perceived as challenging are seen as crises when one is dealing with many role problems concurrently. After assessing the nature, impact, and number of role changes you are facing, move on to action.

Action Plan Guidelines

In assertively managing role changes, follow these general guidelines and implement the specific suggestions presented in the following section of this chapter. Be sure to correlate specific actions with specific types of role problems. Role conflict, role overload, and role discontinuity each demand different types of corrective actions. Also, choose actions that are compatible with your values. Every problem or challenge can be resolved in a variety of ways. The most successful solutions and actions are those that not only yield results but also achieve them in a way that harmonizes with your values, personality, and problem-solving style.

It is extremely important that you follow through and carry out the actions that will resolve your role conflict, overload, or discontinuity. Failure to act or acting according to the values of others has negative consequences. These consequences are felt in the here and now, as well as in future phases of your career. Avoiding action prolongs and intensifies the discomfort that you experience in a nursing role transition. Poor mastery of the career challenge that lies before you undermines your developing professional self-concept. Rather than a developmental gain, this situation is perceived as a loss, a loss of the opportunity to develop professional competence and confidence.

Because your future nursing career is built on the mastery of what you have done and what you are now doing, success or failure in meeting this career challenge has an impact on how your career develops in the future. Failure to act constructively to meet this challenge leaves you weakened in meeting future challenges; you are likely to approach those situations with less insight, capability, and self-confidence. Successful completion of this role transition bolsters you and encourages you to face future career challenges with greater knowledge, professional competence, self-awareness, and assurance.

What Are Specific Strategies I Can Use to Master the Challenges of This Role Transition?

As you face the challenges of the role transition from student to practicing nurse, here are several things to keep in mind. These approaches are useful in handling any of the role problems associated with being a new nurse. First, be prepared for periods of discomfort. As in any growth process, the axiom "no pain, no gain" holds true. Remember, the painful periods don't mean that there is something wrong with you; they show that you are engaged in growth.

Second, take control of your career. It is yours to shape and develop as you see fit. The choice of values that guide your professional practice is up to you. The task before you as a new nurse is to begin to discover your own guiding principles. Some principles you learned in school will no doubt remain very important to you. Others will not fit the environment in which you work, or will not mesh with your sense of self. In that case, look around for other values that do facilitate your professional practice. Observe what other nurses do. Listen to what they say, and be sensitive to how you react to your observations.

As you assume control and ownership of your career, work hard, do your best, but don't try to be perfect. Expecting perfection of yourself leads only to frustration and disillusionment. Allow yourself to be human, to be imperfect, and to learn from your mistakes. Learn to let go, loosen up, relax, and flow with the events in your life. It is impossible for you to be in control of every situation or to be in control of yourself every minute of your life. In addition, you cannot control other people, the way they feel, what they believe, their values, attitudes, or life priorities. Attempting to recognize and live within the limits of your control helps you to deal with the difficult situations you encounter as a new nurse.

Finally, don't try to deal with the transition into nursing on your own. Develop and use support systems in both your personal life and your professional life. Going it alone increases the pain of this life transition and hinders your progress through it. Use the people in your support systems for a variety of different kinds of help. Go to them when you need encouragement, information, insight, feedback, alternatives, or just a little human closeness. If you are embarrassed to ask for help, remember how gratifying it is as a nurse, a helping professional, to know that you have been able to care for another human being. Other people feel that way too.

Role Conflict: Choose Among Alternatives

After 6 straight days of working on this 36-bed stepdown unit, you finally have a long weekend, starting this afternoon. You are anxiously anticipating your old roommate's wedding. You are all packed and ready to go to the airport as soon as your shift is over. However, all of the excitement must be put on hold because you have two patients who need to be admitted before you will be able to leave the hospital. You were halfway through the nursing assessment and admission note on your first patient when someone in the emergency department telephones to say that an unexpected admission, the second one this afternoon, will arrive in the unit in 10 minutes. Wouldn't you know! Both patients admitted to the unit are on your team, and consequently it is your responsibility to admit them.

You are beginning to get annoyed and agitated. You paced yourself through the first admission expecting that it was the only one you would have to do before the end of the shift. You were doing a thorough job, as you were taught in school. Now, however, it looks as if it will be impossible to complete this assessment as you know you should. If you try to do both admissions thoroughly, you will have to stay even later and probably miss the only plane that could get you to the wedding on time. If you do them quickly and leave on time, it will be a job below your standards, one that you will not feel proud of. Since you will be away for 3 days it is not possible to leave the nursing assessments incomplete. So, what are you going to do?

Facing this situation, you feel pulled in two different directions. You are experiencing role conflict, a clash between your role as nurse and your role as friend. As a nurse, you expect yourself to perform high-quality work according to your professional standards; as a friend you expect to join in the wedding celebration. In this situation you cannot do both. You must find a way to reconcile this conflict.

In this or or any role conflict, begin by clarifying your priorities. Identify your values in the situation, as well as your values in the larger scope of life. These have an impact on the choices you must make. Consider your values as the context in which you will analyze and weigh your options. For each of your options, identify the cost and benefits associated with each choice. In dealing with role conflict, choosing to fulfill one role expectation entails letting go of another. You must decide what to do with the role expectations—which you will fulfill and which you will not.

In some cases, you can simply not do what is expected of you and the consequences will be acceptable. In others, failure to do what is expected of you has dire consequences, and you then need to use time or enlist other people to help you with the dilemma. Postponing action on one role expectation until another is completed is a very effective way to resolve role conflict. Sometimes postponing action, however, is not a viable option. If this is the case, turn to your support systems, people in your environment who are able to help you. Use *negotiation* and *delegation* to assist you. When engaging in negotiation, define the situation as a cooperative process, one in which you seek a win-win solution to your problem. Determine the outcome that you seek. Be flexible and creative; list as many options as possible that will help you to achieve the outcome you seek. Explore interests with your negotiating partner. Offer solutions that meet their needs as well as yours. Avoid threats, pressure, and defensiveness. Be willing to compromise and to make trades.

In addition to negotiation, delegation is another key skill in resolving role conflict. Whereas negotiation is a useful tool in dealing with peers or superiors, delegation is useful in dealing with subordinates. Delegation is vesting organizational power in a subordinate by a superior. That is, when you delegate you turn over a task to a subordinate. You give your subordinate the authority or power to complete the task and you assume the responsibility for seeing that the task is accomplished appropriately. Delegation is useful in role conflict situations when the task or role expectation that you have decided not to fulfill is within the capabilities of a subordinate. Be sure to select the person carefully. Define the assignment and delegate authority in light of results you expect; state behavioral outcomes when delegating. Be receptive to different approaches. Be willing to let the other person do the job in his or her own way, as long as the outcome is according to standards. Recognize and reward successful completion of the delegated task. Praise and recognition reward the person for a job well done and increase the likelihood that, in another role conflict situation, this person will help you out again.

If you place yourself in the role conflict situation just described, you need to identify your most important values as a nurse and as a friend. You need to consider whether it is more important to complete the nursing assessment thoroughly or to catch the airplane and be on time for your friend's wedding. In weighing your alternatives, you need to consider the worst and the best consequences that could be associated with both of those choices. You also need to consider which outcome is most likely to happen and which consequence you can best live with.

After considering the pros and cons of your options, you need to choose a course of action. Since leaving the nursing assessments incomplete is not an option in this case, you should consider negotiating with other nurses on the unit to assist you in completing your task. You could delegate some tasks to an LPN or aide working with you, or you could use both strategies. Alternatively, you could consider taking a later plane or you could find another method of transportation. There are many options, many ways to resolve this role conflict. The way you choose to solve this or any role conflict is a matter of personal preference. Use the preceeding guidelines to help you deal with difficult decisions such as this.

Role Overload: Manage Your Responsibilities and Time

Boy, has it been a busy day! Of course, it's hard to remember one that hasn't been busy. Life is full of opportunities and interesting situations, but sometimes, just once in a while, it would be nice to live at a slower pace. Take today, for example. As a primary nurse on postpartum, you had five mothers and babies in your care. It seemed as if everybody needed some special attention.

Mrs. Johnson had some soreness in her stitches and every time you went to get the sitz bath set up it was occupied. How frustrating! Mrs. Turner, worried about breast-feeding, was having a hard time with the baby and needed some special coaching. Young Susan Edwards was very ambivalent about her decision to give her baby up for adoption and needed a lot of support. Mrs. Myer and Mrs. Adams, who were feeling "blue," also needed some reassurance and guidance. Along with your patient care responsibilities, you faced some additional pressures. You presented your first patient education class, a 30-minute session on bathing a baby. It only added to your "new-teacher jitters" knowing that your head nurse was observing you. At the end of the shift, a desperate peer asked you for a ride home. How could you say no? As you expected, the detour caused you to miss half of your much needed exercise class. You left sweaty but not relaxed and rushed home to shower, change, and grab a quick supper before running out to an evening continuing-education program.

If your life ever seems like this, you know the overwhelmed and overextended feeling of experiencing role overload. In this situation, as in role conflict, it is imperative that you clarify your priorities. You must identify what is most important to you, what must be done, and what the situation demands of you, because in role overload you cannot do everything. It is essential that you recognize and accept your limitations. If possible, use negotiation or delegation skills to let go of some role expectations that you cannot or do not want to fulfill.

Consider totally withdrawing from some role, on either a temporary or a permanent basis. Remember that certain of your roles are acquired, that is, you choose them. You can choose to let go of roles that you are unable to fulfill at a given time or that no longer fit appropriately into your life. Remember that *you* obligated yourself in the first place, so give yourself permission to let go of dysfunctional roles. In the same vein, think before you say yes and obligate yourself. Being too willing to volunteer your time is a sure way to create role overload.

Identify, respect, and live within the limits of your energy, resources, and time. When you live beyond your limits, you experience the pressure associated with role overload and experience less satisfaction in your daily life. Only you can know where your limits are; no one else can set them for you. As a result, it is also up to you to defend those limits. You must assume responsibility for identifying situations in which you are asked to go beyond your limits. In these situations, you must define for yourself and for others what is reasonable to expect of yourself. At times, this means saying no to requests and at other times it involves negotiating a compromise with other people. It is very important to give yourself permission to set your limits and to live within them. If you feel guilty about this process, remember that living within your limits is self-protection. It allows you to maintain your energy and the quality of your performance, whether in your personal or professional life.

When dealing with role overload, the stresses of work can frequently contaminate your home life and vice versa. A technique that will help to protect you against the wearing effects of role overload is called a *decompression routine.* This is a 15-, 20-, or 30-minute period of demand-free relaxation time. Insert this decompression time between work and home (if you're working during the day shift) or between home and work (if you're working a 3–11 or 11–7 shift). The value of the decompression routine is that it helps you to relax and unwind after meeting the demands of one aspect of your life. This allows you to approach the other aspect of your life refreshed and capable of responding effectively.

Think of your need for a decompression routine like that of a deep-sea diver who is surfacing from the depths. The diver must stop midway in the ascent to balance the nitrogen in the bloodstream and to avoid getting the bends. Like a deep-sea diver, you need a decompression break, a pause between work and home, to adjust to changing pressures in your life.

How you go about doing this is up to you. Each person has restful and relaxing ways to decompress and no one way is the right way. Also, be flexible. On some days you have more time for a decompression break than on other days. Take the time you have and use it in a way that is relaxing and nurturing to yourself. You might want to lie down, jog, attend an exercise class, take a luxurious bath, put your feet up and read the newspaper, or go window shopping. Do whatever works best for you. If you have children who need you when you come home, teach them that you need 10 or 20 minutes to yourself after a long day. If you have a babysitter, ask her or him to stay an extra 15 or 20 minutes with the children. If you can't get quiet time at home, take it before you go home—stop in the chapel, library, snack shop, or park. It's up to you to make sure that you get this time for yourself. No one is going to do that for you.

Don't wait until your shift is completed to give yourself a break. Be sure to take time out at work, especially on busy days. Making time for a short break and for eating lunch allows you to relax and helps minimize the pressure associated with role overload. When you do take time out at work, avoid spending the time in conversation about patients and work problems. Focus your thoughts on discussing current events, a movie, or other pleasant realities. This helps you to feel as though you really have gotten away from the pressures of work.

Role Discontinuity: Master the Challenges of Role Transition

Think back to the story of Donna Duncan at the beginning of this chapter. If you are a student nurse, can you imagine being in her position and feeling as she did? If you are a new nurse, can you recall experiencing situations or feeling as she did? At these times when you feel bothered by change, as Donna did, you experience role discontinuity. Whenever you change roles, expect to experience periods of discomfort. A natural, uncomfortable transition phase is a part of every role change. This is the essence of role discontinuity, and there are some very practical things you can do to help yourself master the challenges of role change from student to practicing nurse.

First, begin with yourself. Look inside yourself and evaluate how your feelings, attitudes, and expectations are helping or hindering your progress through this transitional phase. It is common to have feelings of anger, sadness, depression, and ambivalence when dealing with role discontinuity. What Donna Duncan, you, and every other new nurse experiences is a loss, the loss of all that characterized your student days. As in any loss, you must mourn and grieve the loss of your old student life before you are personally, emotionally, and professionally able to embrace the new aspects of life as a practicing nurse. Therefore, it is very important that you allow yourself to experience the feelings associated with the loss you have incurred. It is also important to express those feelings. You must allow yourself time to adjust to the loss you have experienced to reopen yourself to the new reality of being a nurse in the work world.

As part of the grief process that you studied in school, expect that anger and resistance to change will emerge in your transition from school to the work world. Some attitudes that you have reflect your interest in bargaining with the "system" to avoid facing the reality of your change. Some attitudes reflect your anger at being "forced" to change. To become clear about your resistance to change, ask yourself the following questions: "What don't I want to let go of?" "What are the consequences of not letting go of my old student life?" Don't make the mistake of believing that your discomfort in making the transition from school to the work world is solely the fault or responsibility of the system. Although there are some system factors, it is primarily the divergence between school-bred and work-world values that causes your discomfort and resistance to change. The conflicts in your attitudes, feelings, and expectations lie at the heart of role discontinuity. Identify what aspects of the student role you like and enjoy. Reminisce about the good times and good relationships you had while in school, to help you get in touch with aspects of the student role you are trying to retain. Then consider the rewards and consequences of hanging on to these old relationships and values. Undoubtedly, you will find some for which there are positive consequences.

However, maintaining certain attitudes, standards, or expectations has some very negative consequences associated with them. Holding onto the past can hinder your growth, diminish your enjoyment of present experiences, and block the development of supportive new relationships. Retain aspects of your old role that work for you, but take action to surrender those that work against you.

To help you in this process of surrendering the old and adapting to the new, identify and use your support systems. Work at developing functional relationships with people in the work setting. These people should include nurses on your unit, your nurse manager, staff development instructors, and other new nurses as well as people in different departments of the organization. Those in your support system offer you many types of help—moral support, insight, problem-solving ideas, an ear to bend, a shoulder to cry on, someone to laugh with. The list is endless. Before approaching your helpers, identify what you need. It is your responsibility as an adult to clarify your needs before approaching your supporters. It is not their responsibility to anticipate your needs or to interpret your vague hints. Be clear about what you need from your support system and ask them directly and clearly. Also, ask others for what they have to give. Some resource people are good problem solvers in clinical situations; others are effective in interpersonal problem solving. If you need someone to listen to while you blow off steam, be sure to go to someone who is comfortable with anger. If you need someone to let you cry and weep away your frustrations, be sure to seek a supporter who is comfortable with tears.

Don't expect a few supporters to be all things to you. Diversify. Develop a wide support system, and don't use the same few people to help you out in every situation. Expanding your support system is a form of self-protection. By diversifying, you avoid overworking those closest to you, ensuring their continued support. You also gain different perspectives on situations, which ultimately enhances the quality of your problem solving. Finally, diversifying is self-protective because it keeps you from being overly dependent on a few people. Because you receive support from a variety of sources, when you lose a key supporter you are not isolated and alone. You have others to whom you can turn if you lose someone by death, divorce, relocation, or a job change.

Use your support system as you adjust to your new nursing role, to help you clarify the expectations of this new role. You can begin to clarify new role expectations by looking at your job description. Use these categories to focus your inquiry. Talk with your nurse manager to identify what she or he expects you to do in order to fulfill the objectives listed on your job description. Be specific. Go to that meeting with questions to help you clarify any aspects of the job that are confusing to you. If there are aspects of your new role with which you feel uncomfortable or that you think you are incapable of fulfilling, devise a program with your nurse manager to help you begin to acquire the necessary skills. It takes time to develop competence and comfort in fulfilling new skills. Set time deadlines, dates when you plan to be able to perform a particular skill.

The new skills required of you are not only professional. In order to fulfill a nurse role successfully, you need to have interpersonal, organizational, and political skills as well. Unfortunately, there is no job description to examine to guide you in the development of these skills. Although they are acquired informally, they are no less important to your success than are your developing professional skills. Experienced nurses who have been in the system for a number of years have observed organizational and political processes and have gained insight into the issues that underlie them. Seek out a few trusted, experienced nurses. Ask them to share their experience and insight with you. Go to them for feedback and validation of your own behavior in the system and your observations of the system. Never automatically discount or blindly believe another person's interpretation of political reality. Rather, consider what others have to say and form your own judgments. If you work at it, in time you will develop an awareness of organizational and political issues. This understanding is an important aspect of becoming acclimated to your new role.

In addition to developing professional, organizational, and political skills, it is important that you work to develop your interpersonal skills. Working with colleagues in nursing and other professional groups and with patients and their families requires strong interpersonal skills. You must be able to *empathize* with the feelings of those around you, patients, co-workers, and other professionals. It is important that you learn to communicate effectively, *sending messages clearly* and in a timely fashion. *Conflict resolution* skills are invaluable. Also, learning to *speak assertively* helps you resolve, as well as avoid, interpersonal problems. The *active listening skills* you learned in nursing school should be used not only with patients, but with everyone in the working environment. *Respect* is the thread that links all of these skills and should be an underlying theme in every interpersonal exchange. Chapter 7, Acting Assertively: Practical Solutions to Problem Situations, examines all of these interpersonal skills in depth.

Adjusting to role discontinuity is a challenge for you as a new nurse. When attempting to deal with it, be sensitive to yourself and to other people. Be open to what others can teach you. Work to develop the skills required in your new role. Take care of yourself both physically and emotionally so that you have the stamina and insight to endure during this process. Finally, don't take yourself too seriously. You are not the only nurse who has had to face this role change. Some situations which seem devastating today will be laughable or at least understandable 2 years from now. Look for the laugh and open yourself up to the understanding. Use the strategies outlined in subsequent chapters to help you make it through.

Bibliography

Ashley J: Hospitals, Paternalism, and the Role of the Nurse. New York, Teachers Press, 1976

Benner P, Benner R: The New Nurse's Work Entry: A Troubled Sponsorship. New York, The Tiresias Press, 1979

Grissum M, Spengler C: Woman Power and Health Care. Boston, Little, Brown & Company, 1976

Healey C: Career Development: Counseling through the Life Stages. Boston, Allyn & Bacon, 1982

Kramer M: Reality Shock: Why Nurses Leave Nursing. St Louis, CV Mosby, 1974

Kramer M, Schmalenberg C: Path to Biculturalism. Wakefield, MA, Contemporary Publishing, 1977

Masson V: Nurses and doctors as healers. Nursing Outlook, pp 70–73. March–April 1982

Schmalenberg C, Kramer M: Coping With Reality Shock: The Voices of Experience. Wakefield, MA, Nursing Resources, 1979

Exercises

EXERCISE 1-1   NURSING SKILL DEVELOPMENT

Part 1: Job Assessment

Directions.   As a new nurse the expectations of your nursing role are outlined in your job description. This contains a listing of the major areas of responsibility included in your nursing position. Your nurse manager uses this when evaluating your performance. You should use the job description to help you clarify what is expected of you in your new nursing role. Also, use your job description to help you identify job skills that you have difficulty fulfilling. Devise a plan to remedy these difficulties and develop your skills.

Using the following job assessment, write the major responsibilities of your job (as listed in your job description) in the left column. In the right column, identify specific skills or duties you should perform to carry out each major job responsibility. Expect to write several performance criteria for most major responsibilities. Check this with your nurse manager to ensure an accurate and complete list. Check the circle next to each performance criterion that you do not, as yet, fulfill satisfactorily.

Major Job Responsibilities
(Broad Categories or Job Functions)

Performance Criteria
(Nursing Skills: Specific, Observable Behavioral Examples of How to Fulfill Major Job Responsibilities)

E X A M P L E	*Carries out an initial and an ongoing assessment of the nursing needs of assigned patients*	○	*Completes nursing history within 24 hours of admission*
		○	*Develops initial care plan based on assessment, within 24 hours of admission*
	_____	○	*Revises care plan as patient's condition changes*
	_____	⊘	*Includes assessment data when documenting nursing care*

Major Job Responsibilities

Performance Criteria

_____   ○   _____

_____   ○   _____

_____   ○   _____

_____   ○   _____

_____   ○   _____

_____   ○   _____

_____   ○   _____

_____   ○   _____

_____   ○   _____

_____   ○   _____

_____   ○   _____

_____   ○   _____

_____   ○   _____

_____   ○   _____

_____   ○   _____

_____   ○   _____

_____   ○   _____

_____   ○   _____

_____   ○   _____

_____   ○   _____

_____   ○   _____

_____   ○   _____

_____   ○   _____

_____   ○   _____

Part 2: Skill Development

Transfer the performance criteria you checked in Part 1 of this exercise to the column below marked "Skills I Must Develop." With your nurse manager, discuss specific ways to learn or improve your performance of these skills and list these specific approaches in the column labeled "How I Will Develop My Skills." Finally, set a realistic time deadline for accomplishing each learning objective and write it in the last column. It takes time to learn and develop, so pace yourself. Spread your completion dates out over several weeks or months depending on the number of skills you have to develop.

Skills I Must Develop	How I Will Develop My Skills	Completion Date

Part 3: Follow-up

Meet with your nurse manager to evaluate completion of your learning objectives defined in Part 2. If any have not been completed successfully, return to Part 2 and again list skills that need development, suggestions for developing them, and dates for completion and reevaluation.

If you have successfully completed Part 2, recognize your achievement. Congratulate yourself for a job well done. Don't stop here, though. Look for aspects of your job that you could fulfill more effectively or efficiently. Identify areas of nursing care that you want to know more about. List growth goals, ways to accomplish those goals, and deadlines in the appropriate columns below. Remember, your career is developmental and dynamic. To remain vibrant and vital you must continue learning and growing throughout your years in nursing.

Growth Goals	Specific Ways to Accomplish Goals	Completion Date

EXERCISE 1-2   MOURNING AND REINVESTING

Directions.   In order to come to terms with a loss, you must mourn. The act of mourning or grieving allows you to disengage your energy from roles and relationships that are lost so you can reinvest yourself in new relationships, roles, and experiences. Graduation from nursing school constitutes a major change; many losses are involved. You lose the student life-style, frequent contact with friends, senior-level status in a familiar organization, and in some cases, living in a familiar community.

1. *What aspects of student life and the student nurse role* change when you leave school? Which are easy to let go? Which are difficult to let go?

Easy to Let Go	Difficult to Let Go

2. *What aspects of your student life can you maintain* after graduating and entering the work world?

3. Recall that the phases of mourning include denial, anger, bargaining, depression, and acceptance. *What behaviors, attitudes, and feelings reflect that you are mourning* the loss of your student life or student nurse role?

4. *What are the consequences* (personal and professional) for holding onto the student life or student role after you have entered the work world?

5. *Who can help you* to mourn the loss of your student role or reinvest in the practicing nurse role? How can they help you?

6. *What are some things you can do* to help yourself mourn the loss of your student role and invest in your new work world roles?

EXERCISE 1-3   *DEVELOPING A DECOMPRESSION ROUTINE*

Directions.   As you deal with role overload, work pressures can sometimes interfere with your personal life, and personal stress can impair the quality of your professional performance. Regular use of a decompression time can help you to separate the pressures of work and home so you can be your best in both aspects of your life.

Call to mind the relaxing practices that help you unwind. Use these daily for a brief time after work and before assuming home responsibilities. If you work a P.M. or night shift, follow your routine after doing home-related tasks and before going to work. Chart your progress and the benefits gained. Writing this plan helps you make a decompression routine one of your healthy habits.

1. Options: How can I relax in 15-to 30-minute time spans?

2. Blocks: What or who keeps me from having and using a decompression routine?

3. Removing blocks: How I can overcome the blocks that stand in the way of my regular use of a decompression routine?

4. Action: How did I make a decompression routine a regular part of my life?

Date	Relaxing Practice I Used Today	Duration	Positive Results

EXERCISE 1-4   DELEGATION ACTION PLAN

Directions. Many new nurses experience role conflict and role overload. Delegation is a skill that can be helpful in dealing with certain cases of role overload or discontinuity. It helps you use your time more effectively.

Using this worksheet, set a specific goal for using delegation in your work. Identify what to delegate and to whom, when, and how you plan to teach or explain the delegated task. Write our your action plan on the worksheet to delegate more effectively.

A. Delegation Planning

I will delegate this task:

_____

I will delegate it to:

_____

Steps for Teaching or Explaining What Must be Done	When I Will Complete Each Step
1. _____	_____
2. _____	_____
3. _____	_____
4. _____	_____

B. Delegation Follow-through

Date
Accomplished   Event

_____   Tell the person about my plan.

_____   Teach the skill.

_____   Observe performance.

_____   Evaluate performance. (Continue supervision until performance is satisfactory).

_____   Tell the person I am turning the task loose but am available for help if needed.

C. Benefits of Delegating

How I will feel about myself:

_____

How I will use the time created:

_____

EXERCISE 1-5   SOCIALIZATION INTO NURSING

Directions. Socialization is the process whereby you learn to appropriately perform the expectations associated with the roles you fulfill. Socialization into nursing begins in school and continues to some extent throughout your career. Some of the difficulties encountered by new nurses relate to differences between school and work-world socialization. Developing an awareness of how school and work-world socialization contrast helps you understand important facts about your new environment. More important, it helps you to operate more comfortably in your new world of work.

To enhance your understanding of the work world and your ability to function comfortably within it, answer the following questions about socialization into nursing. Write your responses in the space provided.

Questions and Directions	School	Work World
Agents of socialization Who are the people who tell you what is appropriate role behavior? Identify specific people who are your agents of socialization. List their names in the appropriate column.	Examples: instructors, peers, patients, school administrators, or professionals encountered during clinical experiences	Examples: inservice educators, nurse managers, peers, patients, support personnel, physicians, hospital administrators.

Questions and Directions	School	Work World
Methods of socialization		
How do these people communicate their ideas about what is role-appropriate behavior? Identify methods and specific examples of how your socializing agents used those methods. List your responses in the appropriate column.	Usually formal, i.e., transmitting skills and knowledge by such techniques as: Lecture Demonstration Discussion Rules and regulations Sometimes informal, as described in column to the right.	Usually informal, i.e., transmitting values, priorities, and attitudes by such techniques as: Doing nothing; ignoring your ideas Nonverbal cues Work assignments Questions; focus of questions reveals priorities. Confrontation; designed to break down old values. Sometimes formal, as described in column to the left.

Questions and Directions	School	Work World
Content of socialization What are the messages about nursing that your socializing agents have transmitted? Identify the "shoulds," which you have been told by various agents of socialization. List your responses in the appropriate column.	Examples: attitudes, values, norms, priorities, and appropriate behavior. Nurses should meet the psychosocial, as well as the physical needs of their patients.	Examples: attitudes, values, norms, priorities, and appropriate behavior. Nurses should complete all patient care during a shift and should not work overtime.

EXERCISE 1-6   INTERVIEW GUIDE

Directions.   Identify a nurse who holds values, attitudes, priorities, and skills that reflect the type of nurse you want to be. Interview her or him, asking the following questions.

1. Describe your career in nursing. How long have you been a nurse? What jobs have you held? What key experiences have shaped your professional development?

2. What values that you learned in nursing school did you keep? What values did you let go of after you left school? Why did you make these choices?

3. If you were starting over as a new nurse, what would you do differently? What would you do the same? Why?

4. After the interview is completed, review the nurse's responses and think of yourself. What did you learn from this interview that can help you make the transition from student to professional nurse?

EXERCISE 1-7   CAREER PLANNING

Directions.   To maximize your potential, increase career satisfaction and capitalize on career opportunities, spend time on career planning. Career planning should be done throughout your career. Use the following guide to assist you.

Part 1: Where Am I Now?

1. Using the pattern of a business progress chart, draw a line that depicts the past, present, and future of your career.

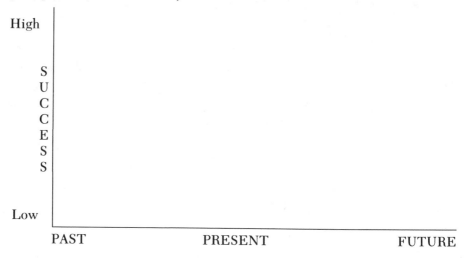

2. Write a brief explanation of the career line you have drawn.

3. List 20 adjectives that describe yourself most accurately in regard to your career.

1. _____	11. _____
2. _____	12. _____
3. _____	13. _____
4. _____	14. _____
5. _____	15. _____
6. _____	16. _____
7. _____	17. _____
8. _____	18. _____
9. _____	19. _____
10. _____	20. _____

(Adapted from Pfeiffer J, Jones JE: A Handbook of Structured Experiences for Human Relations Training, Vol 2, pp 101–112. La Jolla, University Associates, Inc., 1974. Used with permission.)

4. Regroup your list of adjectives into the following categories.

Positive	Neutral	Negative

Part 2: Where Do I Want to Be?

1. What is your conception of ideal attainments in your career? Be as free as possible in selecting these goals. Summarize them below. Example: 1. I want to become Vice-President for Nursing or Director of Nursing in my hospital.

    _____ 1. _____
    _____ 2. _____
    _____ 3. _____
    _____ 4. _____
    _____ 5. _____
    _____ 6. _____
    _____ 7. _____
    _____ 8. _____
    _____ 9. _____
    _____10. _____

2. Using the following four-point scale, assign a value to each of your goals by writing the appropriate number in front of each goal you listed in Item 1.

    1. Of **little** importance
    2. Of **moderate** importance
    3. Of **great** importance
    4. Of **very great** importance

3. List the goals you marked with ratings of 4 or 3 in descending order of importance.

    _____

    _____

    _____

    _____

    _____

    _____

Part 3: How Do I Get to Where I Want to Be?

1. From your preceding list of goals, select at least three for detailed planning. Establish a program, with specific steps and deadlines for attaining each of these objectives. Commit to writing your career development plan using the following format.

Goals	Specific Steps To Meet Goals	Available Resources	Blocks	Ways To Remove Blocks	Deadline

2. Establish a written contract with someone you know to help you fulfill your commitment to attaining your goal.

Person with Whom I Will Contract	Date Signed	Date Accomplished

EXERCISE 1-8 **FOR YOUR CONSIDERATION . . . OR . . . FOR GROUP DISCUSSION**

Directions. Use the following questions to reflect on key points covered in this chapter. Answer these questions individually or in a group.

1. Significant people

   A. Of all the people instrumental in your socialization into nursing, who are the most significant?

   B. What socialization messages did/do these most significant people convey?

   C. How well do these messages mesh with the expectations of your present nursing role?

D. If these messages mesh with the expectations of your present nursing role, how does this affect you?

E. What can you do to resolve any role conflict that might exist?

2. School vs. Work Socialization
   The formal socialization process associated with school is frequently much clearer and more explicit than the informal socialization of the work setting.
   A. How can you learn important priorities, norms, values, and behaviors in an informal way?

B. How can you obtain feedback regarding your work performance in an informal way?

3. Dysfunctional school values
   A. Which school-bred values, attitudes, priorities, norms, and behaviors are dysfunctional in the work world?

   B. Should you let go of any of them? Why?

C. Should you let go of *all* of them? Why?

D. Which work-world values do you believe in? Why?

2 Values Clarification: Making Choices

After working in a primary-care surgical unit, Ellen is ready to broaden her clinical skills. With the increasing focus on early hospital discharge, Ellen decides to seek a position in the home care department of the hospital where she is working.

Ellen is enthusiastic about again providing individualized family centered nursing as she did in nursing school. She looks forward to expanding her knowledge. She also fears that she will not be able to identify all of the needed resources or that she will miss a subtle clue to the status of a patient. Despite this fear, she is excited about being independent. With a mixture of emotions, Ellen begins her orientation as a home care nurse.

Ellen's preceptor is Virginia. Virginia was a public health nurse for 10 years prior to joining the home care department at the hospital a year and a half ago. Following a morning of making calls together, Ellen and Virginia are having lunch. Virginia begins to discuss her frustrations with the current expectations outlined by the director of the department. Each nurse must make seven calls a day, no less than 35 calls a week. There is to be a written plan of care following each initial visit, with documentation of each visit dictated and on file in the office on a daily basis. All physician's orders are to be filed and current within 72 hours, or the nurse is considered to be functioning without a written order. Any equipment available to the patients through the office is to be charged to the patient, and the nurse is to keep account of supplies by a special coding procedure. Arrangements for services or supplies outside the department are to be documented with an authorization form signed by the director. On a random basis, charts will be evaluated by an audit committee composed of three community health faculty members from an affiliated university and three hospital supervisors. Virginia says she doesn't know if she can continue to provide the kind of care to patients she values when she is on a time pressured schedule and is required to follow extra procedures. She feels that her independence and autonomy are being violated. Virginia wonders whether the director values her years of experience.

Even before talking with Virginia, Ellen was feeling overwhelmed with the unfamiliar routine. The conversation with Virginia seems to intensify her doubts. Ellen wonders if she will be able to adapt to the expectations of the department and her supervisor. The value framework of the department seems to use quantity of work as a yardstick. Independence is expected, but authority lies with the director. Effectiveness of practice and performance is judged by educators and hospital nursing service personnel, rather than practicing community health nurses. Ellen wonders if she is ready to expand her skills and function in an independent role. Ellen begins to wonder if becoming a home care nurse was a good decision.

What are Values?

Your *values* are reflected in your likes and dislikes. Your values are what you believe in and devote yourself to, because they feel genuine and true. The decisions about what is significant for you to value or believe are influenced by many factors. Remember when you applied to nursing school or began your first nursing course, and were asked to give reasons why you wanted to be a nurse? Your answers to the questions probed your values.

You may wonder how values differ from attitudes. The primary difference is that *attitudes* reflect a mental perception or a feeling about a particular situation, person, or way of behaving. Values, on the other hand, reflect a deeper spiritual response to these things. Values are the principles or standards that govern your attitudes, preferences, or emotional responses. Think of yourself wholistically, considering social, physical, intellectual, emotional, and spiritual aspects (described in Chap. 3, Power: A Way of Practicing Nursing). Values are influenced by all five of these aspects, but are a specific reflection of your spiritual component. Your values come from the core, or center, of your being.

You are cognizant of some of your values, and less conscious of others. The values clarification process, discussed later in this chapter, is a way of bringing your values into your awareness. Take some time now to write down what you think is important to you in your nursing role. What are your positive and negative preferences? What do you consider worthwhile or desirable? Developing this list takes some time and energy. Don't rush through the process. Be as specific as you can. Your list should reflect both likes and dislikes, as well as the principles and standards that guide you in your nursing practice.

Where Do My Values Come From?

Why does your list of values contain the items it does? What are the sources of the preferences and beliefs you devote yourself to and that cause you to behave in a certain way? Your preferences, or values, have two origins—*external sources* and *internal sources*. The external sources include parents, teachers, religious mentors, co-workers, peers, and other influential people. External sources of values are incorporated into your value system because those values help you gain approval from significant others. Internal sources for values are your own social, physical, intellectual, emotional, and spiritual senses. Internal values arise out of your personal preferences and are based on your needs, interests, and desires. Knowing the origins of your values helps you to differentiate what is truly important to you.

External Sources

Soon after you were born, the values of others were easily incorporated into the value patterns that direct your life. In order to receive love and approval, you adopted a large number of values from others. Because these values are not based on your own preferences that is, on what is of worth and significance to you, they tend to be fixed and rigid. These introjected values are more like rules or edicts and are accepted as your own without going through your own internal evaluation process.

What your parents value became of interest to you very early in your life. As you sought love, affection, and approval from them, you learned to behave in a way that assured you of having their warm, caring responses. If cleaning your room was what was required by your parents to allow you time for watching television, you came to value a clean room. If bringing home A's and B's on your report card was responded to with hugs and praise, you developed a value of doing well in school. If your parents welcomed and encouraged you to have friends of a certain culture, you came to value people from a specific culture. You may continue to live out the values of your parents.

Another powerful external origin of values is teachers. Not only do teachers bestow knowledge and stimulate learning, they also give grades and promotions. During the educational process the priorities and behavior of your teachers influenced and helped form your values. In nursing school, an instructor with a focus and emphasis on pathophysiology may have influenced you to develop a value for the physical impact of illness on a patient. If the director of your school of nursing expected that nursing students belong to a professional organization in order to be recommended for honors at graduation, you may have developed a value for membership in professional organizations. If your nursing instructor evaluated a process recording between you and a psychiatric patient as excellent, you may have come to value communication with a patient. Taking on the values of your teachers is a way to avoid punishment (failure) and receive rewards (high grades and promotions). The values of your nursing instructors influenced your values more readily because your thoughts, ideas, perceptions, knowledge, and understanding about health and illness were in a formative stage. Like your parents, your nursing instructors had a significant impact on the development of your values.

Some of your values also may have been influenced by religious practices and teachings. After being told that only men are religious leaders, which implies that men are superior to women, you may have difficulty valuing women in authority as highly as men. As a result of being instructed in your religious teachings that sexuality is for the sole purpose of procreation, you may not value sex for recreation or as a way of sharing intimacy in a relationship. If you were taught that spiritual experiences occur only in organized services in designated settings, you may minimize the spirituality of birth in a delivery room or restoration of life after a cardiac arrest in an intensive care unit.

Your co-workers and peers are another main external source of your values. In nursing school, if the students who were your friends usually worked on assignments together, you may have come to value studying and working on projects in a group, although you usually do well and like working independently. During your orientation as a staff nurse in a cardiac unit, the preceptor tells you it is more efficient to chart all of the medications you administer at the end of the shift. As a result, you come to value the efficiency in charting everything at one time, rather than documenting data as it occurs. The head nurse on the unit where you are working feels patients should have visitors only during designated hours. You instruct patients to limit visitors to those assigned times and you come to value the limitation of visitors. In addition to parents, teachers, religious groups, peers, and co-workers, social messages influence your values. The media and public figures send messages, some of which you accept as your own. Whatever their origin, your values from external sources are incorporated into your personality, although they are really from other persons.

Internal Sources

When your values are expressions of principles or standards regarding likes and dislikes influenced by your *own* senses, rather than those of others, they originate from internal sources. Wholistically, the internal sources of your values consist in all of your social, physical, intellectual, emotional, and spiritual experiences. You place high value on some of these experiences because they support or enhance who you are or who you want to be. Others you reject because they are useless, unpleasant, or otherwise unimportant to you. These values develop in a process of weighing, not always consciously, what is occurring at a given moment, and selecting or rejecting it depending on whether it is right for you. You are not at this point influenced by what parents, teachers, church authorities, or by what the latest "expert" said you should prefer. The value choices lie totally within yourself in response to your senses. You listen to intuitive internal messages rather than external messages from others.

As you interact with people on a social level, you discover that different social, physical, intellectual, emotional, and spiritual characteristics have different impacts on you. Certain mannerisms, speech patterns, attitudes, or interests cause you to have either a positive or a negative response to another person. Such reactions are not necessarily related to the similarities or differences the other person shares with you. It is more a "chemical" reaction to the qualities exhibited by the other person. As one acid may or may not mix well with another acid or with a base, what you like and dislike about other people is a combination of what you like and dislike about yourself. Your social nature, that is, your need for belongingness and contact in community, causes you to interact with others. As a result, people and their ways of interacting influence the formation of your values. Certain characteristics of others stimulate responses in you that reflect the values you have already formed.

In addition to social interactions, your five physical senses also form and help you to experience your values. What you hear, see, smell, touch, and taste give you information to evaluate. As you interact with a patient, you listen to the words, tones, and pauses and the meanings behind these signals. You look at a patient's color, movements, and posture. You are alert to the scents and odors emitted from a patient. You feel the patient's skin for temperature and moisture and palpate for turgor and muscle tone. The information you gain through your physical senses as a nurse is also obtained in your personal life. You evaluate your encounters as a nurse against your nursing knowledge and against your personal likes and dislikes. Your response to these experiences influences, and is influenced by, your values.

On an intellectual level, what you know and learn influences your values. After completing a nursing education, you may think your brain is the most overworked processor of data. During nursing school, you are in a process of values formation as well as intellectual development. What you see, hear, and discuss is weighed through the valuing process to determine what is right or wrong for you. Your intellectual development fosters the development of values. Through the cognitive process your brain is a conscious perceptor of information. All of the facts and fictions go into the database to help formulate your values.

Emotional experiences, both pleasant and unpleasant, allow you to become aware of and to influence your values. Your feelings, or gut responses, furnish good indications of how an experience fits with your value system. To know what your emotional response is to a situation, you need to tune out the extraneous signals and ask yourself, "What am I feeling right now?" In considering the question, you must turn inward and wait for the answer from your gut, not your head. The emotional indicators of whether a situation makes you feel mad, sad, glad, or scared registers in your value system. it is important to be honest and specific about the emotion you experience.

Although a spiritual experience may occur during a religious ritual, it can also be found in a less traditional setting. While bathing an elderly patient whose skin shows signs of age and toil, when interacting with parents and their newborn baby, or after seeing new buds on the trees on your way home from work you may have a profound internal response. Through your spirituality you experience a sincere awareness of what is true for you, your values or truths. Truths are the bottom line, the essence of what you know to be genuine and real for you. When you remove social responses, tune out physical senses, ignore intellectual awareness, disregard feelings, and get in touch with the crucial elements of what you believe, you are experiencing your values through your spiritual sense. Some truths may include knowing what love is, acknowledging that a person has worth, seeking a balance in life, or pondering the purpose of your existence. Through these spiritual experiences, your value system develops depth.

When taking on values from external sources, you chance losing contact with the potential wisdom of your own functioning, and consequently losing confidence in yourself. You risk experiencing internal conflict when the values of others do not reflect your own Truths. Ways to resolve this conflict through the values clarification process are described later in this chapter. Sometimes it takes a while to recognize the two different sources of values because the influence of others is remarkably strong and well ingrained. Begin now to differentiate what you value because you "ought to" or "should" from what you value as a result of your internal senses. As will be discussed later, when your values are influenced by internal sources, they are more subject to change and refinement and are less rigid over time. As you grow and change, so do your values.

Why Is Knowing My Values Important?

The significance of knowing your own standards, principles, and preferences is that it allows you more fully to be the person you are. When you differentiate the should's and should not's of others from your internal signals, you are able to respond to your own process of experiencing. As a result, you are able to be more self-directed, more aware of your internal responses, and more accepting of the feelings of others. At the beginning of this chapter, Ellen went through the process of identifying what she values as a nurse in making the decision to leave the staff nurse role and take a position as a home care nurse. She values individualized, family-centered care; expanding her knowledge; and being independent. As she begins to experience conflict with the new job expectations, she is able to differentiate her difficulties from Virginia's and to be more aware of her own responses. Then she can be self-directed in changing her behavior to be consistent with her values.

Being Self-Directed

When you know what you like and dislike, you are able to make decisions in response to those preferences. When you are unclear, what you decide is more likely to be directed by the preferences of others. Think of Ellen. She has already defined her career choices. She has determined what is important and worthwhile to her about nursing. But as a home care nurse, what are her principles and standards? What is right for her in her role as a community nurse? Although she is beginning to find answers for herself to these questions, initially she is strongly influenced by Virginia and the director.

As a new nurse, until you identify your values, you may find that your decisions, thoughts, feelings, and beliefs are directed by others. However, as you become more aware of what is important to you, your standards and principles, you will become more autonomous in choosing your goals. Your behavior will be guided more internally and less by the values of others. You will decide which activities and ways of behaving have meaning for you and which do not. You will make choices, and when they are wrong, you will learn from the consequences. When you are self-directed, you are using the wisdom of your own functioning and developing confidence in being the person you are.

Experiencing Inner Response

As you become aware of your values, you are less influenced by the values of others. You are open to your internal feelings and senses, whether they are social, physical, intellectual, emotional, or spiritual. In her role as a beginning community health nurse, Ellen knows she prefers providing individualized, family-centered nursing care. She likes expanding her knowledge and having an independent role. She does not like being unfamiliar with community resources and lacking confidence in her assessment skills. Virginia's concerns about the quantity of work and documentation requirements generates anxiety in Ellen. She feels afraid. Her eagerness to learn the new role is bombarded by feelings of inadequacy. Having some understanding of her values in nursing allows Ellen to be open to the conflict going on within herself during her conversation with Virginia. When you listen to different aspects of yourself, you begin to sense what responses are truly your own. You know what you are feeling and experiencing and how you are reacting. These experiences can then be used as opportunities to form accurate self-concepts and to guide your behavior. As you are more and more open to daily experiences, you are able to experience your feelings more freely. As a result you become a richer, more complete, more fully developed person.

Accepting the Feelings of Others

When you come to know your own values, the boundaries between your feelings and those of others become more clear. You are then better able to respect the individuality of another person, to accept different or mutual feelings, and to be open to the value framework of the other person. While you interact with a patient who is expressing his anger about being ill and searching for ways to cope with the changes, you can be more supportive when you are aware of your own values regarding health and illness. When you are confident about what you believe, you may even identify areas in which your values are similar to those of the patient. Furthermore, because your mind is not wildly searching for personal clarification and your emotions are calm, you are able to learn the value structure of the patient. You can then evaluate the effect your behavior has on the patient because you understand his value structure. Having an understanding of the boundaries between her own feelings and those of the patient will help Ellen to establish a more therapeutic relationship. If a patient says he fears having a terminal illness, Ellen will be more appropriate in supporting the patient if her personal values about being terminally ill are clear. When a patient talks about dying before having a chance to have a family and make a contribution to society, Ellen may be able to listen in a supportive way and also recognize similar values of her own. In another situation of the same nature, Ellen may find herself getting angry and sending nonverbal messages for the patient to stop talking. She could be totally unaware of the effect of her behavior on the patient because she is no longer responding to the patient's value framework, but the confusion within herself. The more she understands and develops comfort with her own values, the better Ellen will be able to accept the feelings of others.

By acting on the basis of your values, principles, preferences, priorities, and beliefs, you are able to interact with others confidently and therapeutically. As a result, you are self-directed rather than directed by others. This self-directedness gives you freedom to experience your internal responses without being threatened by the feelings of others.

Refer back to the exercises at the end of Chapter 1 and review what you listed or defined as your preferences and what you identified as important and worthwhile to you. Refine what you wrote and further clarify your values by addressing the question of what you spend your time doing. Is this what you want to be doing? With whom do you spend time? Is this the person you prefer to be with? On your list of values, put an asterisk (*) beside those values that came from an internal source. Consider now why knowing about these values helps you to be self-directed, free to experience your own feelings, and not to be threatened by the feelings of others.

What Is the Valuing Process?

The valuing process is a method for determining your principles, truths, likes, and dislikes. It is a way of ascertaining what is significant or important to you and of using this information to guide your behavior. As discussed earlier, there are external and internal sources for your values. Because of the strong influence of others, you may be out of touch with your internal signals. In the valuing process, each experience is weighed and accepted or rejected depending on whether or not the experience is significant to you at a given time. Your response is based on who you are at the particular moment, and therefore will be flexible and change from time to time. The steps of the valuing process are as follows:

Step I   Listen to your responses (social, physical, intellectual, emotional, and spiritual).

Step II   Differentiate internal sources from external sources.

Step III Take time to experience full awareness of your internal responses.

Step IV   Listen to your internal responses.

Step V   Evaluate your alternatives.

Step VI   Establish behavior patterns consistent with your senses.

Step VII Trust your beliefs, preferences, likes, and dislikes.

Step I: Listen to Your Responses

Begin the valuing process by learning to tune in to your own senses as you interact with others and have experiences. Your senses are internal responses or conscious realizations and are different from internal sources that are used to differentiate self-directed values from other-directed (external) values. Think wholistically, and identify your social, physical, intellectual, emotional, and spiritual responses. Listen to your intuitive reactions, going beyond a conscious level. When you discover a storm is generating within you, pay attention. Consider the following situation: During lunch two of your co-workers are discussing a recent television program about nuclear power plants. One of the nurses is enthusiastic about the energy potential of the power plant, while the other nurse is becoming angry about the potential dangers. As the discussion progresses into a personal confrontation, you become tense and anxious. You feel your face flush. You look at your watch and suggest it is time to return to the unit. Back on the unit, you find a place to be alone for a few minutes. You reflect on your feelings of discomfort in the cafeteria. You recall that when you were growing up, mealtime was a pleasant occasion and not a time to argue. You also recognize that at lunch you had a need to rescue your friends from negative feelings. And you feel ignorant because you didn't know enough about the subject to contribute to the discussion. These actions are part of the first step in the values clarification process. You are tuning in to your physical, emotional, and intellectual senses and developing conscious realization.

Step II: Differentiate Internal Sources from External Sources

Differentiate whether what your senses tell you comes from internal sources or from the external sources of shoulds and oughts. You will recognize that some responses are your own and some are more like those of persons who have made an impact on you. When you hear yourself say something whose words and tone sound like those of a former nursing instructor, take note. At another time you may recognize that your facial expression and mannerisms are similar to those you observe in one of your parents. In yet another experience, you may be surprised with what you say and do, but recognize how good you feel about it afterwards. These are ways of listening to your responses. Don't be evaluative or judgmental; just be aware of your response. Be sensitive to the reality that some of your responses are influenced by external sources and some are from internal sources.

When you do not know whether the values taken on from others are important to you, you may feel uncomfortable with or insecure about what you think you believe and prefer. This discomfort or insecurity tells you that your values are being influenced by external sources. It also signals the need to clarify your own internally induced values. Learn to listen to your internal responses to a situation. Tune out the externally created rules or quotes that come to your head. Listen for clues that tell you what you think, say, or do has a rightness for you. Clues might be a sense of confidence, relaxation, or optimism. You may not be able to explain your response, but you know it is genuine when the values that give rise to it spring from within.

Beginning a new position is often a time for reflecting on your values. Use this opportunity to distinguish the internal voices from the voices that originated from parents, instructors, or other external sources. Learn to listen for the honest responses that come from inside you. You may recognize that your response is a reflection of values from an external source, but also find that the response is in agreement with your internal source of values. Many values from external sources have a rightness for you and become an internal source of values. Your values may be similar to those of people significant to you.

Step III: Take Time to Experience Full Awareness of Your Internal Responses

After you listen to your responses to a situation and differentiate internal sources from external sources, allow yourself to be open internally. Take time to process the interaction fully in order to discern your internal responses. Don't be an observer; pay attention to your reactions. You may share this experience with another person or reflect on your responses by yourself. The experience will continue to replay or rerun through your thoughts, telling you to pay attention and process what happened further. During this step it becomes clear if your response or reaction is not consistent with your values.

You will hear yourself say, "that's not what I wanted to say (or do)." This is a time for recognizing what your values are and acknowledging that your words, thoughts, or behaviors are not what you want them to be in order to be consistent with your personal standards and preferences. Obviously, there are many experiences in your daily activity that are not of particular significance at a given moment. Your internal reactions to a person or to an event are more significant than the actual situation or who the person is in telling you what is important to you, and what you want to process further.

Step IV: Act on Your Internal Responses

At this point, the values clarification process becomes a little scary. It's as though you are in the middle of having abdominal surgery, and the anesthesiologist wakes you up and tells you to take a look inside. Maybe you don't *want* to know what is inside. Maybe you won't understand what you find. And, what about the pain? But you need to recognize that this is a critical juncture and muster your confidence and desire for self-understanding so that you can proceed.

This is a time to be clear about your values and to accept the need to change. You are willing to give up the value, attitude or behavior that is no longer desirable and acceptable. As you listen to your responses you recognize the grieving process going on as you let go of what you have outgrown or no longer find applicable. To listen means to heed what you are telling yourself and to take responsibility for making choices. Ask yourself, "What am I feeling?" Wait patiently to hear the answer and look inside yourself to focus on the image that evolves. Then, accept the challenge to make the changes necessary to be consistent and to have internal congruency.

Step V: Evaluate Your Alternatives

What behaviors and attitudes are consistent with your values? Evaluate your response in terms of alternatives. When have you felt like this before? What did you learn from the experience then? What did you do the last time you felt like this? How could you respond differently now? What are your choices? How does what happened before influence what is happening now or what will happen in the future? How would you like to react? You keep changing as a person, and how you respond to a particular moment may be different from how you did at another time. Keep your options open—think of them as fluid and flexible. As your own best friend, be supportive and permissive in allowing yourself to consider all possibilities.

In evaluating, "try on" your various alternatives. Think of yourself in a situation in which you are expected to provide only physical care for patients, and it becomes clear that you value a wholistic approach. If you want to make a change so you can respond in a way consistent with your values, ask yourself what your alternatives are. You can adopt the attitude that you will learn as much as you can about physical care although you still value a wholistic approach. You can find a different job. You can become so efficient in physical care that you are able to incorporate a wholistic approach. In considering each of your options, you find one solution feels right and is the one you have the interest in and energy for implementing now.

Step VI: Establish Behavior Patterns Consistent with Your Values

Establish behavior patterns that are consistent with your internal responses and that reflect your values. Now is the time to try out new words when speaking, different behaviors when interacting, and fresh ideas when thinking that feel right for you and reflect your preferences and principles. This is a learning process. You begin to respond differently. At first the newness seems strange and uncomfortable. Soon your responses become familiar and automatic. You know you are consistent when you feel genuine and in harmony.

As a new nurse, you have numerous choices for how to respond to your professional role and job expectations. Consider your choices by listening to your internal responses. Take the initiative to develop behavior patterns that are consistent with your values. If you value primary nursing, seek a position in a primary nursing setting and role. If you value autonomy, build your skills and your knowledge base so that you can practice independently. If you value praise and acknowledgment, strive for excellence or find opportunities that get you what you want. Be patient with yourself as you learn the behaviors necessary to be congruent with your values. Learning new attitudes and different behaviors is a slow process and takes time.

Step VII: Trust Your Beliefs, Preferences, Likes, and Dislikes

Trust your beliefs, preferences, likes, and dislikes. Trust yourself, your feelings and intuitions. At first, the process of changing and living your values is a little scary. You wonder what will happen and how others will respond. Instead of thinking about being unsure, imagine you are taking a journey. Have a spirit of adventure. You will meet a wonderful friend: yourself! Together you explore new territory. You have familiar experiences, but with your trusted friend, you respond to them in a different way. Follow a course directed by your internal sources rather than a preplanned trip directed by external sources. Be the captain of your ship. Weigh your alternatives in light of what you have done, how you feel, and where you want to go. Believe in yourself.

Walking through the steps of the valuing process and coming to know your values is a matter of weighing choices with uncertain consequences. There are risks. The saying "nothing risked, nothing gained" comes to mind. There is a lot to be gained by listening to your internal rhythm. You develop confidence in yourself. You improve or enhance yourself. You know more clearly who you are as a person, your strengths, and the areas you would like to change. You become more independent and self-directed in making those changes.

The values clarification process involves immersing yourself in the immediacy of what you are experiencing, endeavoring to sense and to clarify all of the complex meaning. Included in the present moment is also the meaning growing out of similar experiences in the past. The process involves dealing with both the old and the new. The valuing process is not an easy or simple thing. It is complex, the choices are often perplexing and difficult, and there is no guarantee that the choice you make will in fact prove right for you. However, if the course of action is not true, you will sense it and make the necessary adjustment.

How do the steps of the valuing process work for Ellen, from the case at the beginning of this chapter? During the first days in orientation, Ellen finds herself seeking time alone. She needs to be away from the stimulation and reactions of Virginia so that she can listen to her responses. Sometimes her verbal responses to Virginia clash with what she feels. Ellen tells Virginia that the director has a right to set expectations, but feels uncomfortable about her own inability to meet those expectations. At other times, Ellen recalls messages from class discussion in the community health course she took as a student. As a student those ideas for care seemed creative. Now, they seem unrealistic.

As she listens to her internal responses to the expectations of her new position, Ellen hears herself repeating words of her father, who had a strong work ethic. She hears phrases such as, "you can always do more than you think you can." As she listens to her thoughts, she also hears a question, "Is this what I think?" Because she was directed always to have a care plan on each patient as a nursing student, she continues to follow the practice as a staff nurse. As she processes the expectation to have a written care plan in the office for each patient, she questions whether she thinks this practice is necessary. Why should there be a care plan in the office when she is in the patient's home implementing the care? Perhaps the values of Ellen's father and nursing instructors are valid for her, but until this point they have not gone through her internal evaluation. They are values from external sources. What is her internal voice saying? Ellen needs to listen to this voice to be able to answer this question.

During her lunch with Virginia, Ellen is aware of internal responses to what is said. This is a significant experience. Following the interaction, Ellen reflects often on the conversation. During quiet times, she begins to experience full awareness of her internal responses. The expectations of her job are requiring a lot of time. Just driving to the office takes an hour, plus the time spent to do the necessary documentation. Each of the patient's visits requires at least 30 minutes, often more. Next semester Ellen wants to take a physical assessment course to build her confidence. How much of her life does she want to give to her work and professional development? How is she going to have enough time and energy for her personal life?

When reflecting on her internal responses following the lunch with Virginia, Ellen listens to her senses. She enjoys her job and knows she is a hard worker. In fact, she places high expectations on herself to do more than is usually expected by others. However, her own limitations and the demands of the job are requiring so much of her time and energy that she does little else besides work and sleep. Each evening and on weekends she dictates her nursing notes, write plans of care, and studies from her nursing textbooks. Just prior to making the job switch, Ellen had begun to date Michael, whose company she enjoys. During the past weeks she has had no time or has been too tired to see Michael. He is questioning her interest in their continuing their relationship. Ellen likes Michael and her work. She recognizes that a professional often puts in more than an 8-hour day, but dislikes not having any time or energy for other things. She is afraid she has too many personal limitations for the job. She also feels sad about not spending time with Michael and misses the fun times they shared.

As a staff nurse, Ellen used to feel afraid and inadequate when she was assigned to charge responsibility for the unit on the evening shift. However, after a couple of weeks, she found she learned the tasks that needed to be done, was able to set priorities, and established a routine that made the responsibility rewarding. She perceives now, in her present situation, that she again is afraid of additional responsibility. As she recalls the experience with charge responsibility, she recognizes that more time is needed to learn and adapt her skills. It is too soon to expect the level of performance that Virginia has. In regard to her feelings about Michael, it becomes clear she values an intimate relationship. She wants to plan time with Michael to validate how important he is to her. Not seeing him is inconsistent with her values. While in nursing school she did not pursue a consistent relationship, so learning to allocate her time requires thought and planning.

As Ellen begins to consider her new role a challenge and an opportunity to expand her skills, her behavior also changes. She asks Virginia how to locate community resources, then organizes them for easy reference. She writes a weekly work plan, and meets with the director each Monday to help her to be more efficient than the previous week. Her behavior patterns become consistent with her values. She feels less afraid and inadequate, and more confident and enthusiastic. She and Michael set a time to spend together each weekend. Ellen knows she also wants to see Michael during the week, and as she becomes more effective in her work, she anticipates there will be more time available.

With each additional day, Ellen realizes she is making choices consistent with her senses. She looks forward to beginning each day. Although she comes home from work tired, she has a sense of accomplishment. She likes the way patients respond to her. Her organizational skills are improving so that she can complete six calls a day, and sometimes seven. She has developed a file of resources and so spends less time looking in the yellow pages. Most of all, she feels a renewed commitment to nursing. The relationship with Michael is again an enjoyable part of her life, and confirms her value of having an intimate relationship with another person. Going through the values clarification process helped Ellen to determine what is significant to her, and then to use the information to guide her behavior.

What Are the Consequences of Values Clarification?

The values clarification process as already discussed is a difficult, perhaps painful and scary experience. The outcomes of knowing more clearly what you value and of behaving in a consistent manner may cause you to stand alone, face yourself, or change aspects of your life.

Standing Alone

Picture yourself standing in the middle of the nurse's station on a hospital unit. A physician comes up to you and directs you to call the laboratory for the latest blood sugar results on a patient. After a number of similar experiences in the past, it is clear to you that you value a professional relationship with a physician, but this does not include doing secretarial functions. As a result, you respond to the physician by providing the number to call to obtain the information. Although there are numerous other professionals in the area, activity is stilled and voices are hushed. The physician repeats the request. You repeat the response. As the tension rises, one of the nurses goes to the phone and calls to get the information for the physician. Your co-workers give you looks of disbelief. At that moment, you wish you could evaporate.

Knowing what your values are and making a decision to behave accordingly, may cause you to stand alone. In the aforementioned situation, as a nurse you clarified your values regarding professional relationships. When the occasion arises to act on your values, your co-workers are not supportive. You experience isolation. This is difficult. Depending on the responses of your other resources and how you are feeling at the moment, you may go back through your values clarification process. On the other hand, you may recognize the "rightness" of acting in agreement with your values and you may be more firmly committed.

Facing Yourself

Becoming aware of your values requires you to face yourself and to accept who you are. This process is painful, frightful, and arduous. Maybe you don't want to know or are afraid to learn who you are. Perhaps you resist putting in the effort required to get yourself to the point where you can say, "This is me." There may be discrepancies between the fantasy and the reality of who you are. Merging the two involves pain in giving up an idealized self-image. It also creates fear of what you might learn about yourself. No matter what you find, values clarification is not done quickly and it is usually hard work.

Reflect back to the scenario described in Step I of the values clarification process. Following the lunchtime experience with your two co-workers you become fully aware of your internal responses, and then need to face what you discover. First, you have to consider that your value about acceptable meal-time behavior may not be in agreement with that of others or what currently feels right for you. Second, you realize your behavior was that of a rescuer, and that is not a characteristic you value in others or yourself. Third, you are aware that you value intelligence and take pride in being informed. However, the discussion of a current events topic found you uninformed. Moving through the valuing process to clarify your values in each of the three areas and then behaving in a manner consistent with your values will not be easy. Often a given situation requires you to reevaluate more than one value or aspect of who you are. The clarification takes time and patience with yourself.

Changing Aspects of Your Life

When you move through the valuing process, a third consequence occurs in the sixth step. Establishing behavior patterns consistent with your values means change. Along with experiencing the grief process that is part of changing, you also need to develop and adjust to different attitudes, life-styles, and social expectations. For most people, change is painful, slow, and scary, even when self-directed.

Changing behavior is also risky. Will people like or dislike you when you behave differently? Could the different behavior cost you your job or the loyalty of professional colleagues? Will you be put in a position to choose between your self-esteem and the job? The answer to each of these questions could be yes. There is risk in behaving in a manner consistent with your own values rather than the values of others. This is especially so when the "other" is your boss.

The values clarification process generates anxiety and has consequences. At first, the prospect of standing alone on an issue, facing yourself, and changing some aspect of your life seems like a negative experience to be avoided. True, the process is painful, frightening, and often difficult. However, in a supportive, caring environment, it is possible to achieve both personal and professional growth from the consequences of values clarification.

How Will the Valuing Process Be Helpful?

Everyday people behave on the basis of their values and beliefs, whether from internal sources or through the influence of others. Everyday nurses make choices in the clinical setting based on their values and beliefs. As a nurse, you want to develop confidence, improve or enhance yourself, know yourself, become independent, and be self-directed in making those choices. The steps of the valuing process will help you accomplish these goals. They also help you to be committed to nursing, make decisions, direct change in your behavior, and bridge the transition from student to practitioner.

Increasing Your Commitment to Nursing

Nursing is a demanding profession. It requires a wholistic approach and utilization of all five aspects of your being. Effective nursing calls for commitment. What does being committed mean? It means having a willingness to invest your time and energy in developing and using your skills. There is a sense of duty and obligation, with a personal pledge to be knowledgeable and skilled in providing a specialized service to others. The valuing process is helpful in reaffirming that you are committed to the nursing profession in order to function in your fullest capacity and meet these expectations. Through your insight into your personal value system and knowledge that those values are best met by practicing nursing, you develop a commitment to your profession.

Recall the days before you began nursing school. You went through a self-assessment in deciding what kind of education you wanted. For some people this is an individual process. Others are influenced by family or friends. If you decided that being a nurse was your career choice, you were able to begin nursing school with a sense of confidence and enthusiasm. If you were significantly influenced by other people, and not sure yourself, you may have begun with uncertainty.

At the end of the first weeks of learning what nursing is about you may have questioned the rightness of the nursing profession for you. By midterm, you may have become preoccupied with the thought of dropping out of school and reconsidering your options. If you went through the valuing process and in response to your own senses and choices decided that nursing education was right for you, you were probably able to finish the term, and the rest of your education, with more confidence. However, if your parents or spouse or

Aunt Helen (who is a nurse) conspired to convince you nursing was the best choice for you, you may have succeeded in completing the term, but with little self-confidence and much questioning about your career choice.

As you pursued the clinical experiences, the questioning and uncertainty may have continued. During each course you hoped the answer would emerge. In each experience you wished you would discover that you really were meant to be a nurse. The thought of failing a course at times was a welcome possibility for resolving the dilemma.

Finally, you approached graduation. You no longer questioned whether you wanted a nursing education. You knew you were capable of completing the program; all you needed to do was persevere a bit more. In school you met some interesting classmates and even had some valuable experiences. You began to think about what you would do after graduation. You wondered what you could do with a nursing education.

Your classmates talked about where they would like to get a job. Some seniors requested transcripts so that they could pursue further education. You felt both admiration for, and frustration with, their sense of purpose. You asked yourself, "Why do I want to be a nurse?"

Return to the present. Tune in to your senses and answer the question for yourself today. Continue to walk through the steps of the valuing process. If you hear yourself say nursing is not right for you, consider your alternatives. Life is too short and too precious to spend it not doing what you want. Nursing is too demanding to practice with uncertainty. The nursing profession is too important to have uncommitted members.

If, given all the choices, you conclude that nursing is right for you, and it took until you completed your education to clarify your commitment, celebrate! It is not how long it takes, but establishing behavior patterns consistent with your values, that is important. Now, trust your feelings and be confident in your role, as you continue to be the nurse you are meant to be.

It is vital to you as a person, as a nurse, and as a professional to be committed to your career. Becoming committed is a process filled with highs, lows, and many plateaus of questioning and knowing. The valuing process is a way to progress through each of these layers of uncertainty. It is important that you find nursing a way of outwardly expressing who you are and what values you hold.

Guiding Your Decisions

In your personal life, as well as in your nursing practice, you continually need to make decisions. Effective life choices and quality nursing care are based on sound decision making. Should you get an apartment or live with your parents? Should you get a job or go to school? Should you change jobs or stay put? Should you get married or stay single? In your nursing role, you contemplate the decision to inform a patient of the effects of his treatment. You feel unsure about babies being kept alive on respirators when brain damage is certain. You question the use of heroic measures when a patient requests to die in peace. Should a patient be subjected to a 3-day hospitalization for a procedure that could be done as an outpatient? Does a woman need a hysterectomy after one episode of prolonged bleeding because the doctor said she was menopausal anyway? Such predicaments involve decision making.

The values clarification process described in the seven steps already listed assists you in making decisions. As you clarify your values you develop standards and principles for your choices. Also, the valuing process causes you to consider alternatives in the decision-making process. Decision making is an intellectual process. Decision-making models are helpful as a guide through the maze of possible choices. However, before you initiate the decision-making process, walk through the steps of the valuing process. Listen to your senses, consider your alternatives, and clarify what is significant to you. In collaboration, decision making and values clarification can guide you in dealing with ethical dilemmas in your nursing practice, as well as with setting goals and priorities for patient care.

Directing Changes in Your Behavior

The first steps of the valuing process help you to look at your behavior, listen to your thoughts and words, and feel your emotions. As you reflect on these responses to your experiences and interactions in respect to your values, two things happen. You become more clear about what you value and you learn what behaviors or attitudes are not consistent with your values. Both of these insights provide direction in making changes in your behavior.

When you finish school and begin to practice, the fantasy of a nursing role collides with reality. You feel out of control because you are assigned rotating hours that leave little opportunity for a social life. You can't get a position you like, so you are not challenged or excited about your job. Before you use these sources of dissatisfaction as reasons for leaving nursing, clarify your values. You may recognize that being a nurse is consistent with your values. The conflict you are experiencing is not with your values but with the difference between the fantasy of nursing practice and the reality. Being clear about your commitment to nursing helps you to focus more specifically on changing your behavior and attitudes about hours and beginning job possibilities.

Changing your behavior is a painful process. However, the desire to resolve the conflict causing you to clarify and validate your values provides strong impetus for change. You feel better, happier, and able to be more effective when you have inner harmony and peace. The rewards of having values that reflect who you are and of having behaviors and attitudes consistent with your values are worth the price of change.

Helping to Bridge the Transition from Student to New Nurse

Possibly, the ultimate worth of the valuing process is in helping a new nurse adapt to nursing practice. Adjusting to a nursing role is a two-way street. Your superiors, co-workers, and subordinates need to be satisfied with you, and you need to be satisfied with your work environment and co-workers. Managers and staff nurses expect several things of new nurses. New nurses are expected to be calm, mature, and confident and to adapt to the value framework of the work setting. New nurses repeatedly want to be appreciated, to have an opportunity to expand their skills, and to feel rewarded for their contribution. How does the valuing process achieve these ends?

When you experience conflict between your internal feelings and your outward behaviors, it is difficult to conceal. When what you would like to be doing and what you are actually doing are incongruent, you experience distress. As a result, you are not calm either inside or outside. When a patient or family is receiving treatment in the health care system, they are in some stage of crisis. What they need is a calm and mature care-giver. The clearer your values are to you, the more likely it is that you will reflect a demeanor of calmness and maturity in your practice.

As discussed previously, an outcome of the valuing process is increased self-confidence. Self-confidence, as opposed to arrogance or egotistical behavior, is trusting your ability and knowing your limitations. As a result, you ask questions when unsure. Because your behavior says you trust yourself, your supervisor and co-workers are more likely to trust you as well.

Another expectation of managers and staff members is that a new nurse can adapt to the values of the work setting. Each work environment has its own culture and expectations. What is covertly important is learned through trial and error, experience and observation. "This is how we do it here" are key words in telling you how informal rules and procedures are being used to judge you. There is no procedure guide or policy manual that spells out the informally expected behavior. It is learned in the "school of hard knocks." When you have an awareness of your personal values, you are less threatened and confused by the expectations and values of your work setting and can better adapt to the expectations. For example, in your work setting, getting tasks done and filling out flow charts is the behavior valued by your manager. However, you value the opportunity to incorporate health teaching into your care plan and supply patients with alternatives for care. With the two sets of expectations, you proceed to identify for yourself ways to meet both sets of expectations. When your needs and those of the staff are met, you are seen as adapting. Remember to differentiate internal values from external values of the work setting, so that you remain clear about what is important to you.

You want to be appreciated. What makes you feel appreciated? While there are some threads of continuity, each person answering the question has a different response. A story comes to mind about a woman who loved flowers. Each year for her birthday her husband gave her a flowering plant. When the couple was in marital counseling, the woman stated in her list of grievances that she never received flowers, a gesture that would have meant a great deal to her. In utter amazement, the husband reminded the wife of the plants he selected and gave her for each birthday. It was then she said she valued cut flowers to put in a vase. A potted plant reminded her of a funeral and depressed her. The moral of the story is not to expect others to know what makes you feel valued and appreciated unless you let them know specifically. Before you can let others know your needs, you must identify them for yourself. You create a lose–lose situation when you expect others to know what makes you feel appreciated when you don't even know yourself. The valuing process helps you become aware of what is important to you.

In order to expand your skills and be rewarded for your efforts you must be selective. You need to choose a work setting consistent with what you expect. If you want to do patient teaching, don't choose a task-oriented, intensive care setting. On the other hand, if you enjoy practicing manual skills in a fast-paced environment with a focus on pathophysiology, don't work in a community mental health setting. Through the valuing process you come to identify what you like so you can better select alternatives. If you want to progress along a career path toward a supervisory role, don't get a job in a clinic that has one nurse and a clerical staff. If you become impatient and are intolerant with helplessness, avoid infants and debilitated patients. Find a position in an environment with a philosophy consistent with your values and with managers whose expectations allow you to expand your skills and grow professionally.

The valuing process is helpful to you as a new graduate in preparing you for nursing practice. Clarifying your values assists you in affirming your commitment to nursing. In making decisions, knowing your values contributes to your ability to make choices that are right for you. Proceeding through the steps of the valuing process is an aid in bridging the transition from student to new nurse.

Bibliography

Billings C, Quick M: Does your job work for you? Am J Nurs, April 1985, pp 407–409

Binder J: Value conflicts in health care organizations. Nursing Economics, September/October 1983, pp 114–119

Brink P: Value orientations as an assessment tool in cultural diversity. Nurs Res, July/August 1984, pp 198–203.

Coletta S: Values clarification in nursing: Why? Am J Nurs, December 1978, pp 2057–2063

Noble D, King J: Values: Passing on the torch without burning the runner. J Contemp Soc Work, December 1981, pp 579–584

Simon S, Howe L, Kirschenbaum H: Values Clarification. New York, Hart, 1972

Smith H: How hospitals can respond to changing values. Hospital Topics, January/February 1984, pp 13–17

Uustal D: Experiences in valuing. AORNJ, February 1980, pp 188–193

Uustal D: Values education: Opportunities and imperatives. Nurse Educator, Spring 1984, pp 9–13

Exercises

EXERCISE 2-1   ASSESSING PERSONAL VALUES

Directions. What is important to you? What do you consider worthwhile or desirable? What are your preferences and dislikes? The answers to these questions help you to determine your values. Knowing your values helps you to be more confident and self-directed in your actions. There are no right or wrong answers, other than what occurs inside of you.

Step 1: In the left column, list twenty things you enjoy doing.

Step 2: Indicate in the remaining columns what is involved with each activity or behavior by placing an X or comment in the box.

Money: The activity costs money.

Risk: Some risk is involved, either physical, intellectual, or emotional.

Solitude: You like doing the activity alone.

Togetherness: You like doing the activity with others.

Parents: Your parents also do or did this activity.

Date: Indicate the last time you did the activity.

Activity	Money	Risk	Solitude	Togetherness	Parents	Date

Activity	Money	Risk	Solitude	Togetherness	Parents	Date

Step 3: Explore your answers to the following questions:

a. What does this list reveal about your values?

b. Are you surprised by anything you have written?

c. Are you disappointed by anything you have written?

d. Is there anything you would like to change in the future?

e. What would the change involve?

EXERCISE 2-2   ASSESSING PROFESSIONAL VALUES

Directions.   Sometimes there is conflict between what you consider worthwhile and important as a nurse and what you think you should like or dislike. Clarifying your values and making choices consistent with your own values leads to more job satisfaction. The following exercise will aid you in determining what is important to you and what you value as a nurse. There are no right or wrong answers, other than what occurs inside of you.

Step 1: In the left-hand column, list ten things you like to do as a nurse.

Step 2: Indicate in the remaining columns what is involved with each thing you like to do.

Independence: You carry out the activity independent of other nurses or professionals.

Teamwork: You do the activity as a member of a team.

Risk: There is risk involved with doing the activity.

Setting: Indicate where the activity is or could be carried out. (e.g., hospital, home, community)

Fee: Determine whether a specific fee for service is or could be charged.

Activity	Independence	Teamwork	Risk	Setting	Fee

Activity	Independence	Teamwork	Risk	Setting	Fee

Step 3: Explore your answers to the following questions:

a. What does this list reveal about your professional values?

b. Do you prefer to practice nursing independently or as the member of a team?

c. Are you willing to take risks in what you do?

d. In what kind of setting are the activities you listed done?

e. Is there a specific fee charged for what you like to do?

f. What ideas does your list of activities and responses give you for practicing nursing?

EXERCISE 2-3   USING YOUR VALUES AS PRINCIPLES

Directions.   Your values are the principles or standards that govern your attitudes, behaviors, and emotional responses. What you value the most will have the strongest influence on you. Listed below are 21 values. As a nurse, arrange these values in order of their importance to you as guiding principles in your practice. Read through the list carefully. Then place the numeral 1 to the left of the value that is most important to you. Place the numeral 2 next to the value that is second most important, etc. The value that is least important, relative to the others, will be ranked 21.

Rank Order	Value	Important to Superior
————————	Appreciation	————————
————————	Autonomy	————————
————————	Broadmindedness	————————
————————	Competence	————————
————————	Courage	————————
————————	Decision-making ability	————————
————————	Dependence	————————
————————	Freedom	————————
————————	Helpfulness	————————
————————	Honesty	————————
————————	Independence	————————
————————	Intellectual ability	————————
————————	Interdependence	————————
————————	Job security	————————
————————	Obedience	————————
————————	Power	————————
————————	Recognition	————————
————————	Risk taking	————————
————————	Self control	————————
————————	Sense of accomplishment	————————
————————	Wisdom	————————

Think of your present work or educational environment. Place an X on the right-hand side of the values you think your head nurse, manager, or instructor considers most important.

Compare your list with those most important to your superior. Are the X's next to the values you think are most important? If the X's are next to your least important values, how does this affect you?

Is the comparison between your most important values and the X's reflective of the satisfaction or dissatisfaction you experience in your present nursing role?

EXERCISE 2-4   EXPANDING YOUR OPTIONS

Directions.   When you know what you value, sometimes it is hard to think of options that best reflect your beliefs. This exercise helps you to expand your awareness of those things that have meaning for you and to discover new areas of interest. Use the job classification section of a recent nursing journal or the newspaper and scan the job opportunities. Select 10 jobs that are of interest to you. Give each possibility a number, and evaluate it according to elements that are attractive to you, what qualities you have that fit the expectations and what you would need to acquire before you would be considered for the position. Evaluate the repeated patterns and consistent responses.

Position	Attractive Elements	Qualities You Have	Qualities You Need
1.			
2.			
3.			
4.			
5.			
6.			
7.			

Position	Attractive Elements	Qualities You Have	Qualities You Need
8.			
9.			
10.			

EXERCISE 2-5   TAKING ACTION ON YOUR VALUES

Directions.   Although you are able to verbalize your values and take pride in what you believe, putting them into action is difficult. This exercise is designed to help you determine and remove barriers to action that block you from living your values more completely. In the space below describe a decision you would like to make or an action you would like to take. On the left-hand side list barriers you experience, both real and perceived. On the right-hand side list steps for removing the barriers. At the bottom, write a plan of action for removing the barriers. This exercise may be done individually or in small groups, with each member sharing and receiving feedback from the group.

Decision or Action

Real and Perceived Barriers	Steps for Removing Barriers

Plan of Action for Removing the Barrier

EXERCISE 2-6   **CHOOSING AMONG ALTERNATIVES**

Directions.   In the values clarification process it is often necessary to choose among alternatives. By completing this exercise in a group setting, you will gain practice in choosing from among alternatives and explaining your choices to further clarify your values. Each of the following questions is followed by three alternative choices. Rank these choices according to your value-influenced preferences. After each individual in the group ranks the answers to the question, the group leader directs a discussion, with each member or selected members explaining the reasons for their choices.

1. Which of the following gives you the most satisfaction in a nursing career?

   _____ Salary

   _____ Patient response

   _____ Working with other professionals

2. Who has the most influence on your values system?

   _____ Nursing instructors

   _____ Nurse managers

   _____ Co-workers

3. What aspect of your nursing role do you enjoy the most?

   _____ Physical assessment

   _____ Patient/family teaching

   _____ Coordination of resources

4. How are you best able to perfect and learn nursing skills?

   _____ Formal academic setting

   _____ Informal continuing education

   _____ Clinical practice

5. Which age of patient do you *least* like to care for at present?

_____ Pediatric

_____ Young adult

_____ Elderly

6. What is the hardest for you to do?

_____ Complete a written plan for patient care

_____ Conduct an inservice for your peers

_____ Incorporate discharge planning for each patient

7. Where would you prefer to practice nursing during the next year?

_____ Home care setting

_____ Hospital setting

_____ Community health center setting

8. Which nursing role would you rather achieve in the next five years?

_____ Head nurse

_____ Staff nurse

_____ Nurse practitioner

EXERCISE 2-7 **FOR YOUR CONSIDERATION . . . OR . . . FOR GROUP DISCUSSION**

Directions. Use the following questions to reflect on key points covered in this chapter. Answer these questions individually or in a group discussion.

1. Think of a decision you made recently about patient care. What is your underlying value that influenced the decision?

2. What values of co-workers are most in conflict with your own?

3. What choices have you made lately that surprised you, but felt right and true afterwards?

4. How do you respond to a patient whose behavior reflects values different from yours?

5. Which of your values do you have the most difficulty discussing with others?

6. What is there about you that makes your friends like you?

7. Of all the people you know who have helped you, who has helped the most?

8. Is there something you want very much, but can't have right now? What? Why?

3

Power: A Way of Practicing Nursing

During her final weeks in school, Karen, a senior nursing student, reflects on her soon-to-be realized accomplishment and contemplates her role as a graduate nurse. In her nursing trends class, there is a discussion about power in nursing.

During her clinical experiences in both hospitals and community agencies, Karen witnesses more helplessness among nurses than power. She sees nurses wanting to dominate their subordinates. They want to be right all of the time and are irritated when proven wrong. She witnesses the staff members on a unit guard their domain jealously and prevent anyone from learning their procedures and policies. She hears nurses who were former change agents and risk takers say they are running out of energy. Some nurses say they want to leave the profession. The lack of effectiveness and professional strength seems frightening and contagious.

Karen values her personal power. She set the goal to become a nurse after a degree in anthropology didn't fulfill her interests. She had control over charting a course to meet her goal, or as much control as nursing students can have. She knew how to gain access to people and resources that could help her. She established a support system of individuals who were helpful and interested in her reaching her goal. So far, Karen has lived her life with a sense of personal power. But her observations of experienced nurses are causing her concern. Karen wonders whether she will experience her familiar feeling of power in her unfamiliar role as a graduate nurse.

Why Is Power Important for the New Nurse?

Many times the notion of power evokes an emotional response rather than a reasoned one. An emotional response to power is especially predictable in two groups of people—women and nurses. Since 97% of nurses are women, it is not surprising that the response is the same for both groups.

The emotional reaction to the word *power* may include feelings of fear, anger, helplessness, submission, conflict, coercion, dominance, or control. This indicates a belief that power is something to be reacted to, rather than exercised. The negative emotional responses demonstrate that some people think of power as bad and something to be avoided. In reviewing the social history of both women and nurses, it is not difficult to understand why power creates negative feelings and defensive reactions. Women and nurses have been less powerful than many other professionals, because they have received low pay and little recognition and have had little decision-making control or influence.

However, power has a positive, constructive use in personal and professional roles. Nurses who have a positive view of power and are comfortable with its uses say they feel assertive, capable, energized, and in control, and have a strong sense of self-esteem. There are benefits to you, as a new nurse, in understanding power and learning ways to establish and use it in your personal and professional roles. Power will help you reach your goals and have more effective interactions with superiors, peers, and subordinates. Power is the tool to use in your advocacy of high-quality patient care and in enhancing your professional image. As a new nurse, you will find power useful in promoting change in your practice and profession.

After recognizing the continuum of emotional responses that may be triggered by the definition of power, a more rational definition can be considered. Let's look at the definition of power on both the personal and professional levels.

On a personal level, power is the drive within a person to overcome both internal and external resistance in reaching one's goals. Power is having control and the capability within oneself to affect change and influence others on the journey toward the goal. This drive is not a desire to exercise control *over others*, but to have control within one's self. Power is having the energy and the means to utilize what is needed to reach the "pot of gold." Power is a way of living, not a way of responding.

On a professional level, power connotes the ability of a nurse to reach goals with patients, to function autonomously, and to effect change within a work setting. Power is knowing how to work within the system and to use the system to reach one's goals. Nursing's desire need not be to dominate the health care system, but to make decisions regarding expectations and policies for nurses. It is interesting to note that both personal and professional power have essentially the same definitions—to have the ability to utilize internal and external resources to reach one's goals. The primary difference between personal and professional definitions of power lies in the difference between its individual and its collective use.

What Are the Sources of Power?

The bases for power come from a variety of sources. For nurses, sources include their numbers, the wholistic approach of nursing, the Nurse Practice Acts, support for cost containment, and a professional power base.

Numbers of Nurses

The largest professional group within the health care system is nursing. In fact, the number is well over a million and a half in the United States. Nursing is represented by many voices. Nurses occupy every corner of the earth and will someday be represented in outer space. Nurses are present in families, work settings, communities, national organizations, and international councils. There is no question of the power of numbers when a job needs to be done and nursing comprises a large number of individuals. The power of numbers is decreased, however, when not all are going in the same direction or addressing common goals. Conversely, power grows with a cooperative effort.

Because nursing has the largest number of health professionals, nurses have the collective power to create an impact on a specific work setting and on the health care system as a whole. To do so, they must work together. Nurses are notorious for working against each other and allowing the profession to be fragmented by various educational backgrounds, geographical divisions, clinical specialties, organizational affiliations, and cultural orientations. Instead, nursing must bring together the contributions of each person and subgroup to exert a united influence. What nurses accomplish in a unified way may be like the pebble dropping in the pond—the ripple spreads throughout the system. Chapter 4, Working Together: Building Effective Work Groups, and Chapter 5, Networking: Developing Professional Support Systems, will discuss more about nurses working together.

The Wholistic Approach

Nursing comprises the greatest percentage of health care professionals, and also is the professional group that relates to people in a wholistic way. Nurses are oriented to the total needs of people 24 hours a day, 7 days a week, and 12 months a year. In their interaction with patients, nurses relate to their social, physical, intellectual, emotional, and spiritual aspects. The nursing process begins with a history and assessment of each of these five aspects, and continues with a wholistic plan, intervention, and evaluation of care. The wholistic approach is the unique contribution of nursing. No other profession takes this approach.

A closer look at the *wholistic approach* emphasizes the value of this method in meeting health care needs. Each individual has five interrelated components: social, physical, intellectual, emotional, and spiritual (Fig. 3-1). The outer circle is the social aspect and is the most superficial, while the spiritual component is the center or core of an individual. When a person is interacting with others, the contact begins on a surface level and progresses to the center. Attempting to interact otherwise would be ineffective and undermine the person's power base. As illustrated in Figure 3-1, the outer layer is *social*. The least intimate interaction with another person is the social acknowledgment, "Hello, my name is. . . . " As acceptance grows, the next level of interaction is *physical*, perhaps a handshake or touch. Then the contact becomes more personal and is performed on an *intellectual* level by asking questions or teaching. As intimacy grows, the response is expressed in

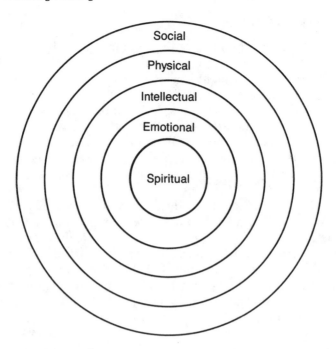

Fig. 3-1.   Wholistic health.

an *emotional* way. When interacting in the most intimate manner, the sharing takes place at the most guarded and vulnerable level, the *spiritual* aspect. At the core are the person's values and beliefs.

When caring for others in a wholistic way, it is important to remember to care for oneself and value the significance of the contribution. Nurses are unduly modest, even self-deprecating about their accomplishments. Along with learning how to give wholistic care, nurses must be equally good at knowing and learning how to care for themselves. Think of a wooden bucket that shrinks and becomes like a sieve when all of the water is emptied out. The same thing happens to people when they pour out their concern and compassion so completely and totally to others that their ability to care eventually vanishes. Ideas for how to keep from totally emptying the bucket and ways to replenish it are discussed elsewhere in this book.

The wholistic approach used by nurses is a source of power in the health care system. Consumers are less willing to accept a "body-shop" approach that deals only with the physical or emotional aspects of illness. Instead, they place value on being evaluated and treated as a whole person. As nurses continue to demonstrate the kind of care demanded by the public, the power nursing has grows.

Nurse Practice Acts

Nursing is one of the professional groups in this country whose general job description is legislated by the state governments. Nurse practice acts give each nurse the definition and parameters of nursing practice. Because of the legislative process, the nurse practice acts provide nursing with an additional source of power in a number of ways.

First, because its definition and description are legislated, nursing practice will be upheld in a court of law. For example, consider a staff nurse in a 200-bed community hospital in a state that has a practice act supporting the teaching role of the nurse. If the physicians in the hospital make it known that they don't like nurses teaching their patients, the nurse could continue to teach patients with confidence that she is practicing within her legal boundaries. The practice acts can be used in addressing the specific policies of the hospital regarding nurses teaching patients.

Second, nurses can expand the definition of nursing practice or the educational requirements for registration through the legislative process. The process of changing a state's act generates power for nurses by unifying their efforts and clarifying the preparation and practice of the profession. While there is need for consensus and agreement by the members, the effort to change one practice act results in benefit to all nurses in that state regardless of their work setting. The change will also be enforced by the power of the state law. For example, school nurses often work alone or as a minority group of health professionals in a school district. They may have great difficulty working with a school board or teachers' union to expand their practice. However, as part of the nursing profession, their practice can be expanded through legislation. The result of the hard work of a few leads to benefits for many. The legislative process makes it more clear what nurses are prepared to do, and enhances the power nurses have in practicing.

Third, while the state practice acts are passed by elected legislators, the wording is usually proposed and directed by nurses. Since many nurses work for employers who may not be nurses, this allows nursing to create its own general job description. Nursing as a profession has more power when the definition and parameters of practice are described by their own members. When a job description specified for a given position is prepared by a non-nurse, it can be evaluated in relationship to the wording of the practice act.

Many times nurses take their state practice acts for granted. They may not even know its content. As a beginning practitioner, it behooves a nurse to know the state practice act, and use it to build the professional power base. It gives the nurse authority to know what behaviors are upheld in the court of law. It can be a vehicle to upgrade and expand the profession. And, it provides guidelines for evaluating job expectations.

Cost Containment

Nurses do not enter the profession to become wealthy. While they are interested in adequate pay and appropriate monetary compensation, nurses' salaries fit into a cost containment program. This is a real strength and a source of power for nurses in an organization.

A new nurse will probably receive a beginning salary between $15,000 and $20,000. This amount is comparable to other beginning professionals such as social workers, physical therapists, and nutritionists. However, unlike the limited contribution of other professionals, nurses provide a broad range of services, including those of many other groups. For a similar salary, a nurse has more potential earning power for the organization. To do more with less fits the definition of *cost containment.*

Look at what nurses contribute to the organization. How much money do nursing services make for the organization? In most cases the cost of nursing care is grouped in the room charge of the hospital bill or office visit in a clinic. Find out how much money patients pay for nursing care in your organization. This information can build a power base in two ways. First, it makes an employer aware of charging too little for the high-quality care rendered by nursing as compared with other professional services. Second, it helps nurses judge more accurately whether the salaries are a fair share of the revenue received for services. In either case, having the financial information helps nurses to enhance their power base when confronting an institution about the amount of money received for nursing service and paid in salaries. Cost containment efforts are enhanced with nurses, and employers benefit from this reality.

Professional Power Base

There is continuing discussion both within and outside the nursing profession about whether or not nursing possesses the power base necessary to achieve recognition as a major force in meeting the nation's health care goals. Some people question whether nursing even has the capability to obtain power, and if nurses know how to use power to influence others. While the nursing profession has problems as the result of the ways people have used, misused, and abused power, individual nurses throughout history have demonstrated power in their nursing roles.

There are two ways a nurse exhibits power: through influence and through control. A nurse has power to influence others' (patients' and co-workers') attitudes, ideas, and decisions. A nurse has control of patients, health care resources, and the environment. However, the amount of influence and control an individual nurse has depends on the power base established in a particular setting or situation. A *professional power base* is generally derived from four origins: reward, expert, referent, and positional power.

For nurses, *reward* power is gained by giving patients high-quality health care for their health dollar. These rewards are exemplified by explanations of the plan of care, a few minutes spent listening to fears and concerns, an unrequired phone call to an anxious family member, a suggestion of community resources, or some helpful teaching materials. This kind of care is valued and eagerly accepted by the health care consumer. It is coming to be expected in health care, and nurses are prepared and available to meet it. Health care consumers are seeking services that extend beyond physical intervention to acknowledge their individual needs, validate their self-worth, and treat them with dignity. It is difficult for consumers to find health care providers who respect their right to make informed decisions and value their ability to use information. As the competition within health care grows, institutions are eager to employ professionals who provide the kind of care consumers want. When a person is sick, the need is for someone to help select the best care, to evaluate the effects of treatment, to support and nurture throughout the period of crisis, and to educate and explore options for treatment. What professional group in American society besides nursing is prepared to respond to all of these needs? The service nurses provide is comprehensive and unique. Nurses are the patient advocates, and the interventions of the nurse greatly influence the course of events for a patient and family. For these reasons, nurses have rewards that build their power base.

The *expert* power of nurses is a second base for power. As identified earlier, most nursing programs provide the nurse with a broadly based education in the biologic, behavioral, and social sciences. The clinical experiences that coordinate with the academic component help the student to apply theory when working in a variety of settings. Many nursing students also seek concurrent employment as a nursing assistant or in a related role in a health care setting. As a result of these classroom and clinical experiences, nurses have expert power from two sources—knowledge of nursing and knowledge of the health care system.

The first source of expert power for nurses lies in the breadth and depth of nursing knowledge. Nurses care for people in a total way, and are aware of the medical problems, the social conflicts, the learning needs and abilities, the emotional strengths and limitations, and the values and beliefs of the person. Of all the health professionals with whom the patient interacts, it is the nurse who is the expert on the person as a total being. The skill of a nurse practitioner is based on a wholistic approach to patient care. This approach is the essence of nursing, and is what sets nurses apart from other health care professionals. This expertise increases the dependency of an employer on nurses because the needed service is not available from other professionals. This dependency increases the power nurses have.

The second source of expert power for nurses is their knowledge of the health care system. Through the educational experience, nurses are acquainted with other disciplines and with institutional and community agencies. If a patient problem is related to finances, nurses know whom to contact. If the need is for supplies or services, nurses know where to find them, or know someone who can. From their contacts with numerous health care professionals, nurses can suggest resources to support the patient and family. Nurses develop power based on the knowledge of individual health care providers and of how the system works.

A third base of professional power, *referent* power, is based on the psychological process of identification. If a nurse has physical or personal qualities similar to those of someone with power in a patient's life, the patient transfers the power to the nurse. To many patients, nurses are most often associated with a parent or a nurturing, caring person. How often have you heard a patient say that you remind him of a person by whom he felt cared for or loved? This association with a loving, concerned person provides the nurse with an additional power base. The nurse becomes significant, trusted and valued, and a referent base of power is established.

Furthermore, while nurses are educated to their careers, they are socialized to be parents. From infancy, children learn to be nurturing, understanding, and able to respond to the needs of others. They cuddle their dolls and are sympathetic or empathetic with their playmates. They also learn to be self-reliant and aggressive. The qualities of compassion and strength may be demonstrated by the same person. Toughness and tenderness are opposite sides of the coin, but not mutually exclusive behaviors. One suggestion here is to acknowledge the perception of nurses as surrogate mothers or parents, in addition to being strong and tough, and build a power base from that source.

Another suggestion is to interpret the parent role in a positive way. Like a supportive parent, the nurse provides reassurance and concern at a time of crisis. As a knowledgeable protector, the nurse provides explanations, suggestions, and alternatives. Like a parent who fosters self-esteem and personal growth, the nurse helps a patient through the problem-solving process without taking over. Not unlike a parent who guides a child through the stages of growth and development, the nurse fosters personal growth and maturity. Even if much younger than the patient, the nurse gains a power base from a nurturing role. The key is to ascertain that the patient is in a dependency role, but not to encourage or force the person into a submissive position.

Positional power, a fourth base of power, is based on the position held within an organization or on authority inherent in that position. Positional power is also known as *legitimate* power. Positions in our society often designated as having legitimate power include president, general, and supreme court justice. The position of a physician also carries with it positional power. What about that of a nurse?

When this question was asked of a group of senior nursing students, the room was silent. Then, an insightful student stated that a nurse does not have the same amount of power as a physician in ordering procedures and prescribing treatment for a patient, but as a means for communicating with the physician and within an organization, a patient and family may see the nurse as having a significant amount of power. As a patient advocate and guide through the health care system the nurse is in a power position.

Nurses are in a position to have an impact on health care costs. As health care benefit costs have escalated for employers, companies are looking to resources to help eliminate unnecessary medical and surgical treatment, decrease the length of hospital stays, and provide high-quality, low-cost health care alternatives. In response to this need, companies are developing and marketing this kind of service. The most effective organizations utilize nurses to educate, counsel, and suggest health care alternatives to employees. In this role, nurses have a tremendous amount of power with hospitals, agencies, and physicians in controlling the amount the third-party payer of the medical plan will pay. Nurses today have an opportunity to be on the cutting edge of establishing positional power within the profession to provide lower-cost, higher-quality health care.

Traditionally, nurses have not wielded a great deal of power within institutions or with physicians. The stereotype of the nurse as a handmaiden and subordinate is still present. However, on an individual level, as a patient care coordinator and in specific settings, nurses may have legitimate authority in their positions. The present trend in health care management is expanding the positional power of nurses. As health care dollars are being controlled by nurses through employee benefit programs and through increasingly efficient patient care delivery, nurses are beginning to develop a stronger power base with the public and the health care industry.

Referring back to the beginning of this chapter, how much of a professional power base does the new nurse, Karen, have? Although a newcomer, she just completed some short but first-hand experience in a variety of health care settings. She provides quality health care with her knowledge of both wellness and illness and her ability to respond to the wholistic needs of patients. She is keenly aware of the problem of care that is less than adequate, and is eager to help patients find high-quality resources. Her expert power base has both a strong and weak component. She is strongest in having the most current and broadest knowledge base she will ever have in her career. The weakness results from a limited amount of experience to enhance and strengthen her knowledge. The strength of her referent power base is dependent on the association patients have with her being a nurturing, supportive person. Certain of her physical attributes and personal characteristics have a more profound impact than others. How significant a legitimate power base Karen has depends on the environment in which she practices and on public response to her performance. From each of these sources, she is beginning to form a good professional power base.

How Do I Build a Personal Power Base?

The process of building or strengthening a personal power base follows a wholistic approach. As a whole person, you have social, physical, intellectual, emotional, and spiritual aspects. You build your power base in the same manner in which you relate to a patient in a progressive way. Refer back to Figure 3-1 at the beginning of this chapter. As indicated on the diagram, you begin on the social level, the most superficial, and continue toward the central or spiritual level.

Social Level

As you establish the outer aspect or social level of your power base, build relationships. Develop friendships with people you value, who value you and contribute happiness and joy to your life. Choose friends who validate your worth and help you maintain a strong sense of self-esteem. Establish relationships with others that have a balance between giving and taking, fun times and serious discussions, closeness and separation. Find out what others need, and when possible provide it. Networking with other nurses is a valuable way to build professional relationships. Although you are an individual, it is also important to foster significant personal and professional relationships. Developing social skills and contacts expands your power base by giving you a support system, a source for validating who you are, and an opportunity to interact with others whom you value.

Physical Level

Having a strong body supports a strong power base by giving you the appearance and an internal sense of health, strength, and well-being. However, maintaining and developing your physique takes some effort. One way is to practice the familiar triangle you teach to the diabetic patient. The triangle illustrated in Figure 3-2, illustrates how to build a strong, powerful body.

Have a regular plan of physical exercise. At least three times a week, for 20 to 30 minutes, do some kind of physical activity (run, swim, bicycle, jump

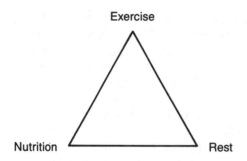

Fig. 3-2. Foundation for physical health.

rope, or dance) to stimulate your cardiovascular, respiratory, and musculoskeletal systems. All through your life cycles your body needs physical stimulation. The end of childhood does not herald the end of the need for your body to run, jump, and play. Fuel your body with foods from the basic four food groups. Avoid salt, sugar, fat, and junk food as much as possible. Remember the analogy of not expecting your car to run on inadequate fuel, so why expect that of your body? Be sure to rest as well. Not only do you need an adequate amount of sleep each day, but you also need to take measures to release stress and tension. As with a rubber band, a certain amount of stress is necessary for you to function optimally, but too much can cause you to snap. (Specific ways to deal with stress and tension are discussed in Chapter 6, Stress Management: Self-Care Skills for the New Nurse.) Your body is priceless; you can't go out and buy a new one, so don't abuse it. Your body is a powerhouse; make it an example of health and physical fitness. Caring for your body empowers you with both an external look and an internal feeling of personal power.

Intellectual Level

The educational program of most nursing schools produces a graduate with a strong understanding of the physical, biologic and behavioral sciences. New nurses have skills in nursing process, research, teaching, and coordination of resources. But don't let your learning stop with your basic educational curriculum. Further your knowledge in both formal academic programs and informal continuing education in order to strengthen your mind. When possible, go to the library to read the literature from other professions, so that you can relate to co-workers with insight and understanding. Round out your general knowledge beyond the professional resources and be familiar with what the public is reading, so you will be able to respond to questions or concerns. Keep up with what is going on in politics, economics, international affairs, the theater, and music. One requirement of a professional is to have a broad general knowledge base. Read a fun novel or a scholarly assay; be aware of all kinds of writing. There is power in words and ideas.

Learn how to acquire and implement power in your life by observing powerful people around you. There are splendid examples of power in the academic and clinical worlds that you can apply to your nursing practice. The successes of nurses are described in the professional publications, as well as daily newspapers and lay magazines. Consider how nurses whom you know are emerging into power positions. Study what they do and learn something from each of them. Learning expands your sense of power by making you knowledgeable in nursing and intellectually informed about the people and world around you.

Emotional Level

The first step in developing a strong emotional power base is to be aware of your emotions. You can achieve this in several ways. Some people are reflective and introspective enough to be able to learn about their emotions independently. Others utilize group process and join a consciousness-raising group to develop emotional insight. Still others seek professional guidance from a therapist or counselor. Some are fortunate to be in relationships that provide helpful feedback and constructive confrontation. All of these are means to developing insight into one's own feelings, whether they be anger, sadness, gladness, or just fear.

Your experience in nursing school was a continual educational process of discovering the emotional responses you had to cancer, surgery, birth, death, rape, resuscitation, abortion, neglect, and other experiences. (It is no wonder a nursing education is so emotionally draining—it is like going through years of intensive therapy!) By knowing your feelings, you can stay in control in adverse situations. It helps others to see you calm and capable under stress. Knowing your own emotional responses to circumstances cultivates your ability to deal with complex situations. It doesn't matter what position you are in; if you cannot cope, you cannot influence others! Being aware of your feelings and developing emotional control confers power. When you are familiar with your feelings and accepting of what you feel, you are able to support and be a resource to others.

Spiritual Level

When the spiritual aspect is discussed, it is frequently equated with a specific denominational group or religious affiliation. However, the focus here is on the core of your being that is described and exemplified by your personal values and beliefs. While these values and beliefs may have been greatly influenced by your religious experiences and affiliations, they have also been formed by your parents, peers, political leaders, teachers, and others. You have been influenced by all you have heard, seen, and felt. As a result of all you have known and experienced in life, you develop your individual value and belief systems. (Chapter 2, Values Clarification: Making Choices, expands on this topic further.)

Similar to the way you develop emotional strength, you build a strong spiritual core by knowing what you value and believe. On a personal basis, clarify what is important to you in life. Sometimes a way to identify what is important is to ask yourself, "How would I spend my life if I only had 6 months left to live?" Who would be the significant people I would want to be with? What would I want to accomplish? Where would I want to be? Why would some activities be more important than others?" The answers to these questions provide you with clues to what is important to you.

Another way to get in touch with what you believe and value is to write down what guides your decision making and gives you a sense of direction. You may want to call this writing your philosophy. For many, an understanding of these guideposts is not accomplished on a Saturday afternoon in the sunshine. Rather, with some soul-searching from time to time, or during painful periods, glimpses of truth emerge and a framework develops.

As a nurse, think about what attracted you to the profession. Go beyond such reasons as the ability to find employment, the money you would make, or the desire to please a relative or friend. Although these reasons may tell you some truths about yourself, go deeper. What do you have to contribute to humanity? In what way can you make this world a better place to live? Where do you want your career to take you? Being a nurse may be the avenue you chose because it is the best way for you to exercise what you value and believe. Making decisions and acting on the basis of your values and beliefs increases your power base. It results in consistency in your behavior, personal and professional growth, and commitment to what you think and do.

Looking back on Karen at the beginning of this chapter you gain a sense of a part of her personal power base. Socially, she has relationships with people who provide help and support. Physically, she must have a strong body or she could not make it through the clinical rotations of a nursing program. Intellectually, she has a broad knowledge base gained from her nursing education and a previous degree in anthropology. Emotionally, she is in touch with her fears and joys. Spiritually, she seems to value control and self-direction. Her education in both anthropology and nursing is strongly suggestive of an interest in people and a belief in their value and dignity. Her personal power base has balance, as she begins to expand her professional base.

How Do I Use Power?

The preceding definition of power and discussion of what power is, served as a framework for exploring the most important thing to know about power, *how to use it*. As identified at the beginning of this chapter, power is an internal drive that motivates all aspects of your being to be in control of your goals, to utilize resources, and to influence others. The following discussion begins with how to use power within yourself, with your supervisors, and with your subordinates. Then the use of power with physicians, health care administrators, and the public will be examined.

Using Power within Yourself

The first step in using power is knowing what you want and how to get it. As a new nurse, Karen is using her power when she makes a commitment to a career path. By determining where she wants her nursing career to take her, what clinical areas will give her the experience she needs, what position will move her toward the one she wants to attain, and what additional education will qualify her for the desired status, she is using power. When you have this kind of insight, you have power. In order to figure out what you want, do some soul-searching and consider your options and alternatives. By being honest about your fears and desires and exploring the implications of each possibility, you learn more clearly your sense of direction. When your goals are clear, you can proceed to take action to meet them. Determine what motivates and helps you to move toward your goals. Put your internal and external resources to use. Power comes from knowing where you want to go and how to get there.

The second step in using power is to package yourself as a person with power. How you look to others and the effect you have on them influences how you feel about yourself. It also influences how others feel about you. In most clinical settings, nurses wear uniforms. The uniform may be the traditional all-white attire from head to toe or an adaptation such as a colorful top with white pants or skirt. However, a person dressed in either of these fashions does not represent a power figure in our society. There are two approaches to this problem. If your organization permits, wear a clinical lab coat, as physicians and many other professionals do, over sensible street clothes. Or, if you must follow a dress code that requires a traditional nursing attire, be meticulous. Wear a tailored uniform or a white blazer; wear simple jewelry. Although a nursing uniform is not equated with power, dress in a way that reflects your personal sense of power. When you work in a clinical setting that does not require you to wear a uniform, dress in ways that reflect authority and influence. Again, wear tailored clothes and subdued colors, and avoid looking as though you are going to a party or, at the other extreme, an athletic event.

In addition to dress, another part of your package is your nonverbal communication. Several aspects of body language communicate power. Think of an oak tree, and have your body move with the tree image in your mind. Plant your feet firmly whether you are standing, doing a task, conversing, or sitting. Regardless of your position, your body should be in balance and your posture erect. Also, as a tree moves in response to the breezes, your gestures should be graceful and appropriate. Like a tree on a windless day, you should be calm and imposing, reflecting control, while being alert to what is going on around you. By mirroring the oak tree your body language communicates power.

The third step in using power within yourself is adapting. No matter how clear your goals, and strategies for meeting them, in the real world there are many forces that are beyond your control. Therefore, like the captain of a ship, it is important that you be flexible and adaptive. As a ship goes out on a voyage, the captain has a course charted. However, storms and other circumstances and events may interfere and cause the course to be altered.

Adaptation takes many forms such as assertiveness, acceptance, and directness. A nurse with power strives to demonstrate adult behaviors. Interactions with others take place on an adult-to-adult level whenever possible. As discussed in the chapter on assertiveness, a powerful nurse uses assertiveness skills much of the time. While submissive or aggressive behaviors may be chosen in some circumstances, these are not the most often used. A powerful nurse is proficient in the use of assertiveness skills, and has a firmly established belief in the right to be assertive. However, in the real work world, there are two groups of people who often require different kinds of adaptation: her supervisors and subordinates.

With supervisors, the nurse frequently manifests power by adapting in a more accepting way. You may frequently find supervisors and head nurses who have been socialized and acculturated to relate as an authoritarian parent. They expect those beneath them to be obedient. Being able to adapt to the authoritarian style in an accepting way, with awareness of and a choice in what you are doing, is using power within yourself. More ways of using power with supervisors are discussed later in this chapter.

With subordinates, the nurse often manifests power by adapting in a more direct way. Those under you may expect you to relate to them in a more aggressive way. If you can adapt to this more authoritarian role when subordinates expect it, you have more power with them. This is explored later in terms of leadership skills with subordinates.

Using Power with Supervisors

Your supervisor is the person to whom you report, who tells you what to do, and who evaluates how well you did it. It may seem contradictory to talk about using power with your supervisor when the organizational structure and job descriptions make it very clear which position has power over which. There are some ways, however, that you can use power with your supervisor. These strategies help you utilize the resourcefulness of your boss to reach your personal goals.

One way to use power with your supervisor is to be supportive. When you are interviewed in applying for the position, you have an opportunity to learn what the person who is hiring you wants to accomplish and believes to be important. One consideration in deciding whether to take a position is to decide if you can be supportive of the philosophy, goals, and expectations of your supervisor. These expectations are reflected in the questions, "What causes you to be absent from work? How do you work with others? Have you conducted inservices? What tools do you use in patient teaching?" You also learn what is expected by asking your own specific questions about when assignments and schedules are made, how charge responsibility is determined, how conflict is handled, what committee work is designated. By knowing what your boss is trying to accomplish and what is expected of you, you are in a position to help him or her to succeed. By having a mutual interest in the goals your supervisor is trying to reach, and by making suggestions for ways to meet them, you become more valued. Because you are willing to cooperate, there is less need to directly monitor what you do. More independence means more power.

Another way to be supportive is knowing when to back off from your individual goals or your own ideas. You must be ready to support your boss and recognize when to redirect your focus back to what he or she thinks is important. Needless to say, this whole process is easier when you have a manager who knows his or her own goals. If your manager's goals are unclear, help clarify them by asking what is expected of you. Ask what special committee or projects you could work on. Identify problems on your unit and suggest possible solutions. Offer suggestions for ways things could go more smoothly in your work setting. If your ideas are not agreeable to your boss, drop them. Give your boss praise when her or his efforts are on target. Remember, you are learning how to work the system when you help your superior to look good, and that increases your power.

Another way to use power with your superior is to indicate you have an interest in learning. Managers like people who want to learn, and managers are often good people from whom to learn. As mentioned earlier, many people in management positions feel they have a parental role. They want to pass on their wisdom and insights gained from many years of experience to those worthy. You should profit from using this resource to meet your learning needs. *Power is knowing your goals and utilizing resources to meet them.* Ask your head nurse for ways you can become more proficient at conducting inservices. Acknowledge when your patient assessments are not as thorough as you like, and ask your supervisor to support ways to build your assessment skills. When you have a problem, ask your manager for suggestions or alternatives. A boss wants to be seen as an authority figure and a valued resource. The more your manager sees you as a learner interested in what she or he is teaching, the more power you have to utilize with your boss.

Establishing a record for yourself as a successful employee, is another way to have power with your superior. Become known as a person who can cope well with critical problems. In all work settings there are times of crisis, and a boss looks to the person who can respond knowledgeably, and in a calm, confident manner. Be an employee who gets your work done thoroughly and on time. Let your manager see that you are productive and that, when given responsibility, you accept it. The better your record of accountability, the more power you have with you boss.

You also exercise power with your superior when you develop relationships with others. This is a form of referent power. Network with recognized authorities and people in power positions. While the discussion of networking is in another chapter, the importance of it is worth mentioning here. Establish these relationships by being on committees and making appointments with key people to learn more about their area of expertise. Power is also present in the relationships with people you know. The connections you have made are useful to both you and your supervisor.

Using Power with Subordinates

As a nurse, you may think it incredible that you have subordinates in your first position. However, there are most likely nursing students, nurses' aides, orderlies, and unit secretaries looking to you for direction. And, before you know it, there will be new staff members whom you will be asked to orient or precept. How do you effectively use power with subordinates? The power you have to meet your goals through the resourcefulness of your subordinates is gained by means of giving praise and suggestions, using the art of delegation, and setting some personal restrictions.

First, look at the power that comes with the title of nurse. This is your positional power. Power is most apparent when the position is recognized in the organizational chart to be superior. As a staff nurse, you are in the superior position to a nurse's aide, and unquestionably you have more power. Avoid any inclination to use your influence in a negative way. Do not allow your nursing role to become one of an autocrat who maintains control over those who are subordinate. While power rests in having control, that control becomes negative or destructive when used without regard for the impact it has on others. Some characteristics of the destructive use of power are listed below. Avoid:

Making statements such as "Just do as I said!" or "This is the way we do it here!"

Developing antagonistic feelings toward your superior or subordinates, thus draining energy that could be directed more productively

Coercing people into doing what is demanded rather than encouraging them to be self-directed

Inhibiting creativity so that the staff is task oriented

Encouraging subordinates to become dependent rather than independent

If you manifest these characteristics, it is usually a clue that you are using the power of your position without a strong base of personal and professional power as described at the beginning of this chapter. In contrast, if you manifest the opposite, more positive behavior, it reflects that you are practicing from a firm power base. Even in a beginning staff position, you can use your power with subordinates in a positive way. Some of the positive ways include giving praise and suggestions, and developing the art of delegation. In addition, recognize ways subordinates can progress in their positions, and be supportive of their development.

It was mentioned earlier that some of your subordinates will probably place you in a parentlike role. While you will be more successful as a nurturing parent than an authoritarian one, your two broad areas for using power with subordinates are in indicating your expectations when you need assistance and in giving praise when it is earned. The style you develop in helping your subordinates to improve their performance and grow into more responsibility will be strictly your own. Through both praise and constructive criticism, you help your subordinates to feel secure because you relate a sense of being in control. Your expectations must be clear, so the subordinate's energy isn't wasted on guessing, and the personal and professional growth of subordinates is guided. Working together or brainstorming with your subordinates to define what you want them to do can promote creativity in their behavior and increase their commitment to the desired task. As you nurture the growth of subordinates, your power grows also.

Delegating authority is another use of power with your subordinates. You have goals to reach and responsibilities to meet, but you have a limited amount of time and energy. Power is gained by using the resources assigned to you to get the job done. However, people will not necessarily do what you expect unless you clearly communicate your expectations to them. The steps to delegating are as follows:

1. Define the tasks that need to be done.
2. Identify the staff members available and their skills.
3. Communicate clearly what results you expect in the assignment.
4. Give a specific time framework for completion of tasks.
5. Provide feedback—suggestions and praise—as progress is made in implementing the delegated tasks.
6. Evaluate the results of the assignment at its completion.
7. Document what was done.

As a new nurse in a clinical setting, one of your job expectations is to make out assignments for your subordinates. In doing so, things to consider include the following:

Match the assignment with the skills of the staff person.

Balance the assignment between familiar patients and new and challenging ones.

Recognize individual preferences and areas of expertise.

Be reasonable about what to expect in a given time frame.

Expect others to accomplish what they are asked to do.

When defining the tasks to be done and determining the available staff members and their skills, incorporate all of the considerations above. This requires thorough assessment. Listen to reports. Ask questions of both patients and staff prior to planning how the work for the day will be done. After assessing, it is best to put the work plan in writing and supplement it with verbal explanations. This way, it is clear exactly who is accountable when you evaluate what is accomplished.

The time required for completing work is usually well understood by the staff members who work on a unit. However, occasionally there are people who are not familiar with the usual routine, or the usual expectations are changed. In such cases, stating when to do various tasks is helpful.

As staff members are progressing with their assignments, it is important to provide them with feedback. Let them know what they are doing well. It is a source of support and motivation. Your interest in their work also conveys the message that you think what they are doing is important. In addition to recognizing high-quality performance, provide subordinates with suggestions for ways to improve their work. Take advantage of opportunities to teach your subordinates something new.

During the course of the day, or of your shift, evaluate the effectiveness of the work. This helps others see the need to be flexible as the situation demands, and prevents people from getting into a rut. Is what is being done consistent with the work plan and specific care plan for each patient? Is the activity of the day consistent with the overall focus of the unit? Is what is expected to be accomplished getting done? Once authority is delegated, the staff person is responsible for getting it done. In evaluating the effectiveness of the work, it is also good to consider if changes need to be made. If the condition of a patient changes or the subordinate cannot care for all of the patients originally assigned, be ready to adapt your plan. A plan of action is not written in stone, but rather in pencil.

The last step in delegation is to document what was done. This includes updating care plans, patient records, and log books. Documentation should not be regarded as a tedious, boring nuisance; it is a key part of your job. The law does not recognize that care was given unless it is documented. Insurance companies bill hospitals but do not pay for charges when nurses do not document the follow-through of ordered care. One hospital was not paid for 90 of the 139 IVs ordered for a patient, because the insurance company could only find 49 IVs documented. The saying "no job is complete until the paperwork is done" is certainly true of delegation.

As the person delegating, you must remember that you are accountable for what you delegate. Although you assign patient care responsibilities to a subordinate, you are responsible to see that the care is given. When delegating you must expect your staff members to do what they are assigned to do. This requires confidence that the person to whom you delegate can succeed with the assignment. As you become more effective in implementing the steps of delegating, your power grows and you are more able to utilize your resources to meet your goals.

In using power with subordinates, it is helpful to consider some personal restrictions. To maintain a power position with those working under you, it is best to limit relationships to a professional, working level. Having social relationships with those you direct weakens the authority and influence you have over them in the work setting. This does not eliminate friendly interactions, but they should be limited to the workplace.

Finally, when interacting with your subordinates, limit the amount of information you disclose regarding your personal life. Again, power is weakened when working relationships become personal rather than professional. Focusing on work and professional matters while on the job helps maintain the power you have. Effective nurses are willing to divide their attention between personal and professional matters. On the job, the attention is directed toward attaining work goals and developing effective professional relationships.

Power is a means of exerting control and influence over your individual as well as your work-group goals. The preceding section focused on the individual goals of the nurse. Now the subject is the use of power in meeting goals of nursing practice as they relate to groups of nurses.

It is often said that nursing has failed to progress as a profession because nurses are a fragmented group. Disputes over basic educational requirements, the absence of commitments to nursing careers, and the socialization process of women are some of the factors contributing to the fragmentation. In order to win recognition and respect from physicians, health care administrators, and the public, this splintering must be replaced by groups of nurses working together on common goals. Although it is important that nurses develop individual power bases, it is groups of nurses sharing goals and working the system cooperatively to meet their common goals that gives the nursing profession power.

Using Power with Physicians

Consensus would not be difficult to obtain if you were to ask any group of people to decide who are the most powerful, physicians or nurses. Because of their current status in our society, physicians would readily be acknowledged as having more power than nurses. This does not mean that nurses are powerless. We do have power to use with physicians; we just need to acknowledge it and use it.

As a nurse, you are educated to do a wholistic history and assessment of the patient and/or family problem, and make a nursing diagnosis. You are prepared to make a plan for ways to resolve the problem, implement the plan, teach the patient, and evaluate your effectiveness. Do you feel that the medical diagnosis or prescription for a patient's problem is more important than your nursing services in helping the patient get well? Public opinion probably would answer in the affirmative. Knowing nursing's impact on healing and keeping people well to begin with, why do we allow this preception to continue? Granted, for approximately 10% to 25% of people with complex medical problems, a physician is probably best prepared to intervene. However, in diagnosing early symptoms of illness, you as a nurse are well prepared to intervene.

In collaborating with physicians in the work setting, you need to establish and use your clout. By asserting your capabilities and demonstrating your skills, your prestige and the prestige of nurses in general increases. Physicians respond well to nurses who have such attributes of power as knowledge, sensitivity, initiative, poise, and diplomacy. You consistently need to use these characteristics in your practice. Recognize that not all physicians have been jointly educated with nurses, nor have they had an opportunity to work in a joint practice with nurses. Some physicians carry a tainted perception of nurses as handmaidens dependent upon or less professional than physicians. As an individual nurse, you increase your influence with, and recognition from, physicians by interacting confidently in your role and by practicing in an accountable way. When you deal with physicians in this complimentary fashion, your personal power is augmented.

As the public becomes increasingly sophisticated in matters of health and disease, there is heightened personal awareness of changes in the body. Often, if the early signs and symptoms of stress due to any social, physical, intellectual, emotional, or spiritual cause are prevented or recognized and treated (as nurses are well prepared to do) the person avoids becoming so ill that the services of a physician are necessary. Think of wellness and illness on a continuum. As Figure 3-3 indicates, the opportunities for nurses to be the primary professionals helping an individual move back into a state of wellness are significant and numerous. Figure 3-3 indicates areas where nurses effectively make an impact on keeping people well or on helping them to reverse the progression toward illness.

Moving along the continuum, we find those people who are not enjoying wellness, but who are not really ill. They are experiencing early signs and symptoms of illness. These are people who have tests done, but no cause can be found for their problem. They act out of sorts or verbalize complaints. They may be abusing themselves in some way. Because of the wholistic orientation of nursing, a nurse is the ideal health professional to respond to these early signs and symptoms. If the person enters into the health care system, such as a clinic, the services of a nurse are probably sufficient to resolve the problem

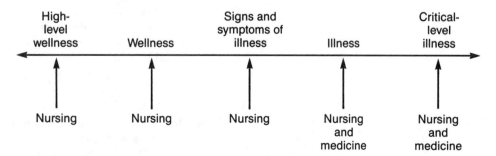

Fig. 3-3. *Wellness-illness continuum.*

without further medical intervention. A challenging way to expand nursing power is to identify nontraditional settings where nurses can meet these needs. A senior citizen center, a day care center, or a factory are some examples of places where nurses can "set up shop." Or, how about in a company, focusing on the health care management of a specific group of employees? Being assertive and creative in reaching the patients who manifest early signs of illness develops the power and visibility of the nursing profession.

In the illness section III are those people who enter the traditional illness-care settings, such as a clinic, general hospital, or skilled or extended-care facility. Nurses are the principle care providers in these settings, with medical support. While these are the areas in which the nurse-doctor games are played, it is apparent that nursing and medicine have different and complementary roles. When nurses identify professional goals and are accountable for meeting them, nursing power is more evident to the physician with whom they work. If you work in a traditional illness-care setting, enhance your professional power by clarifying your nursing role, demonstrating nursing skills, and being a knowledgeable health care provider.

The critical illness group is at the far right of the wellness-illness continuum. This group includes people who are in intensive care and acute care settings. Here again, the traditional roles of nurses and physicians can cause some tension, and power struggles can be intense. Physicians often have a more primary role in diagnosing and treating, and nurses are more supportive by implementing physician's orders. However, as nurses develop confidence in nursing's contribution to the care of these patients, a better balance of power between medicine and nursing results.

As you consider the broad scope of patients' health care needs, remember that there is a lot of territory left for nurses to pioneer. As a new nurse, it is wise to initially get a job in a traditional setting to help you build your skills and confidence and define your career goals. Then join with other nurses who share your goals, and start moving in the direction in which you want to go. Utilize all the resources you can find, including those in the traditional health care system. Physicians are your partners. Your roles are different, but they are complementary. Expect recognition and respect. If you don't encounter it, continue to assert your capabilities and demonstrate your skills. Use your power as a vital link in the health care system.

Using Power with Health Care Administrators

Because most nurses are employees of large organizations and do not practice autonomously, they often feel vulnerable and controlled. Individual nurses exercise little control or influence in determining policies, employment benefits, salary, or environmental conditions. However, as the largest group of professionals usually employed in a health care setting, nurses can work collectively with each other to exercise power in their place of employment.

What is your opinion of unionization in nursing? Some people think of unions and work contract negotiations as unprofessional or simply "bad." However, by joining together and utilizing these processes, nurses exert a significant amount of power as employees. Power is activated when individual nurses join the nursing organization and participate in the collective bargaining process. Recognize that belonging to an organized union reinforces your role as an employee, but the unified effort produces power to use with the employer.

In nonunion settings the collective effort of nurses can also be effective with administration. For example, if your job description is ambiguous and nonsupportive of the kind of practice you value, or there is an inconsistent process for approving attendance at seminars and conferences, a way of dealing with these problems is for those of you affected to join forces. Through group process and functioning as a task group, you can determine what steps to take in initiating a change. In a united effort, the plan for change or clarification is presented to your supervisors. While an individual voice is often ignored, the united voice of a group is more difficult for an administrator to discount.

There is a growing number of nurses in administrative positions who also have masters degrees in Business Administration or Nursing Administration. The dual background of nursing and business prepares these nurses for administrative positions in health care institutions. When functioning effectively, the master's-prepared nursing administrator is eager to utilize the high-quality, cost-effective services of nurses to develop a productive nursing department. As a new staff nurse it is to your benefit to have a nursing executive who understands nursing process from experience and who values the nurse-patient relationship. However, concern with efficiency and productivity can be taken to extremes, so be aware of your vulnerability to abuse. Be alert to expectations to practice in an expanded role that impinges on medical jurisdiction. Decide whether your job description supports a wholistic approach to patient care, and not just a list of tasks to meet physical needs. Also, consider whether your salary reflects adequate payment for the quantity and quality of care expected. When you encounter nursing administrators who have forgotten their nursing roots, it may disturb you. Don't let the advanced degree intimidate you in responding. Clarify the boundaries of your professional practice. Be assertive about your wholistic approach to patient care. Confront the issue of an equitable and appropriate salary. Suggest to the administrators that they foster the advancement of the nursing profession in the business of health care.

Through membership in the American Nurses' Association, nurses are represented in a professional way with employers and with legislators who decide on laws that control nursing practice. As a new graduate, join your professional organization. Become active in supporting the political activities of the organization. With health care administrators on the national, state, local, and institutional levels, a nurse has little power alone. However, as a professional organization, nurses can use their collective power in the employment and legislation processes to influence employers and legislators.

Using Power with the Public

People are greatly influenced in their perception of nursing as a profession by what they see in the media. It is well documented that television, newspapers, magazines, and novels do little to enhance the power image of nurses. People develop a more realistic image of the power of nurses when they encounter them in real situations. In the sheltered moments of birth, death, pain, and need, patients see nurses as confident, competent care givers. The challenge for nursing is to transfer the image of power associated with patients' experiences to the public mind. Nursing must rise to this challenge by having confidence in the value of what nurses contribute, in order to convince the public of the power of the profession. Then initiative is needed to portray the reality of nursing practice more accurately in films, in the theater, and in literature.

Before others will acknowledge your individual power, you must acknowledge it yourself. Power is an internal force and a part of your personality. It is manifested in your professional performance. Knowing your job and doing it well is a key component of a powerful image.

Although you may not do this during your first year in nursing practice, you may wish to consider ways to practice nursing independently of physician and institutional controls. Support legislation that funds independent nursing care and third-party payment for nursing service. You may think of becoming a partner with a physician in a joint practice, making an equal contribution and taking a share of the profits. Be as influential as you can with your legislator by keeping him or her informed about health care issues and your positions on these issues. Work cooperatively with physicians, neither as their subordinate nor as their superior, but as a partner in providing high-quality health care.

The traditional work setting for nurses is hospitals. The acute and critical care provided in a hospital continues to furnish excellent opportunities for a new nurse to learn, develop, and hone professional skills. Staff nursing allows you to deal with the total needs of patients and their families during the crisis of illness. However, the hospital is not the only setting in which to find people who need nursing care. Treating illness is also not the only role for nurses. You can exercise creativity in choosing how to carry out your nursing role. One means is to educate the public about wellness and find a role that supports health. You might consider being a nurse entrepreneur in a variety of settings outside the hospital or clinic. Assess possibilities in schools, churches, day care centers, industry, or business. Reflect again on the wellness-illness continuum (Fig. 3-3). Where could you make your best contribution to health care?

Alone, you can certainly accomplish something significant. With others, you may achieve even more. One possibility is establishing a women's health center that provides education and meets the unique health care needs of women from adolescence to senescence. There are important nursing functions not only in treating illness, but also in supporting wellness. Nurses often make effective managers because of their skills in working with people and getting things done. Capitalize on your personal and professional strengths as you explore your options. There are opportunities for practicing nursing in many nontraditional situations.

While planning your use of power in your personal and professional roles, reflect back on Karen at the beginning of this chapter. Will Karen have the power in her nursing role that she felt in her personal life? The answer is yes and no. The day she graduates from nursing school she will not enter a profession known for its power. However, Karen does have the opportunity to set professional goals and practice nursing from a power base. She can seek the positions and additional education that will prepare her for her goals. She can learn to use the health care system to create change. Beginning on a patient-care level, she can influence others to get what she needs to provide the most comprehensive, highest-quality care for her patients. She can join with other nurses for support and to meet the common goals of the individuals and profession. So can you.

Power is not a way of responding to those around you. Power is a way of practicing nursing.

Bibliography

Ashley J: This I believe about power in nursing. Nurs Outlook, October 1973, pp 637–641

Boyle K: Power in nursing: A collaborative approach. Nurs Outlook, May/June 1984, pp 164–167

DeSantis G: Power, tactics, and the professionalization process. Nurs Health Care, January 1982, pp 14–17, 24

Diers D: A different kind of energy: Nurse-power. Nurs Outlook January 1978, pp 51–55

Garant C: Power, leadership, and nursing. Nurs Forum 20:183–199, 1981

Grissum M, Spengler C: Womanpower and Health Care. Boston, Little, Brown & Co, 1976

Janik A: Power base of nursing in bargaining relationships. Image, Summer 1984, pp 93–96

Kanter RM: Power games in the corporation. Psychology Today, July 1977, pp 48–53, 92

Levenstein A: Power, realism and compromise. Nurs Management, May 1983, pp 51–53

McFarland DE, Shiflett N (eds): Power in nursing. Nurs Dimensions 7(2):1979

O'Rourke K, Barton S: Nurse Power Unions and the Law. Bowie, MD, Robert J. Brady, 1981

Persons CB, Wieck L: Networking: A power strategy. Nurs Econ, January/February 1985, pp 53–57

Storlie FJ: Power—getting a piece of the action. Nurs Management, October 1982, pp 15–18

Exercises

EXERCISE 3-1   BUILDING A PERSONAL POWER BASE

Directions.   Building or strengthening a personal power base is necessary in order to establish a firm professional power base. In considering yourself wholistically, it is necessary for each of the five aspects to be developed to generate an internal sense of balance. While each of the five aspects is interrelated, the social level is more superficial and the spiritual has more depth. Determine what you already do and would like to do to support each aspect of yourself. On the lines on the left side of each circle, list what you already do. On those on the right side write what you would like to do.

Evaluation

1. In which areas are you strongest and in which areas weakest?

2. Are the things you do and want to do by yourself or with others?

3. What can you determine keeps you motivated to do what you do? What blocks you from what you want to do?

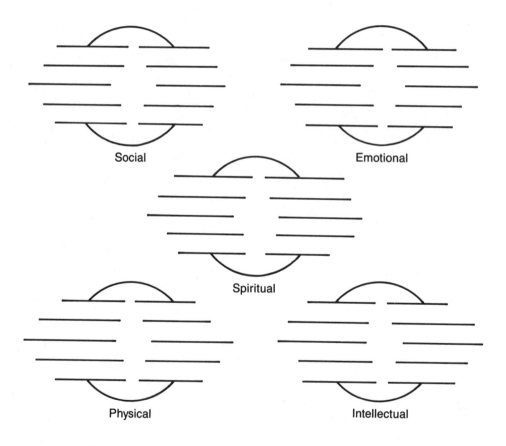

EXERCISE 3-2   BUILDING PROFESSIONAL POWER STRATEGIES

Directions.   As a nurse, you exhibit power by influencing others' attitudes, ideas, and decisions and by controlling patient care, health care resources, and the environment. However, the amount of influence and control you have depends on the power base you establish.

Part 1: Assessment

Review the four bases for professional power. List what you are able to do in your present role and work setting that enhances your professional power base in each area.

Reward power—

Expert power—

Referent power—

Positional power—

Part 2: Plan

Consider the power you have in each of the four areas and clarify the professional goals you want to achieve in your present position. List the short term objectives and steps that will take you toward your goals. Determine the people you will need to influence and the resources required.

Goals	Objectives	Action Steps	People to Influence	Resources to Use

Part 3: Implementation and Evaluation

Develop a work plan to guide you in building your professional power base.

Goal(s) for building reward power

Date Initiated	Activity	People Involved	Resources Used	Date Completed	Comments

Goal(s) for building expert power

Date Initiated	Activity	People Involved	Resources Used	Date Completed	Comments

Goal(s) for building referent power

Date Initiated	Activity	People Involved	Resources Used	Date Completed	Comments

Goal(s) for building positional power

Date Initiated	Activity	People Involved	Resources Used	Date Completed	Comments

EXERCISE 3-3   *USING POWER WITHIN YOURSELF*

Directions.   The first step in using power is knowing what you want and how to get it. In figuring out what you want, do some soul searching and be honest and clear about your desires and fears. You have power when you are self-directed and in control of where you want to go. Think of yourself standing on the landing of the staircase of your career. Follow the steps that take you in the direction you want to go. List all of your options and alternatives.

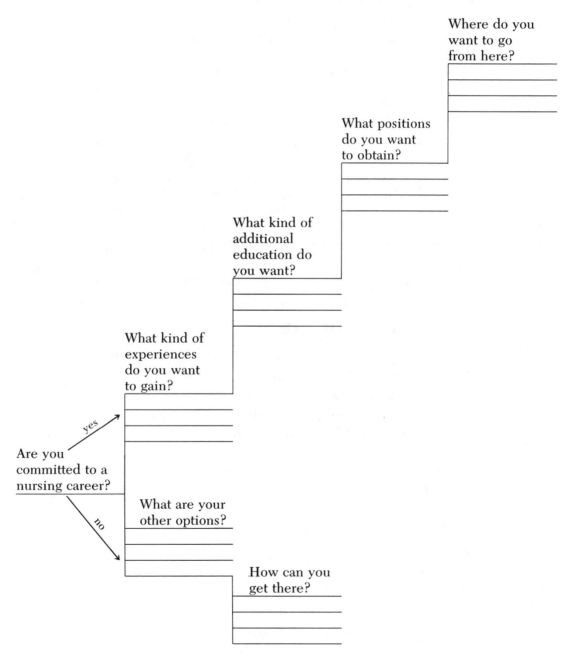

EXERCISE 3-4   USING POWER WITH SUPERIORS AND SUBORDINATES

Directions. In your work setting you have three levels of positions. Along with your peers will be those positions superior to you and those subordinate to you. These three levels have positional power. In meeting your goals and those of the work setting it is important to develop skills in using the power of your position. Designate the following characters to act in a scripted role play situation:

One nursing manager
One to four staff members

In the role play setting, the manager conducts a staff meeting at which an inservice for the next month is planned. The role play will take about 15 minutes.

Use the following scripts for the roles:

Nursing Manager: Has an authoritarian personality and a personal agenda to tell the staff who should do what for the inservice.

Staff Nurse A: Wants to be selected for the assistant manager position and demonstrates the ability to delegate authority and clarify expectations.

Staff Nurse B: Currently is going to school part-time and wants to meet a course requirement by preparing the evaluation tool for the inservice.

Staff Nurse C: Is a new nurse who just finished orientation and wants to help the manager look good.

Staff Nurse D: Has a mutual interest in the goals the manager is trying to reach.

Evaluation of Activity

Following the interaction, discuss the following questions:

1. Who used power most effectively? How?
2. What did each person do to exert power?
3. Were the steps of delegating authority followed?
4. In what way was consideration given to match assignments with individual skills?
5. How were individual goals met in planning the inservice?

EXERCISE 3-5   ESTABLISHING POWER WITH PHYSICIANS

Directions.   Before you can establish power with physicians, it is often necessary to confront your prejudices and past experiences. This exercise is used in a group setting. The total group is broken into pairs, with each pair having an observer. One member of the pair is the "nurse" and the other the "physician." The physician in the pair goes first and gives an idea or assumption about nurses. The nurse then gives an idea about herself or himself as a nurse and makes a statement about the profession generally.

The process and responses are critiqued with the observer.

The roles are then reversed and the "nurse" gives an idea or assumption about physicians. The "physician" then gives an idea about herself or himself as a physician and makes a statement about the profession generally.

The process and responses are critiqued with the observer.

The exercise can be repeated.

We all prejudge, depending on our past. However, the more experienced and reliable your sources of information, the less prejudice will prevent you from establishing a power base.

EXERCISE 3-6   **FOR YOUR CONSIDERATION . . . OR . . . FOR GROUP DISCUSSION**

Directions.   Use the following questions to reflect on key points covered in this chapter. Answer these questions individually or in a group discussion.

1. What decisions or policies do you have power to influence in your present work setting?

2. Thinking of yourself wholistically, which of your five aspects—social, physical, intellectual, emotional, spiritual—is the most balanced? Which aspect is least balanced in giving you personal power?

3. In your present job description, what statements contribute the most to your power base?

4. How do you, as a nurse, build power through cost-containment efforts?

5. What resources are you able to utilize in your present role to reach your goals?

6. What relationships would contribute to your power base?

7. Which of the issues currently being considered in your state legislature could you use the collective power of nurses to influence?

8. What have you done to improve the image of nurses as having power?

4 Working Together: Building Effective Work Groups

To celebrate the completion of their first year in nursing, Jennifer Goode and her classmates are holding a "first anniversary party." Walking into the party, Jennifer reflects on her first year as a staff nurse. The word that comes to mind is "new." She is a newlywed living in a new apartment, in a new town and is working in a new nursing job. She is both excited and a bit nervous at the prospect of sharing stories with her old classmates because this first year has been both positive and painful.

Last September, after spending an exciting summer involved in wedding plans, getting married, honeymooning, and settling into a new home, Jennifer began work on a 32-bed psychiatric unit in the local general hospital. Psychiatric nursing is Jennifer's favorite specialty, and she is particularly pleased that she was able to land a job in this field. The common approach of spending a year in general medical–surgical nursing never appealed to Jennifer. She is eternally grateful to the supervisor who took a chance on a new grad. For Jennifer, starting in the psych unit means she is that much closer to her dream of being a psychiatric clinical specialist.

Belief in her dream has ebbed and flowed this year. Jennifer has had some positive as well as some painful experiences. The first 6 weeks on the psych unit were devoted to orientation. Jennifer learned basic facts about the hospital and the specific unit on which she works. Demonstrating her ability to perform basic functions posed no problems.

Although Jennifer proved to be functionally capable, she began to feel interpersonally incapable. The jitters and discomfort she felt when first going to work did not subside as quickly as she had anticipated. Used to being part of the "in" group, Jennifer felt that after 6 weeks on the unit, the newness should have given way to developing relationships. Since that was not the case, she began to feel excluded.

Two months into her job, Jennifer decided to discuss her feelings with her counterparts. After all, Jennifer thought, this is a psych unit, and who should be able to discuss feelings if not psychiatric nurses? Jennifer raised the issue at a staff meeting. She described her sense of isolation and her belief that the unit nurses, two old-timers in particular, were not open to the inclusion of new staff members. The surprise and supportive reactions she received during the meeting were replaced two days later by hostile and angry comments. The two nurses whom Jennifer named in the meeting accused her of not being receptive to their overtures. They told her that it was she who was closed and that the problem was hers, not theirs.

Following the November staff meeting, Jennifer's optimism was gone. The isolation she described during the staff meeting continued to grow. She felt insecure and depressed. Communication between Jennifer and the two staff nurses was cool, competitive, and sarcastic. She questioned her capabilities and wondered what she really had to give. She became defensive and withdrawn, unable to resolve the problem.

As the year progressed, Jennifer developed supportive relationships with other people on the unit, which helped her to resolve her problem. The social worker, psychiatric technicians, and other new nurses seemed much less critical and competitive. They reinforced her capabilities and helped her develop clinical as well as interpersonal skills. With their support, Jennifer had less need to prove herself. She became more secure and, consequently, less competitive with the two "problem nurses."

Walking into the first anniversary party, Jennifer recalls the pain of her first year in nursing. She also realizes that what she has learned this year is very positive. Her husband, the social worker, the new nurses, and even her two adversaries, have taught Jennifer many lessons. The most important lesson is that accomplishing nursing tasks is just one part of the nursing role. Getting along with co-workers is just as important as providing high-quality patient care. Jennifer also has learned that in a work group there are many different people with many different skills. It is important to respect each of them, to be honest and yet politically astute. Jennifer realizes she has much to learn, but this no longer bothers her. Not only has she regained some of the optimism she had last September; she has also developed a new, broader perspective. As she enters the party, she is anxious to share her new insights with old classmates.

Why Should I Learn about Work Groups?

During her first year in nursing, Jennifer Goode learned much more than hospital policies and procedures. While she tested her capabilities and limitations, Jennifer learned that there is more to nursing than clinical competence. She found that relationships with her co-workers have a tremendous impact on her own ability to practice nursing, on her success and failure, on her happiness and frustration in her role. She discovered that she does not work well in isolation. After many months of pain, she realized that she was sorely lacking in the skills necessary to work with and understand groups of people. Lacking those skills, she encountered problems when attempting to become a part of her work group.

As you make the transition into the work world, you must learn many of the same lessons that Jennifer did. Your success and satisfaction with nursing are related in part to your ability to interact successfully with your work group. Developing an understanding of group dynamics and the skills to work with people in a group helps you in making the transition from school to the work world.

What Should I Learn about Work Groups?

Facts you need to know about work groups are taken from small-group theory, which describes the characteristics of groups and how they function. According to small-group theory, a group is an interdependent collection of individuals who share common goals and needs.

There are four types of groups, distinguished by their major purposes.

The social group, focused on socialization, recreation, or enjoyment
The therapeutic group, designed to help or heal
The consciousness-raising group, dedicated to enlightening or educating
The work group, committed to performing a specific job or task

The group in which you work in your nursing role is the fourth type, a work group. It is dedicated to accomplishing the specific task of providing nursing care to designated patients. This work group is composed of interdependent clinical, managerial, and ancilliary personnel. Being interdependent means that group members must work together to get the job done. It also implies that group goals cannot be achieved unless all members perform their jobs to the best of their ability. All members should know the group's goals and should collaborate in working toward those goals. If you don't know what the group's goals are, the effectiveness of your work group is diminished and group problems easily emerge. Make it your business to find out what your work group's goals are. This helps you to be a more valuable member of the group.

In addition to common goals, groups have common needs. These needs fall into two categories known as *task needs* and *maintenance needs*. Table 4-1 presents the task and maintenance needs that groups experience. In order for a collection of individuals to operate as a group, some of their energy must be focused on performing a necessary task or function. The remainder of the effort and attention must be spent on developing or maintaining effective relationships among group members. Task and maintenance needs exist in every collection of people who are considered a group and remain throughout the entire existence of every group.

These two sets of needs run parallel to each other; neither one can replace the other. At different points in the life of a group, emphasis on meeting task needs or maintenance needs shifts. Sometimes one set of needs takes precedence over the other. In order for a group to function in a healthy way, however, both types of needs must always be satisfied to some extent.

Your work group has task needs and maintenance needs. Your work group, and you as a member of it, must work on providing patient care, as well as on maintaining effective group relationships. As Jennifer Goode discovered, performing tasks is only half of the work of a group. Collaboration with peers is the other half. As a new nurse, you need to develop group skills as well as clinical skills. It is important that you understand the goals and needs

Table 4-1   Group Development

Phase	Correlation with Human Development	Observable Behavior	Task Needs	Maintenance Needs
Forming	Childhood	Polite Impersonal Guarded Watchful, exploring Testing the water	Identify group goals Clarify jobs and role expectations	Test group relationships Decide to include or exclude new member Depend on leader, old members, and standards for structure and guidance
Storming	Adolescence	Overt or covert conflict Interpersonal hostility Power struggles Apathy Poor job performance	Resist task	Resist cohesion, collaboration and commitment to the group
Norming	Young adulthood	Getting organized Establishing procedures Developing skills Confronting issues and problems constructively Giving feedback	Clarify goals of the group Define tasks and procedures for achieving group goals Allow group goals to supersede personal goals when necessary for the good of the group	Develop cohesion, collaboration and commitment to the group Adopt new roles and standards of performance
Performing	Adulthood	Open Mature closeness Collaboration Flexibility Productive and effective performance	Operate productively Produce quality work Use group achievement to stimulate positive feelings about group	Respect and support members Develop role flexibility Use positive feelings about group to motivate attainment of group goals

of your work group. You should develop the skills necessary to work successfully with the other people in your work group, taking into account the dynamics of that group.

What Are Group Dynamics?

Whenever a collection of people come together for a specific purpose, a group is created. The personal qualities and quirks of each member blend together to create group dynamics, much as the ingredients thrown into a stock pot help to make soup. When you alter the combination of people or their traits, you change the group, just as altering the kinds or relative amounts of ingredients dramatically changes soup. The best soup simmers slowly; the flavor develops over time as ingredients blend together. A group is much the same. Its characteristics, atmosphere, and dynamics develop over time as people interact and get to know each other.

By definition, group dynamics are the forces in a group that determine the behavior of the group and its members. Group dynamics explain how a group handles its task and maintenance needs as well as how it communicates. Although the dynamics of every group are unique, some general characteristics are shared by all. Understanding these common characteristics helps you understand and work with your group's dynamics. Develop an awareness of group dynamics by first observing what people say and do. Next, interpret your observations in light of the common characteristics of groups-task needs, maintenance needs, goals, operating rules, communication patterns and leadership. Observe group behavior in the same way that you observe patient behavior, objectively and as dispassionately as possible. The more matter-of-fact your observation, the more effective you are in assessing the dynamics of your work group.

Establish who talks to whom. Identify what people talk about and what they avoid discussing. Identify subgroups: who work together, who is an outsider, and who are members of the "in" group. Identify the goals and objectives of your work group. What is important to your manager, and how does this person communicate the goals to you? Assess the presence of hidden agendas, personal objectives that are unstated but have a powerful impact on the functioning of your work group. Listen for messages from people or from the system at large that define what you should and should not do. Finally, observe the leadership in your work group. Expect to find leadership in people other than the designated leader, who is your manager. Assess the style of leadership used by both designated and informal leaders. Their leadership sets the tone in your work group, and the group members work either with or against that tone.

How Do Groups Develop?

How the group responds to its leadership, goals, rules, and communication patterns reveals important information about the dynamics of your work group. The most positive and effective dynamics are found in groups that are the most highly developed. Every group evolves and develops throughout its life cycle, very much as an individual develops over the human life cycle. The behaviors you observe in your group and its members tell you at what developmental phase your work group is functioning. Group behavior also indicates what actions you should take to work more effectively with your group. Your observations point out ways in which you can help your work group to function more effectively.

According to Tuckman, there are four developmental phases that any group can experience. Table 4-1 summarizes the key aspects of each of the four phases. In each developmental phase, individuals and the group as a whole manifest characteristic types of behaviors. These behaviors are the overt manifestations of how the group is meeting its tasks and maintenance needs. A group's needs are phase specific and so, when a set of needs are met, the group moves on to new behaviors associated with the next developmental phase. As in human growth, group development does not occur in distinct steps. Phases overlap each other, with some members of the group operating at one level of development while others are operating on a different level. Crisis, loss, or change can occur at any time throughout the life of a group. As in human development, any crisis, loss, or change causes the group to regress to an earlier phase of development.

There are many losses and changes that work groups encounter, such as staff turnover, promotions, loss of patients, and new policies or procedures. Because of this, there is a tremendous push towards regression in nursing work groups. In addition, developing the openness that is required for group cohesion and integration is a risky prospect. These two factors, the frequency of loss and change and the risk of openness, make it difficult for nursing work groups to move beyond the forming and storming phases into norming and performing. Consequently, many work groups get stuck in the storming phase. Unlike human beings, who inevitably mature into adulthood, groups are prevented from fully developing when group dynamics are not properly managed.

As a new nurse, you are a member of a work group. Your entry into this group is a change that causes the group to regress to the forming phase. Every member of your work group is dealing with the issue of inclusion, wondering if or how you should be included into the group. Developing an understanding of group dynamics helps you enter your work group and operate more effectively once you are included.

How Can I Persuade My Work Group to Accept Me?

This question is often asked by new nurses. Consider Jennifer's concerns. For more than half of her first year in nursing, she felt isolated from her work group. Her comments at the staff meeting proved unsuccessful in persuading her peers that they should accept her.

Like Jennifer, you as a new nurse are confronted with the challenge of persuading your work group that you are worthy of inclusion. However, you are seeking inclusion not only into your work group, but also into the nursing profession. Attempting entry into two groups at the same time doubles the intensity of the transition and doubles the difficulty of the process.

Your transition into the practicing nurse role is complicated by two other factors. The first is your need for affiliation. Every human being has a need to belong and to feel part of a group. As Jennifer Goode realizes, this affiliation need is compromised, challenged, and left unmet for the person who is outside a group and trying to enter it. The outsider status is uncomfortable at best, and can be a very painful experience at other times. The second factor that complicates your entry into nursing is the mourning process accompanying inclusion. Both you as a new nurse and the long-standing members of your work group face losses at this time. You are dealing with the loss of familiar peers and student role expectations. The established members of your work group recall a departed staff member whom you might be replacing. They miss that person or, at the very least, they miss the comfort and familiarity associated with knowing what that person contributed to the work group. If you are entering a work group but are not replacing a former member, the established members still experience a loss: that of the familiar group structure. The losses that both parties experience complicate the inclusion process by generating ambivalence and resistance in both you and established members of your work group.

As the work group deals with the *forming* phase and decides whether to include or exclude you as a new member, behavior of group members is characteristically polite, impersonal, and guarded. Jennifer Goode's experience shows how established group members test the new person's capabilities. As a new nurse, you evaluate the group and its members also, seeking to understand the group goals. You also attempt to clarify the nursing role expectations and to test group relationships. Although the testing that occurs during the forming phase of group development is uncomfortable, it is necessary. Whether on the professional level or work group level, the forming phase allows a group to evaluate your capabilities as a potential new member. Permitting entrance to only those new members who meet admissions standards enables your work group and the nursing profession to control the quality of its function and product. Quality control is an important concern to the nursing profession and, on a smaller level, to your nursing work group.

Recognize the Dynamics of Groups in the Forming Phase

When attempting to enter a group and gain acceptance, start first by recognizing the dynamics of the forming phase of group development. Remind yourself of the affiliation needs you have, of the mourning that accompanies the process of inclusion, and of the group's need to evaluate you vis-à-vis their standards. Remember that the forming phase is essential to group health and development. So try to maintain your perspective. Forming is just one phase in group development. Be patient and expect this phase to last for a while, but not forever. Remind yourself that the testing that is characteristic of the forming phase is a manifestation of the group's need to evaluate potential members. In some ways it is a positive sign: you are seeking entrance into a group with standards. Try not to personalize the testing that you encounter; everyone entering the group is tested, not just you.

Expect to Feel Some Loneliness

Expect to feel some loneliness, isolation, or distance from the group members when attempting to be included in your work group. It is natural to experience these feelings during the forming phase because your affiliation needs are not being met. It takes time for the group to fully include you into its membership; until then, satisfy your affiliation needs with people outside your work group. Interact with friends and family after work. Keep friendships and socializing for after work hours. While at work, seek to develop collaborative professional relationships rather than personal friendships. This helps you maintain realistic expectations about work relationships. It also promotes effective professional performance and helps to keep the discomfort of unmet affiliation needs in check.

Develop Supportive Professional Relationships

When forming relationships at work, identify several people whom you respect and with whom you feel comfortable. Look beyond nurses and include nonprofessional staff as well as members of other professional groups. Seek out these people and build relationships slowly. Start with informal and casual conversation. As relationships and some closeness develop, then you will be able to move to deeper levels of conversation and sharing. It takes time to get to know another person. Be patient and give yourself some time.

Seek and Use Feedback

As you work your way into your group, you need feedback. Use staff members, nurses in staff development, a clinical specialist and your nurse manager as sources of feedback. Others are often unaware of your need for feedback. Because it is your need, it is your responsibility to ask. Be direct; be assertive. Do not wait for others to volunteer words of praise or constructive criticism. Ask for help in evaluating your performance, clarifying your priorities, and identifying your problems.

Be sure that you listen to what is being said to you. Distorted perceptions and defensiveness are not uncommon for new nurses who are trying to enter a work group. It is very important that you attempt to correct distorted perceptions and let go of defensiveness. These act as barriers to your learning and keep you from being included in the group.

Come to Terms with Back-Stage Reality

When receiving feedback, expect evaluation to include more than that of your technical nursing skills. Your interpersonal and political competence are likely to be evaluated also. Remember, you are being judged by work-world standards now, not by academic standards. In her books, Marlene Kramer discusses a concept called *back-stage reality*. This is the behind-the-scenes behavior, the short cuts, the "tricks of the trade," the unsanctioned approaches to solving problems or to delivering patient care that experienced nurses are privy to. Students do not learn back-stage reality in school. They learn how to operate "by the book." Adaptations of standard nursing procedures are learned on the job; they are a reality of the pressured and imperfect work world. Your ability to perceive, understand, accept, and operate in harmony with back-stage reality is one criterion on which you are evaluated. How you handle this has an impact on how you are included into your work group.

Discuss troubling aspects of back-stage reality with a trusted colleague or with your nurse manager. Maintain an open mind when encountering and discussing this phenomenon; it has value in some circumstances. Withhold final critical judgment until you have a complete picture of the unit and the situations in which it is used. This takes time, experience, and insight.

After allowing yourself adequate time to objectively assess the appropriateness of your unit's back-stage reality, you may find parts of it that go against your value system. Practice nursing based on your own values. You do not have to go along with the behavior of your peers. However, if you choose to depart from it, expect them to react negatively. After all, you are telling them that their behavior is wrong. If you feel strongly enough about it, suggest ways to alter those aspects of the back-stage reality that are in conflict with your values. Do not attempt to do this, however, until you have been included as a member of the group. Attempting to change group standards or behavior before you are included is difficult and can block the inclusion process. Focus on your own professional performance during the forming phase. This is more than enough to keep you busy. Remember, the manager is responsible for the unit. You are responsible for yourself. Live out your values and allow other nurses to practice according to theirs. If you want others to respect your professional priorities, you must do the same.

Share Your Skills

In attempting to enter a work group, the golden rule is a helpful guide: do unto others as you would have them do unto you. Look for ways to be supportive, encouraging, and helpful to your co-workers. Sincerely compliment others on their nursing care, their helpfulness, and their intergroup relationships. Identify a special skill or aspect of theoretical knowledge that makes each of your co-workers shine. Recognize their expertise both by giving positive feedback and by seeking them out when you need assistance in that area. When co-workers extend themselves to you either professionally or socially, be sure to respond positively. Thank them for their interest, feedback, or advice. Accept their social invitations, whenever possible. Return the favor by inviting them to socialize with you. Social connections are often the precursors of effective professional relationships.

Think of what special skill, knowledge or personal capability you have to offer your peer group. Whether it is passing a nasogastric tube, comforting grieving families, or organizing social events, offer to share skills. Find ways to contribute to the group. Your contributions remind both you and your co-workers that you are a capable and talented person. This is easy to forget when you are new and learning so much. When you contribute to the group, you also communicate your interest in moving from the dependent position of the "new person" to full group membership. Advertising your capabilities and interests are very persuasive means of promoting the inclusion process.

Working your way into a group can be a trying experience. Don't blame others for your discomfort. Recognize the pain for what it is, a sign of transition and growth. Work your hardest, but don't expect the impossible. Be realistic. Do your best but don't try to be perfect.

How Can I Persuade People to Work Together?

After only 6 months of working on the orthopedic unit, you are not sure how much longer you can take it. Staff conflict, which is at times overt but more often covert, is personally wearing and is now beginning to jeopardize the quality of patient care. The aides and orderlies are unionized, but the nurses are not. This leads to contention between the professional and nonprofessional staff. In addition, there is ongoing tension between all three shifts.

Because no one rotates, the staff on one shift fails to understand the pressures of other shifts. The common complaints of incompleted work and lack of follow-through are now serious concerns.

Your 75-year-old patient who recently underwent a total hip replacement is developing decubiti, and this is what angers you most. The nursing order you wrote calls for turning the patient on the even hours around the clock. On the day shift you are religious about turning your patient. The P.M. staff complains that they are too busy to turn the patient so frequently. Through the grapevine, you have heard that the night shift orderly will not awaken the patient and refuses to follow the order. Although you don't know if this is true, you suspect that the night nurse fears confronting an experienced orderly who is also the union representative. Whatever the reason, you are frustrated with the unit's lack of follow-up and coordination of patient care. While your co-workers are wasting their energy on the conflict, the patient is not receiving the quality of care he deserves.

Working together is important in any group. Among a nursing work group it is crucial. Without collaboration and cohesion among all members of a nursing work group, patient care suffers. Both the quality of care and the quantity, as measured in productivity levels, is diminished when groups fail to work together. In addition, staff morale also declines. Faced with the environmental pressures that exist in today's health care system, nursing work groups need to work collaboratively and cohesively.

As Table 4-1 indicates, groups that resist operating cohesively and collaboratively are in the phase called *storming*, which is analogous to the developmental phases of adolescence. A large number of groups get stuck in this phase because of the risks associated with operating cohesively and collaboratively.

When your work group is in the storming phase, each member of the group is deciding whether or not it is worthwhile to bond with the other group members. Bonding involves surrendering some control of one's worklife. In a group that is truly working together, the needs of the larger group take precedence over those of individual members. People understand this intuitively, and during the storming phase group conflict and resistance are symptoms of the group's ambivalence and doubts about working closely together.

Conflict and resistance in the storming phase reveal that not all group members are convinced that they will benefit from working together. Individual group members fear that if they allow group goals to supersede their own goals, this sacrifice will yield no positive personal payoff. Because they doubt that giving to the group will benefit them in the long run, group members who are storming focus on meeting their own individual needs and resist meeting the needs of the group. The effectiveness of a storming group is severely limited.

When the group as a whole and its individual members decide that the risks of cohesion and collaboration far outweigh the benefits of resistance and focusing on individual needs, the group begins to move from the storming phase into the more productive and positive *norming* and *performing* phases. The destructive and devisive conflict that characterizes storming is transformed during the norming and performing phases into a more positive, growth-producing force. Instead of confronting people or overtly complaining about others, during these phases, conflict focuses on addressing issues and on solving problems. People work together to develop constructive conflict resolution strategies and mutually satisfying solutions to problems. Strategies for developing a collaborative work group are based first on convincing others that group cohesion is beneficial to their interests and second on developing positive conflict resolution skills.

Build Group Cohesion; Develop Teamwork

As an individual in your work group, you cannot build group cohesion on your own. Group dynamics are very strong and cannot be shaped by you or any other person acting individually. It is possible and advisable, however, for individuals to form subgroups or coalitions and work together to enhance the cohesion of the larger group. Identify other members who are interested in promoting group collaboration and cohesion. Arrange a meeting during lunch or after work. Discuss ways to encourage nurses to be more helpful to each other and to work as a team. Also, discuss the blocks and barriers to your group's working together. These are the people, policies, structures, and behaviors that encourage isolation and discourage teamwork. Identify realistic ways to remove those barriers and to work more collaboratively. Teamwork makes your job easier and more enjoyable. You and your co-workers can develop effective teamwork if you want to. It is not easy to do but it is worthwhile.

Table 4-2 lists characteristics of highly cohesive groups. Use it to assess the cohesion of your work group. Use the examples as a guide for developing group cohesion and collaboration. For example, define difficulties as challenges or opportunities. Share difficult jobs fairly, among all nurses. Socialize with all members of the staff. Communicate honestly and directly. Do not allow group members to speak disrespectfully to one another. Never violate another's confidence. Support your group when outsiders criticize it. There are many other ways to develop teamwork suggested by the examples listed in Table 4-2. Implement those that are applicable to your work group and use them to begin a program of building work group cohesion.

Solve Problems and Resolve Conflicts Constructively

By definition, conflict is a situation in which each of two parties, either individuals or groups, perceive that the other party has violated their rights or has failed to meet their needs or expectations. When rights are violated and needs or expectations go unmet, human beings feel anger. This is a natural response; anger always accompanies conflict. The intensity of the anger varies, more serious violations causing more intense anger.

How an individual or group resolves conflict and anger is referred to as their conflict-resolution style. Groups that are in the storming phase characteristically have a nonproductive or even a destructive conflict-resolution style. To help a group move to a more effective level of functioning, work on helping it to develop a constructive conflict-resolution style. To achieve this, first identify the individual and group forces that block constructive conflict resolution. Within individuals, the blocks that occur are lack of knowledge of effective conflict resolution skills, fear of dealing with conflict, or disrespectful attitudes about the other party with whom they are in conflict. Groups also

Table 4-2   **Characteristics of Highly Cohesive Groups**

Characteristics	Examples
1. Members value group goals.	Members accept long- and short-term group goals. Members accept leader's priorities. Members participate in formulating group goals. Members perceive group and its work as meaningful. Members are willing to work hard to achieve goals.
2. Individual goals mesh with group goals.	Members feel they benefit personally from group membership. Group membership brings individuals closer to long-term career goals.
3. Group works to attain difficult as well as easy goals.	Difficulties are defined as challenges or opportunities. Difficult jobs are fairly assigned to all members. Leader recognizes and rewards successful completion of difficult tasks.
4. Relationships are friendly and enjoyable.	Members socialize at breaks and mealtimes. Subgroups interact easily and amicably. Members enjoy being together.
5. Relationships are trusting and open.	Communication is direct, honest, and respectful. Members discuss controversial issues without fear of reprisal. Confidentiality is honored. Members resolve conflicts constructively.
6. Relationships are loyal and supportive.	Members defend group to outside critics. Members avoid criticizing group or its members in front of nonmembers. Members handle conflict internally. Members receive support when speaking up in a meeting. Help is offered when members need it. Risk taking is encouraged and rewarded. Members praise and recognize one another's accomplishments.
7. Participation is stable, reliable, and consistent.	Turnover is low. Call-outs are infrequent. Use of floats or temporary help is minimal. Members arrive on time, complete work on time. Members follow through on commitments.
8. Participation is flexible.	Members readily accept assigned tasks or roles. Members help those who need help. Members willingly fill in for those absent. Members can all fulfill a variety of roles. Members are willing to adapt to change.

Table 4-2   **Characteristics of Highly Cohesive Groups (Continued)**

Characteristics	Examples
9. Participation is goal directed.	Members understand and fulfill their responsibilities. Leader guides group toward goal achievement. Leader assists ineffective or resistant members to alter unacceptable behavior.
10. Participation is interdependent.	Leadership is democratic. Members cooperate on achieving goals. "We, us" is used to describe the group, not "us vs. them" or "I". Contributions of all members are valued and respected. Members do not compete against each other.
11. Participation is guided by group norms.	Job descriptions specify expected behavior. Rules are applied fairly and consistently. Rules facilitate rather than hinder the work. Policies and procedures are clear and relevant. Violations of norms are censured.
12. Participation is productive.	Productivity levels are achieved. Members manage time effectively. Group functions within budget. Conflict does not consume group energy.
13. Participation yields high-quality output.	Professional standards are met. Quality-assurance audits yield positive feedback. Patients/clients offer positive feedback. Members work to their best ability.
14. Participation improves the security and self-esteem of members.	Members develop technical-job skills. Individuality is respected and valued. Members interact respectfully. Rewards of membership are both tangible and intangible.
15. Participation is satisfying.	Members are proud to be group members. Members praise group to outsiders. Work of the group challenges members to grow. Members feel competent to do job and fulfill roles.

have blocks to effective conflict resolution. Lack of conflict resolution skills among many members in a group can be a severe block to the group's attempts to solve problems. This is particularly crucial if the leader has difficulty in dealing with conflicts. Another group block is failure to make conflict resolution a priority. When groups are focused on getting tasks accomplished and see conflict resolution as a low priority, this hinders effective conflict resolution. The history of the group can also block effective conflict resolution. When a group has a history of destructive problem solving, group members are often mistrustful and afraid to bring conflicts out into the open.

To help your group resolve conflicts constructively and work together effectively, identify any individual or group blocks that hinder group problem solving. Take action to remove or diminish the impact of these blocks so that you can actively proceed to develop conflict resolution skills in the group. Some suggestions for how to accomplish this follow.

Developing a productive conflict-resolution style is based on several key principles. First, conflict consumes group energy. Individual and group energy that might otherwise be focused on productive work is wasted when groups fail to resolve conflicts. Second, conflicts cannot be resolved unless both parties want to resolve them. Third, effective resolution requires that the needs of all parties be addressed; a win–win solution must be devised. Fourth, conflicts should be resolved as early as possible. The longer a conflict remains unresolved, the more complicated it becomes. Fifth, conflict-resolution behavior should mirror the intensity of the conflict. A mild conflict should be handled with a less intense demeanor than a very serious conflict. When mildly angry, respond in a mild way. Sixth, conflict resolution should always be characterized by a respectful approach. Disrespect and nastiness guarantee continued conflict.

The process of resolving conflict involves four steps. Additional information on this topic is located in the section entitled Negotiation and Compromise in Chapter 8, Dual Commitments: Meeting the Demands of Career and Family. *First, bring the conflict to the surface.* Get the problem out into the open and discuss it as directly as possible. Do not assume that you understand the other person's feelings or her or his interpretation of the problem. By its very nature, conflict implies that you see the problem from one perspective and the other person sees the problem from a different perspective. Try to imagine how the other person perceives the problem. Be as clear as possible in describing to the other person how you perceive the problem. Use "I" statements to tell the person how you feel and why you feel that way. To accomplish this describe the behavior of the other person to which you are reacting. Then describe which of your needs is not being met by that behavior or which of your rights is being violated by that behavior. A clear description such as this helps the other person to understand your perspective on the problem. More extensive description of this kind of "I" statement is included in Chapter 7, Acting Assertively: Practical Solutions to Problem Situations. Seek an agreement between both parties on problem definition before proceeding to subsequent stages of conflict resolution. Agreement is needed on defining the problem behavior before you can create successful solutions. So clarify what behavior of yours is causing conflict for the other person. Likewise, determine whether the other person understands and agrees that a certain behavior on her or his part is generating conflict for you.

The second step in the conflict-resolution process involves generating a solution. After the problem behaviors are clear, both parties need to generate a list of possible solutions to the problems. There are always many alternative ways to resolve conflict. The more solutions you generate, the greater is the likelihood that you will identify at least one that satisfies both parties' needs.

When generating alternative solutions, look for ones that satisfy the needs of both parties. Without a win-win solution, the conflict is never truly resolved.

The process of generating solutions is most successfully carried out through brainstorming. Brainstorming is particularly useful in working with groups of people who either have set ways of dealing with problems or who are not very creative in their approach to problem solving. Brainstorming opens up a group to building on one another's ideas and to realizing that there are many different ways to solve problems. The key to the success of brainstorming is that it separates idea creation from idea evaluation. With these two separated, creativity and innovation enter into the problem-solving process, and much better solutions are identified. Whether brainstorming individually, in pairs, or in a group, follow these rules and the steps in the brainstorming process.

The rules of brainstorming are as follows:

Rule 1. Produce quantity, not quality. Present as many solutions as possible.

Rule 2. Do not remark or critique as solutions are created or listed. If working with other people, do not allow jokes, snickering, or responses when solutions are identified. These act as evaluations and block the idea-creation process.

Rule 3. No censorship is allowed. Even far-fetched and improbable solutions should be brought forth.

Rule 4. Producing ideas is separate from evaluating ideas.

In the brainstorming process, there are three parts.

Part 1. Each person writes as many solutions as possible. Whether you are working individually or with others, each person writes on a piece of paper as many alternative solutions to the problem as possible. This takes 5 minutes and, when brainstorming is done with others, it is done individually.

Part 2. Solutions are listed. Each person writes on paper or a blackboard all the problem solutions they generated in Step 1. No critique is allowed during Step 2.

Part 3. Increase the range of alternative solutions by building on other solutions. Look at all the ideas listed in Step 2, and combine ideas to form new ones. To increase the range of alternatives, change the size, frequency, timing, format, or style of delivering a solution.

Following the brainstorming process, you have an extensive list of alternative solutions to your conflict. From these alternatives, choose the best solution. *Best* is a vague term and must be interpreted in light of your own needs—how much time, energy, money, or other resources you have available to you. It also implies the most satisfying alternative to both parties.

Step 3 in the conflict resolution process is implementation. After Steps 1 and 2 have been completed, implementation flows naturally. Each party knows what behavior to change and agrees on the way to change it as defined in Step 2 of the conflict-resolution process. This focus on behavior gives clear outlines for action in the implementation phase. Both parties know their responsibility in solving the conflict. Clear definitions of behavior also help in evaluating the success of the conflict resolution process in the final phase.

During the fourth step, follow-up, both parties evaluate the effectiveness of the conflict resolution process. Discussions during the follow-up phase focus on the implementation of the solution. Determine whether the solution was implemented, how well it was implemented, and whether the results achieved the desired outcome. If during follow-up you identify continued conflict or dissatisfaction with the results of the conflict-resolution strategy, repeat the steps of the process. Return to Step 1 and be certain that you defined the problem accurately, in behavioral terms, and to the agreement of both parties. Next, re-evaluate your choice of alternatives. Perhaps another alternative is more effective. Finally, if your conflict-resolution strategy was not successful, evaluate your implementation. Check that both parties fulfilled their agreement to change behavior. Also, decide whether extension of the implementation step might ensure the success of conflict resolution. During follow-up, evaluate the need for further action that may be needed.

In the scenario at the beginning of this section, you were angry that your patient developed decubiti. To resolve this situation, you plan to use conflict-resolution strategies. You know that you alone are not powerful enough to change the dynamics of your work group. Consequently, you plan to seek the support of your superior in dealing with this conflict. In a meeting led by your nurse manager, you plan to brainstorm with staff members of the P.M. and night shifts to identify ways to minimize the number of patients who develop decubiti. You realize that involving staff members from all shifts increases the likelihood that they will comply. You also know that focusing on better care for patients is much more effective in solving your problem than is criticizing or lashing out at the other shifts. Although you would like to vent your frustration, you plan to keep it in check, since you know that solving conflict in the work setting is difficult and demands responsible, not self-indulgent, behavior. As you and the nurses in this scenario illustrate, dealing with work groups is a difficult but important challenge. If you, as a new nurse, develop an understanding of group dynamics, your transition into nursing goes much more smoothly.

How Can I Develop a Positive Relationship with My Nurse Manager?

You are upset. After 5 months of working on this 36-bed medical unit, you are finally feeling competent and confident. However, you have a problem with your nurse manager. You feel that you do not get much leadership or support from your manager, who is seldom on the unit. The only time you see her is for a few minutes at the change of shifts or when she has some negative feedback. Your nurse manager does not compliment you about your patient care and frequently harps at you about overtime. Just this afternoon, she seemed quite annoyed when you mentioned a diabetic teaching program and post-hospitalization diabetic support group that you want to initiate. You can't understand why your manager reacted so negatively to this idea. Why is she annoyed at a staff member who wants to practice professionally and creatively? You are afraid to approach her and discuss it further for fear that the idea will be squelched. Should you proceed without telling her? Should you drop the idea altogether? What should you do?

Feeling unappreciated, misunderstood, or stifled by your manager is a very unpleasant experience. It colors your perception of your work group and can even diminish the quality of your patient care. When you experience problems with your nurse manager, the pleasure and satisfaction of nursing are often reduced. But as in the scenario above, it is often unclear what, if anything, you can do to improve the situation. Sometimes clashes between you and your manager are transitory and related to external events pressuring one or both of you. It is a good idea to ride these out.

The more serious clashes, however, are those that continue over a period of time. Any strategy for altering a clash between you and your manager must be based on a clear understanding of the reasons for that clash. The label *personality clash* is often used. It is an inadequate designation because it places the root of the conflict in personality only. The problem with this analysis is twofold. First, it covertly supports continuation of the conflict and renders both you and your manager helpless to promote change. Why? Because there is no way to change personality short of in-depth psychotherapy. The purpose of the work group is not to change people's personalities. That level of interaction is reserved for therapeutic relationships, not for working relationships. In a work group no one has the right to ask another person to change her or his personality.

The second reason why *personality conflict* is an inadequate term is that it fails to focus on behavior. Even if you did have the right to ask another person to change her or his personality, that concept is abstract and meaningless in the real world. You know and experience another's personality only through her or his behavior. So, to focus on personality rather than behavior keeps you preoccupied with intangibles and abstractions. Doing so supports the clash rather than promoting its resolution. When you have problems with your manager, do not fall prey to the personality clash label. Dig deeper. Look to behavior, a more tangible factor for guidance in assessing the problem between you and your manager.

To understand the root of the problem, analyze your behavior as it relates to your manager's goals and leadership style. As the designated leader of your work group, your manager is accountable for the functioning of the group. Your manager is responsible for directing the group toward accomplishing its goals and promoting constructive intergroup relationships. The nursing administrator to whom your manager reports evaluates the manager on these two factors. Consequently, your nurse manager has goals and objectives to help guide the group toward effective task and interpersonal functioning. When you have problems with your nurse manager, analyze your behavior in light of her or his goals. If your behavior hinders attainment of your manager's goals for the work group, your behavior is obstructive whether you intend it to be or not. This perceived or real obstructiveness is the basis of the problem between you and your nurse manager.

Another dynamic contributes to problems between superiors and subordinates. In addition to obstructing attainment of your manager's goals, your behavior might clash with your manager's style of leadership. By definition, *leadership* is influencing others toward the achievement of goals. How your manager attempts to motivate the work group to achieve goals is leadership. When you resist, undermine, ignore, or more innocently, fail to recognize your manager's attempt to influence you, your behavior is perceived as opposing leadership. This opposition, whether or not it is real, can be a second cause of problems between you and your manager.

Change Yourself, Not Your Boss

Be assured that you cannot change another person; you can only change yourself. So, when in conflict with your boss, focus on yourself. Recognize that something you are doing or not doing, something you are saying or not saying is contributing to the problem. It always takes two people to make a problem. Don't fall into the trap of blaming a problem you are experiencing on another person. Look at yourself and identify what you contribute to the problem. Check with your manager to be sure that you both agree on what part of your behavior is contributing to the problem. If you alone can't identify what you contribute to the problem, ask your manager for feedback on your behavior. When you recognize your contribution to the difficulties between you, tell your superior that you do. Then change your behavior. Don't expect your manager to change unless you are willing to change. Start changing yourself. This notifies your nurse manager of your sincere interest in improving the relationship. Indirectly, changing yourself has an impact on your manager because, as members of a group, you are interdependent. Working on yourself enhances the relationship between you.

Recognize and Respect Your Manager as a Leader

Every manager is in a leadership position, but not every manager is a great leader. Some managers are indecisive, unsure, mistrustful, poorly organized, bad at delegating, or unskilled at developing their staff. If your manager is a great leader, you are very fortunate. However, if your manager has some leadership problems, make the best of what you have and work with him or her. Although at times you are dissatisfied with your manager's leadership, try to empathize and understand. Your manager is doing the best possible job even though it doesn't meet your expectations. You don't have to like your manager, but you must learn how to work with her or him.

To work with your manager, you need not agree with or like her or his style of leadership. You must, however, respect that person's position as a leader. Respect implies several things. First, respecting your leader means recognizing her or his right to make decisions and to expect that they be implemented. Second, it means accepting that your manager has a broader organizational view than you do. Your manager is aware of organizational dynamics, information, and problems by virtue of the fact that the managerial position is located above yours in the organizational hierarchy. Because of this broader organizational view, some of your manager's decisions may not make sense to you. At certain times, respecting your manager requires accepting that her or his decisions are based on information of which you are not aware. Third, respecting your manager implies acknowledging her or his greater level of experience. As a new nurse, you possess a current body of nursing knowledge. This is a great strength, but not the only strength required for effective nursing. Your nurse manager has several years of experience that can be a practical, useful resource for you. Value and use this experience. Finally, respecting your manager involves accepting personal, clinical, and managerial limitations. It is unrealistic and unfair to expect your manager to know everything or to be an expert in all aspects of the nursing role. Your manager is only a human being with limitations, problems, faults, and foibles. Be realistic and fair in your expectations of your manager; ask only for what your manager is able or willing to give. If you need more or want more, seek other sources of support.

Identify Your Manager's Goals

The job of a manager is to accomplish goals and tasks through the action of others. Your job as a staff nurse is to fulfill the tasks assigned to you and thereby to assist your manager in accomplishing the work group's goals. It is very difficult to help your manager accomplish work group goals if you are unaware of them.

Take the initiative to find out what your manager's goals are. Do not assume that you know what your manager wants. This is a mistake that is commonly made and that leads to subordinate–superior clashes.

Sit down with your manager and discuss unit goals and your part in fulfilling them. This discussion could be uncomfortable for a new manager or for one who is unclear about the goals of your unit. So approach your nurse manager in a nonthreatening manner. Focus on your performance, not on how well your manager can articulate unit goals. Ask such questions as, "What should I be concentrating on? What is a priority for me to be doing? Is there any important aspect of my job that I am not fulfilling?"

Recognize in advance that the professional goals that you set for yourself may not mesh with those of your manager. You may be disappointed to hear your manager request better documentation, organization, or discharge planning. Be prepared to discuss alternative or creative ways to meet your individual goals, while at the same time fulfilling your manager's work group goals. Consider acting on personal goals in other settings, at a later date, or in conjunction with work group goals. Remember, your manager's primary concern is fulfilling work group goals. If you want to work successfully with your manager, discover what her or his goals are and focus your performance on attaining those goals. Do not work against them.

Support Your Manager

Your manager knows you only through your behavior, actions, and communication. Develop a constructive superior–subordinate relationship by being honest when you communicate. Be reliable in your attendance and performance. Don't surprise your manager. Keep your boss informed about what you are doing. Don't wait for performance evaluations to tell your boss what is happening. When you have a good day, or when there is trouble, tell your boss. All of these help to develop trust and openness between you and your nurse manager.

Trust and openness are very important between the two of you because of the interdependent nature of your relationship. You both need each other in order to achieve your goals. While you are important to your boss, do not overestimate your importance. Your contribution to the work group is valuable, but you are not indispensable. Keeping a proper perspective on your relationship with your manager helps you to act in ways that are constructive and supportive of your manager and the work group goals.

The four guidelines for working with a nurse manager can help solve superior–subordinate clashes. Return to the scenario at the beginning of this section to see how these guidelines suggest some practical solutions. First, you must look at your own behavior, recognizing that the problem is not only the manager's but in part is also your own, although your manager gives few compliments and many complaints. You are unaware of the manager's priorities. You should acknowledge that your manager may have a reason for frowning on the development of diabetic classes and a post-hospitalization diabetic support group. You should try to understand what is causing the manager's frown and try to understand the goals your manager has for the unit. After discovering those goals, identify what you should be doing to help achieve them. In dealing with your manager, be honest and squelch any temptation to develop the diabetic class or support group behind your manager's back. However, in trying to work in harmony with your manager's goals, do not automatically surrender your own desire to develop a diabetic teaching program and support group. Look for acceptable ways to implement your own goals. Suggest working on only one of the two options; suggest conducting a pilot study to evaluate the benefits of your ideas; seek a later date to initiate your project or offer to do this work in a community agency. In addition, attempt to convince your manager of the value of your ideas.

Although you are working with your manager on attaining work group goals, your own goals are still important. *Influence strategies* are useful in persuading others to work with you on your goals. These strategies are practical ways to operationalize your power. They are enabling strategies. The Latin root of the word power is *posse*, meaning "to be able." Use the following influence strategies to help you reach your goals.

Use Influence Strategies to Sell Your Ideas and Achieve Your Goals

Influence strategies are useful when you are trying to have an impact on anyone—your superior, peers, subordinates, family members, or friends. The effectiveness of influence strategies varies. What works with one person may not work with someone else. What gets results in one situation fails in others. Knowing which strategy to use in a given situation, with a particular person, is the key to success in influencing others.

Influence strategies, as defined by David Kipnis and Stewart M. Schmidt, are practical ways to use power. By definition, influence strategies are the ways in which you make suggestions or requests in order to obtain the results you want. Any strategy is composed of several specific tactics, which are ways to apply the strategy in real situations. The seven influence strategies are:

Reason
Friendliness

Coalition

Bargaining

Assertiveness

Appeal to higher authority

Sanctions

The first influence strategy is *reason*, the use of data, facts, and information to influence others. Reason is the first choice, the most effective strategy for influencing your manager. Reason involves tactics such as planning your conversation before talking with your manager and preparing detailed action plans to justify the ideas you want to implement. Reason also involves the use of logical arguments, explaining why you want to do things and what the value of your idea is to your manager or to the organization. When using reason, present facts, figures, data, and any information you can to support your position.

The second influence strategy is *friendliness*, anything you do to make others think well of you. Friendliness is the most widely used influence strategy and it is based on the use of interpersonal skills and sensitivity. It is particularly useful in attempting to obtain personal favors or assistance and in trying to influence someone in a position of greater power. Tactics for implementing a friendliness strategy vary. Do things to make the other person feel important, acknowledging her or his skill, competence, or knowledge. Use a respectful, polite approach when asking for what you want. Develop an ongoing rapport so that the other person feels good about you before you make a request. Such factors as effective job performance, responsible attendance, and support of your manager's goals are tactics that help to develop an ongoing rapport. Also, the friendliness strategy can be implemented by timing your request appropriately and acting respectfully while trying to influence the other person.

Coalition is a third influence strategy. This is based on the power of numbers and involves mobilizing others to assist you. Coalitions are useful in attaining personal as well as organizational objectives. When many people speak up, it is often easier to sell your ideas. Develop coalitions by talking with co-workers, gaining their support and commitment when trying to persuade your manager to act on a request. Ask others to speak up in a meeting, to verbalize the same request, or to put ideas into a suggestion box.

Bargaining is the fourth influence strategy. This is negotiation, exchanging favors, or trading. Bargaining is useful in trying to attain personal goals and when you are willing to make concessions to get what you want. Offer to give up something to get what you want or offer to help in one task in order to be free to do another.

Assertiveness is the fifth influence strategy. As a strategy, this means using a forceful manner, making demands, expressing strong emotions, or establishing deadlines. (Note that the connotation of the word *assertiveness*, as Kipnis and Schmidt use it, is different from that discussed in Chapter 7, Acting Assertively: Practical Solutions to Problem Situations.) Assertiveness, as described here, is useful when combined with other strategies or when you want to convince others which course of action should be taken. Assertiveness, however, is a two-edged sword. It can yield the results you desire but can also lead to ill will. Use a forceful manner, demands, and deadlines only when certain that you are right. Tactics for implementing the assertiveness strategy vary. Nagging and making a nuisance of yourself is one. Confronting another person face to face and reacting forcefully to their suggestions is another. Expressing anger directly is still another tactic. Citing organizational rules policies, procedures, or nursing standards is an additional way to operationalize the assertiveness strategy.

The sixth influence strategy is *appeal to higher authority*. This is use of the power in the organizational chain of command, either talking directly to your manager's superior or implying that you will. Appealing to higher authority is a very risky strategy to use with your own manager because it can be perceived as a threat. It can easily undermine any relationship that you have and can backfire. Appeal to higher authority is more effective when you are using your manager to influence peers or subordinates. Useful tactics in operationalizing this strategy are filing reports or memos to generate pressure. Another tactic is talking with a superior and asking that she or he back you up in your request. As a final, somewhat indirect tactic, ask the higher authority to pressure the one you seek to influence in the hope that this pressure will induce that person to respond to your request.

The final influence strategy is the use of *sanctions*. This is positive and negative reinforcement, reward and punishment, to get what you want. This strategy is not successful for influencing your manager. It is somewhat more effective when used with subordinates or peers.

When attempting to influence your manager or others, use a variety of different approaches. Be willing to vary your strategies because this offers you the best chance for success when you are seeking to influence another. Use your resources to help guide your choice of strategies. Your resources are the talents, facts, people, or things that you can use to help you get what you want. When you believe you have few or no resources available to support you, you hesitate to act to influence, or you choose an ineffective strategy. Avoid this trap by identifying the organizational and personal resources that you control. Organizationally, identify what information you possess and what relationships you can tap for support. Also, reinforce the value of your work to the organization. On a personal level, remind yourself of your knowledge, expertise, confidence, or interpersonal manner. When assessing your resources, do it realistically. False modesty reinforces powerlessness; overestimating resources leaves you vulnerable.

When planning your strategies, also avoid the trap of being easily put off by adverse reactions. When you encounter resistance, don't give up quickly. Don't rigidly persist in using the same strategy, either. Also, avoid escalating prematurely to the more radical strategies such as sanctions or assertiveness. When you encounter adverse reactions, remember that other strategic approaches can overcome resistance. Think strategically and look for alternatives to influence strategies and tactics.

Though presented as methods for enhancing your relationship with your boss, influence strategies are useful in relationships with peers, subordinates, members of other departments, patients, and the public. Influence strategies are powerful strategies designed to enable you to reach your goals. Use these in all your relationships because, whether you are dealing with other staff nurses, aides, orderlies, staff from other departments, patients, or a disgruntled family member, you need skills to help you achieve your goals. Used flexibly, influence strategies can help you to see your ideas implemented and to achieve your goals.

What if I Float and Work with Another Group?

During the 7:00 A.M. report, you are assigned by your head nurse to go to 7 West, the maternity unit. This is the first time you have been asked to float. With great reluctance and fear, you arrive on 7 West. After waiting for some information for 10 minutes, you finally meet the brusque charge nurse and receive an assignment that overwhelms you. As the charge nurse hurries down the hall, you decide that you will get little support from her and decide to try to do your best in this difficult situation. You are pleased and surprised at how much you remember about taking care of postpartum patients, something you have not done since nursing school. You are frustrated, however, by the time you waste searching for supplies and by the unavailability of unit staff. At lunchtime you are relieved to have a break and are only mildly disappointed to eat alone. Throughout the afternoon, you think you are doing well considering the unfriendliness on the unit. At the change of shift, however, as you attempt to give a thorough report, you are cut off by the charge nurse and asked to be succinct. In attempting to hurry, you forget to report on some significant information and have to find the charge nurse for a second report. At 3:30 P.M., you leave the postpartum unit feeling fairly good about your performance but frustrated and exhausted. You are angry that you have worked in relative isolation throughout the day. You wish the charge nurse or a staff member had given you some orientation, direction, and feedback on your performance. As you leave the hospital, you hope it will be a long time before you are called to float again.

Floating is the process of supplying temporary personnel to a work group that has a workload that outweighs its staff. Administratively, there are many ways to implement floating as a means to ease staffing shortages. Staff members from temporary agencies or from an in-house float pool are frequently used. At some hospitals both systems are used simultaneously. When temporary staff or money shortages are critical, nursing administrators often resort to "pulling" a permanent staff person from one work group to cover another. Expect that sometime during your nursing career you will be asked to float to another unit.

By its very nature, floating is a critical situation. One unit is short of personnel and therefore has a heavy workload. Consequently, the staff on the receiving unit is frequently tense, stretched to capacity, or extremely task oriented. Added to the situational pressures felt by the receiving unit's staff are the pressures felt by the nurse who is floating. The float nurse is asked to perform in unfamiliar surroundings and without the benefit of a supportive work group. Even with a friendly unit, the float nurse is not part of the work group. The float nurse enters a group that is in a forming stage when she or he goes to another unit. The experience resembles a nurse's first day in any work group. The float nurse has little or no credibility. Although her or his presence is helpful, the float nurse disrupts the dynamics of the group. The float nurse and members of the receiving unit manifest behaviors characteristic of the forming phase. People are polite, impersonal, guarded, watchful, or exploring. The group needs to clarify for all members (including its newest member, the float nurse) what are the jobs and role expectations of each. The float nurse tests group relationships to see who is a source of information, guidance, or assistance. A major cause of the discomfort experienced in floating stems from operating in a group that is in the forming phase of development.

Being separate from her or his usual work group also creates discomfort for the float nurse. All nurses need the support and encouragement of peers. This is particularly true for new nurses or for nurses who are working in a clinical area in which they are not comfortable. Separation from the usual work group is also difficult because the float nurse is concerned about the workload of peers. In his or her absence, the workload of those left behind on the float's own unit increases as a result of her or his absence. Finally, the float nurse is concerned about patients on the home unit. The continuity of care is interrupted when a nurse floats, and the satisfaction of providing regular care to a familiar group of patients is lost. Faced with the pressures inherent in a floating situation, use the following guidelines to help you handle the situation effectively.

Act Professionally

Present yourself to the charge nurse. Communicate your name and usual clinical responsibilities in a cooperative and respectful manner. Use a self-assured voice and maintain eye contact. Demonstrate a willingness to work and a confidence in your ability to be a helpful worker. A confident demeanor indicates to the charge nurse that you are assertive and able to handle yourself professionally.

As introductions are made and assignments are given, assess the charge nurse as a leader and as a resource person. If the charge nurse has a laissez-faire approach or is unavailable to act as a resource, ask for a specific nurse to be designated as your resource. You have a right to request this, for your own ability to function and for the good of your patients. If the charge nurse is autocratic or overly directive about responsibilities you are uncomfortable fulfilling, gently but firmly define your capabilities. Reassure the charge nurse that you plan to maintain contact and offer periodic reports about your work. Don't personalize the charge nurse's need for information because, though the authority to care for patients is delegated to you, the charge nurse is ultimately accountable for what happens on the unit.

Clarify Your Assignment and Communicate Your Limits

Find out as much as possible about the unit's expectations of you and the time schedule of activities for the shift. Get a report on the patients on the unit, at least those assigned to you. Evaluate the appropriateness of your assignment based on your own knowledge and professional skills. If the assignment is not appropriate for you, state your reservations in a reasonable manner and suggest alternate plans. *Never* accept an assignment for which you are not qualified. Protect yourself as well as your patients by making safety your first priority. Call the nursing supervisor when the charge person is unable to renegotiate your assignment.

Get the Job Done

Make the best of the situation; don't blame others for it. Approach co-workers in a spirit of cooperation. Ask someone to act as a contact person to familiarize you with the layout and procedures of the unit. Be prepared to be flexible and to integrate your style of doing things with theirs. Utilize your floating experience to learn new things, to share information, to test your interpersonal and professional skills.

Evaluate How Well You Did under the Circumstances

At the completion of the shift, you naturally have many thoughts and feelings in reaction to your experience. To evaluate how well you did, first consider the dynamics of the situation in which you were asked to function. Consider: "What was the pervading atmosphere of the unit? How could I have been better accepted into this work group? What did I need that I did not get? What was the quality of my patient care?"

If the atmosphere was friendly with supportive leadership and staff, then examine your performance in light of your usual self-expectations. If, however, the situation was tense, chaotic, hostile, or volatile, use less exacting criteria for evaluating your performance. In difficult situations set realistic expectations about the quality of your nursing care and your influence on the unit. Accept the limitations imposed on you by elements in the environment that are beyond your control. Don't be overly critical of a less-than-perfect performance. Use what you learned in this situation to make your next floating experience more satisfying.

As a new nurse, whether floating or working on your home unit, recognizing group dynamics is one key to your success. There is more to nursing than clinical competence. Developing an understanding of group dynamics and the skills to work with people in a group helps you make the transition from school to the work world.

Bibliography

Cohen M, Ross M: Team building: A strategy for unit cohesiveness. J Nurs Admin, January 1982, pp 29–34

Kipnis D, Schmidt SM: Profiles of Organizational Influence Strategies: Influencing Your Manager, Diagnostic Survey and Profile. San Diego, University Associates, 1982

Larson M, Williams RA: Understanding group processes. In Longo D, Williams RA (eds): Clinical Practice in Psychosocial Nursing. New York, Appleton-Century-Crofts, 1978

Tuckman B: Developmental sequence in small groups. Psychol Bull 63:384, 1965

Wilson H, Kneisl C: Psychiatric Nursing. Menlo Park, CA, Addison-Wesley, 1979

Exercises

EXERCISE 4-1   INTERVIEW GUIDE

Directions.   Your inclusion into a work group is eased if you understand and acknowledge the concerns of existing group members. Use the following interview guide to help you empathize with and learn from the more experienced nurses in your environment.

Interview three experienced nurses. Ask each of them the following questions:

1. What are the pros and cons of having new nurses join a work group?

Nurse 1	Nurse 2	Nurse 3
Pros:		
Cons:		

2. What does it feel like to work with a group of people, to lose some staff, and then have new people replace them?

Nurse 1	Nurse 2	Nurse 3
Feelings:		

3. What advice would you give to a new nurse who is just starting out and who is trying to be accepted as part of a work group?

Nurse 1	Nurse 2	Nurse 3
Advice:		

4. After the interview, review the comments. What did you learn?

Nurse 1	Nurse 2	Nurse 3
Conclusions:		

EXERCISE 4-2   *GROUP COHESION ASSESSMENT*

Directions. Use the following tool to assess the cohesiveness of your work group. Next to each of the 15 characteristics, write the number that most closely reflects your assessment. Use the following key to guide your choice of numbers:

0 = Not at all
1 = Infrequently
2 = Frequently
3 = Almost all of the time

Total up your group assessment in the box marked total. Record your number on the graph to see how cohesive your group is.

Characteristics	Examples
___ 1. Members value group goals.	Members accept long- and short-term group goals. Members accept leader's priorities. Members participate in formulating group goals. Members perceive group and its work as meaningful. Members are willing to work hard to achieve goals.
___ 2. Individual goals mesh with group goals.	Members feel they benefit personally from group membership. Group membership brings individuals closer to long-term career goals.
___ 3. Group works to attain difficult as well as easy goals.	Difficulties are defined as challenges or opportunities. Difficult jobs are fairly assigned to all members. Leader recognizes and rewards successful completion of difficult tasks.
___ 4. Relationships are friendly and enjoyable.	Members socialize at breaks and mealtimes. Subgroups interact easily and amicably. Members enjoy being together.
___ 5. Relationships are trusting and open.	Communication is direct, honest, and respectful. Members discuss controversial issues without fear of reprisal. Confidentiality is honored. Members resolve conflicts constructively.

Characteristics	Examples
___ 6. Relationships are loyal and supportive.	Members defend group to outside critics. Members avoid criticizing group or its members in front of nonmembers. Members handle conflict internally. Members receive support when speaking up in a meeting. Help is offered when members need it. Risk taking is encouraged and rewarded. Members praise and recognize one another's accomplishments.
___ 7. Participation is stable, reliable, and consistent.	Turnover is low. Call-outs are infrequent. Use of floats or temporary help is minimal. Members arrive on time, complete work on time. Members follow through on commitments.
___ 8. Participation is flexible.	Members readily accept assigned tasks or roles. Members help those who need help. Members willingly fill in for those absent. Members can all fulfill a variety of roles. Members are willing to adapt to change.
___ 9. Participation is goal directed.	Members understand and fulfill their responsibilities. Leader guides group toward goal achievement. Leader assists ineffective or resistant members to alter unacceptable behavior.
___10. Participation is interdependent.	Leadership is democratic. Members cooperate on achieving goals. "We, us" is used to describe the group, not "us vs. them" or "I." Contributions of all members are valued and respected. Members do not compete against each other.
___11. Participation is guided by group norms.	Job descriptions specify expected behavior. Rules are applied fairly and consistently. Rules facilitate rather than hinder the work. Policies and procedures are clear and relevant. Violations of norms are censured.
___12. Participation is productive.	Productivity levels are achieved. Members manage time effectively. Group functions within budget. Conflict does not consume or drain group energy.

Characteristics	Examples
___13. Participation yields high-quality output.	Professional standards are met. Quality assurance audits yield positive feedback. Patients/clients offer positive feedback. Members work to their best ability.
___14. Participation improves the security and self-esteem of members.	Members develop technical–job skills. Individuality is respected and valued. Members interact respectfully. Rewards of membership are both tangible and intangible.
___15. Participation is satisfying.	Members are proud to be group members. Members praise group to outsiders. Work of the group challenges members to grow. Members feel competent to do job and fulfill roles.

☐ Total

Record the number that correlates with your total on the graph below for a picture of how cohesive your group is.

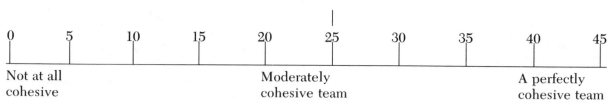

0   5   10   15   20   25   30   35   40   45

Not at all
cohesive

Moderately
cohesive team

A perfectly
cohesive team

EXERCISE 4-3   DEVELOPING GROUP COHESION

Directions.   In order for groups to function effectively, members must work collaboratively and cohesively. Use the following tool to help the members of your group work together as a team. Effective plans must be based on effective assessments. Therefore, if you have not done so, return to Exercise 1 and complete the group cohesion assessment.

Because you cannot alter group dynamics alone and to ensure the validity of your assessment and plan, it is best to work on this exercise with a representative sample, if not the entire collection, of other group members. If this is impossible, complete Part I on your own. Share your thoughts with your nurse manager. Discuss your concerns about group cohesion and how you might work together to enhance the cohesion of your work group.

Part 1: Group Discussion

To check the accuracy of your perceptions and the validity of your group cohesion assessment, it is best to compare your findings with those of other group members. Use the following questions to guide group discussion. If you are working individually, use the following questions to prepare for a discussion with your nurse manager.

A. Which characteristics did you rank highest, as a number 3?

B. Which characteristics did you rank lowest, as a zero?

C. What do you think this assessment reveals about the group?

D. If the group works on them, which characteristics might be *easiest* to develop?

E. Which characteristics are *most important*, the ones most needing improvement?

F. Which characteristics will you work on? Develop consensus among group members about the three characteristics of highly cohesive groups that you plan to work on.

1. _____

2. _____

3. _____

Part 2: Action Plan

In response to question F of Part 1, you identified three characteristics of highly cohesive groups that you want to develop in your work group. Now, work with other group members to plan how to develop those characteristics in your particular work group. Use the following chart to guide you in developing an action plan. Be sure to define behavioral outcomes. These will help you evaluate the effectiveness of your action plan when you work on the final part of this exercise.

Characteristics We Wish to Develop	Specific Ways to Develop this Characteristic	Dates When Steps Will Be Completed	Individual or Organizational Factors That Might Hinder Successful Development
1. _____ _____ _____ _____			
2. _____ _____ _____ _____			
3. _____ _____ _____			

How to Overcome These Hindrances	People Who Will Help in Achieving Our Goal	Measurable, Observable Behavioral Outcomes

Part 3: Evaluation

Follow-through and evaluation is the necessary, final step in any planning process. Use the action plan you developed in Part 2 to guide you in answering the following questions.

A. Were the behavioral objectives achieved? If not, why not?

B. Is the work group operating more cohesively? Cite specific examples to support your evaluation.

C. If you repeated this process, what would you do differently? Why?

D. What additional characteristics of group cohesion would you like to see developed? If you wish, use these to devise a new action plan. Return to Part 2 and repeat the process.

EXERCISE 4-4   BRAINSTORMING

Directions.   The purpose of brainstorming is to creatively generate ideas for conflict resolution or problem solving. Review the brainstorming rules and the parts of the brainstorming process. Then, practice them on a real problem or on one of the hypothetical problems provided below. When working on a real problem, be sure to define it actively. (e.g., Ways to . . . , How to . . .). This puts energy into the process and helps increase the quality of your brainstorming.

Brainstorming Rules

1. Present as many solutions as possible.
2. Do not remark or critique as solutions are listed.
3. No censorship is allowed. Even farfetched and improbable solutions should be brought forth.
4. Producing ideas is separate from evaluating ideas.

Parts of the Brainstorming Process

1. Each person works individually and writes as many solutions as possible.
2. Everyone's solutions are listed on newsprint or a blackboard so all can see. No comments are made during this step.
3. The range of alternative solutions is increased by building on the ideas listed in Part 2. Each person reviews proposed solutions and combines two ideas to form a new idea or changes some aspect of a solution (e.g., size, frequency, timing, etc.) Finally, new ideas are listed along with the other alternative solutions.

Brainstorming Practice

1. Define the problem actively. Write the problem on newsprint or a blackboard so all can see. Choose a real problem or one of the following hypothetical problems:
   a. Ways to support new nurses during the first year in nursing.
   b. Ways to resolve intershift conflict.
   c. How to organize and plan time at work.
   d. How to improve continuity of care.
2. For 5 minutes, individuals write a list of solutions to the problem.
3. The individuals then read their solutions to the group and write them on newsprint or the blackboard.
4. The group expands the range of alternatives and writes them so all can see.
5. Now that idea creation is complete, the group critiques the alternatives and chooses the most effective solutions.

EXERCISE 4-5   FLOATING CHECKLIST

Directions.   Floating can be a frustrating, frightening, or frantic experience. Use the following checklist to help you turn floating into a more comfortable experience for you and for everyone else involved.

Before Leaving Your Unit

1. Check your attitude. Approach the assignment as positively as possible.
2. If you have commitments with patients or other professionals that you must break, notify them of your new assignment. Reschedule or reassign your responsibilities to another nurse.
3. Leave as soon as possible. Delaying only postpones the inevitable and might make your new assignment more pressured.
4. Be sure you are wearing your name tag.

When You Arrive on the Other Unit

1. Introduce yourself to the charge nurse immediately.
2. Clarify your assignment and negotiate an altered assignment if you are unable to do what is asked of you safely.
3. Identify a resource person to whom you can go with questions. Meet that person if you do not already know her or him.
4. Check if there are any peculiarities, unique protocols, or preferences you should honor while working on this unit.
5. Locate key supplies and equipment.
6. Plan and organize your work before you begin.

While Working on the Other Unit

1. Check your attitude. Be as friendly and cooperative as possible. Don't blame the staff for your being here.
2. Be flexible and try to fit in with the staff's way of doing things.
3. Complete your assignment to the best of your ability.
4. Treat this as a learning experience.
5. Ask for help when you need it. Don't be afraid to admit your limitations.
6. Check in with the charge nurse to offer feedback on how your work is progressing.
7. To help retain your energy and to pace yourself, take meals and breaks.

When You Have Finished Working

1. Report off to the charge nurse.
2. Offer feedback to the charge nurse.
3. Evaluate how well you did under the circumstances.
4. Identify what, if anything, you would do differently the next time.
5. Identify what you learned from this experience.

EXERCISE 4-6   **FOR YOUR CONSIDERATION . . . OR . . . FOR GROUP DISCUSSION**

Directions.   Use the following questions to reflect on key points covered in this chapter. Answer these questions individually or in a group discussion.

1. Think of a work group you have tried to enter. List the names of people who were members of the group during your entry. Include your own name. Next to each name, identify things they did or said that reflected that they were including or excluding you. List your own behaviors, too. In conclusion, what kind of behavior facilitates inclusion and what kind hinders inclusion?

Names	Behavioral Examples of Inclusion and Exclusion
1. Yourself	1.
2.	2.
3.	3.
4.	4.
5.	5.
6.	6.
7.	7.
8.	8.
9.	9.
10.	10.

Conclusions:

2. How is the relationship between student and nursing instructor similar to or different from the relationship between new nurse and nurse manager? What impact do these similarities and differences have on you?

Similarities:

Differences:

Impact:

3. What is practiced in the work world is often different from what is taught in nursing education. Marlene Kramer labels these practices "back-stage reality." Cite some examples of back-stage reality and explain why they exist.

Back-Stage Realities	Why They Exist

How do you feel about these back-stage realities? Why?

What, if anything, should be done about these back-stage realities? Why?

5 Networking: Developing Professional Support Systems

Peggy Brindle is in a quandary. As a senior nursing student, she is trying to decide where to work after graduation, a mere 3 months away. The decision seemed easy until this afternoon. Now, everything is confusing and Peggy doesn't know what to do.

Her first choice all along was St. Francis Hospital. In her home town, St. Francis has an excellent reputation for providing high-quality nursing care on a very personalized level. When interviewing at St. Francis, Peggy met the vice-president of nursing, a leader with a reputation that Peggy greatly admires. The nurse recruiter described a very extensive orientation program, and Peggy felt sure that this would meet her needs as a new nurse. Peggy also met the staff members and the manager of the operating room, the people she will work with if she chooses St. Francis. She was interested to hear of the growth in cardiac surgery being done at St. Francis. Peggy's dream is to be part of an open heart surgery team someday. Experience at St. Francis might help her reach that goal. In reviewing her interview at St. Francis, Peggy realizes how "at home" she feels there. Working at this hospital would allow her to live near her family and friends, to work on professional goals, and to work in an environment that is clearly supportive of her and her philosophy of patient care.

This afternoon's interview at Eastern Regional Medical Center (ERMC) has complicated Peggy's decision. On the encouragement of her advisor, Peggy decided to interview with at least one additional hospital. She went to ERMC expecting to dislike the large medical center atmosphere. She sees now that the extensive facilities and programs are quite attractive. ERMC has a fast-paced, competitive, and highly professional atmosphere. Peggy is particularly impressed by the extensive cardiac surgery program. The nurse recruiter assured her that her goal of working on an open heart surgical team could be realized if she worked at ERMC. She would have to spend 1 year on a surgical unit, however, before being considered for work in surgery.

Peggy's dilemma is this. St. Francis Hospital is a known quantity. It is in her home town and has an atmosphere and philosophy with which Peggy feels comfortable. Eastern Regional Medical Center, on the other hand, is an unknown. It is in a town 48 miles from home, and if she chooses to work there Peggy will need to move to a town in which she has no contacts. Peggy is uncertain how nursing is practiced at ERMC. While on the surface everything looks professional and challenging, Peggy knows little about the real workings of ERMC.

Should she play it safe or take a risk? Is ERMC really as fine as it seems? Will she be able to handle the challenges of both moving and acclimating to a new job? Would she like living near ERMC? As Peggy struggles with these questions, she realizes her inability to answer them alone. She needs to talk to other people who can help her analyze the situation and discover which choices will best meet her needs.

After thinking for a moment, Peggy brightens up. She is happy to know that she has several personal and professional friends who can help her analyze her options. Fellow seniors, last year's graduates who work in both settings, and of course her advisor, all are sure sources of support. As Peggy attempts to make this major career decision, she realizes how much her school support system means to her. She wonders also if she will be fortunate enough to find new supporters out in the work world.

Is It Important to Develop Professional Support Systems?

In order to answer this question, you need to identify the nature of support systems and the benefits you can gain from using them. The concept of support systems is described in sociology literature. By definition, a support system is a group of people to whom you are linked, who provide you with resources necessary for living. Because you are a social being and because life is very complex, it is essential to your well-being that you link with other people. It would be nearly impossible and extremely stressful to live or work without the support of others.

There are many different types of support systems, providing different types of resources that you need to survive. The two major categories of support systems are instrumental and expressive. *Instrumental support systems* provide the physical resources necessary for living. They provide things like money, jobs, food, clothing, shelter and physical protection. *Expressive support systems* provide the psychosocial resources necessary for living. These include caring, concern, security, communication, intimacy, and recreation. Some members of your support system provide both instrumental and expressive resources.

The benefits to be gained from using your support systems are many. Support systems actively increase the body's ability to manage stress and to avoid illness. Support systems contribute pleasure and meaning to life. They help you survive when that is a priority and to grow when you have the opportunity. Support systems are necessary for healthy living, in both the personal and professional domains.

During the past 10 years, as women have become more visible and powerful members of the work world, interest in developing professional support systems has grown. The term *network* is often used to refer to a professional support system. By definition, a network is the collection of individuals with whom you interact for the purpose of support, information, and guidance to enhance your professional development. Your network consists of all your contacts and professional associates. When you use your network, you are *networking*. This verb is defined as the process of linking with your professional support system; it is the process of making things happen in your career by reaching out and using the various people you already know or know of.

Whether you call it a professional network or professional support system, as a new nurse you need to connect with these people. Trying to face this major professional transition alone leaves you vulnerable to the stresses you encounter and diminishes your ability to master the challenges before you. As you make the transition from school to the work world, seek both to develop supportive individual relationships and to join supportive professional groups. Look for role models whom you can emulate. Work with a clinical preceptor to develop competence and confidence in your skills. Develop supportive, friendly relationships with nurses as well as nonnurses. If one does not already exist, develop a new nurses' network in your place of employment. Finally, link with professional organizations or informal groups of nurses, to continue your professional growth after graduation.

How Can I Establish and Use a Network?

Your broadest, most extensive professional support system is your network. If you think about all the people you know and all the people they know, you can see that each contact in your professional network is multiplied many times over. There is almost no limit to the resources in your professional network. As Peggy Brindle contacts her advisor at school, she links with one person in her professional network. To help Peggy out, the advisor gives Peggy the names of three nurses from Eastern Regional Medical Center. Peggy's network now consists of four people. By contacting two of last year's graduates who are old friends, Peggy is directed to four other staff members at ERCM. Peggy's network now includes a total of 10 people who can give her information that will help her in choosing a place of employment. This is networking, using professional contacts to the benefit of your career.

If you want to develop your career, you need to develop your skills at networking. Men in the work world have understood this concept for a long time. Historically, men have used the "old boy" network to develop and grow in their careers. Women must have this kind of support system as well. Traditionally, women develop supportive relationships in the personal and domestic domains, but tend to "go it alone" in the working world. Facing career challenges on your own is a risky and often ineffective career development strategy.

Most literature on the supportive process of networking presents it as a tool, useful for women who want to get ahead in the male-dominated professions or business arena. It is also a tremendously valuable tool for women in female-dominated professions such as nursing. There are no men within nursing locking women out of the positions at the top. Women fill almost all of these influential roles. But in the broader arena of the nation's health care system, nursing does not hold as many positions of power and influence as it should. Networking with nurses, as well as with other professionals, will help the profession of nursing to make a more powerful impact on the U.S. health care system and on the quality of patient care. Networking, then, is an effective strategy for individual career development, for developing the profession of nursing, and for influencing the health care system.

Develop the Prerequisites for Networking

There are several prerequisites to successful networking. First, you must have a basic self-interest. This generates a desire to get ahead. Without this, there is no reason for networking. Second, successful networking occurs when the tendency to help others is replaced by a willingness to use others and in turn, to be used. Women and nurses are traditionally taught to be givers and helpers, and for many, being takers and users is quite uncomfortable. In a helping relationship, the giver/helper is in a position of greater strength. This power comes from control of resources that the other needs or wants. The person receiving help has less power because she or he is in a position of relying on another. The imbalance of power in a helping relationship is death to a networking relationship because over a period of time, the stronger, more effective member becomes exhausted by putting out and not receiving as much in return. Networking fails when it is one-sided, when one person gives while the other person takes. In contrast, the second prerequisite for networking suggests a more balanced approach. Called the *mutual-use* approach, it is an enlivening force in networking. Mutual use is a synergistic process in which each networker interacts with others from a position of strength, contributing or using whatever is needed. The personal strength that is the cornerstone of mutual use arises from the third prerequisite for networking, a positive self-concept. In order to be useful and to feel comfortable in using your network, you must think well of yourself and of your capabilities. So, armed with the three prerequisites, a basic self-interest, the ability to use and to be used, and a high self-esteem, you are ready to participate in the process of networking.

Work Individually or in Groups

You can approach networking on an individual basis, as Peggy Brindle is doing when she contacts the people to whom she has been referred. You can also approach networking within the more formal structure of a group. As you join professional nursing organizations, community groups, or other health care groups, you develop contacts and you extend your network.

Use Your Contacts

Whether done on an individual basis or within the structure of a professional group, networking starts with an assessment of the current state of your career and with a definition of your career goals. Remember, the purpose of networking is to help you link with the resources you need to help develop your career. Before you can pursue and connect with those resources, you need to know where you are going. Use the career planning exercise at the end of this chapter to help you focus and to make the best use of your resources.

Once you are clear about your career goals, it is easy to get involved in networking. You already have an existing network. Start networking by first identifying members of your current network; co-workers, colleagues, family members, and friends. Although these people have provided you with the career assistance and support necessary to reach your present position, you need to expand your current network. Keep in touch with this current network, continue to include them and use them for support. Also include new people who can help you move ahead toward your goals.

When Peggy Brindle contacts the seven people who work at ERMC, she expands her current network to include new people. These people can help her in her career decision and will continue to be resources to her in the future as well. To achieve your career goals you need to specifically link the professional skills of your contacts with your goals. Ask those in your current network for contacts. When you get leads, be sure to follow up on them. Set some time aside every week for networking. Meet for networking during breakfast, lunch, or dinner; over coffee or a drink after work. Arrive early at nursing association meetings so that you have time to talk informally with other nurses. When you attend seminars or professional conferences, introduce yourself to new people. Discuss your interests and concerns. When asking for help from people with whom you are networking, be sure your focus is clear and your questions are refined. Don't be afraid to ask for what you need, but only ask for one thing at a time. You don't want to overload your network. When someone is unavailable or brushes you off, don't be discouraged. Your priorities are not necessarily theirs. As soon as possible, however, talk with another network contact so you keep the networking process alive. Finally, remember that networking is a mutual-use process. Make yourself available as a resource to others. Try to give as much as you get from your network. Don't think that just because you are a new nurse you have nothing to offer. Remember that you have many contacts, strengths, skills, and resources that you can and should share with your professional network.

Develop a Peer Support Group

Peggy is now completing her sixth exhausting week as a surgical staff nurse at ERMC. She knew the honeymoon phase wouldn't last forever but she *never* dreamt it would be over so quickly! During the three weeks of hospital orientation Peggy met seven other new nurses, just as excited and nervous as herself. They sat together in classes and ate lunches with each other during orientation. By the end of the orientation program, they jokingly referred to themselves as "the Group." Much to her dismay, Peggy has seen none of them in the past 2 weeks. This is the time she most needs their moral support, but because they are assigned to several units throughout the medical center, they have no regular opportunity to meet.

Peggy knows that a meeting of the Group would help her to become more confident and perform better. She wonders if any of the others are feeling as overwhelmed as she does. Reassuring herself that at least one of the Group must be in the same boat, Peggy vows to phone them tonight and organize a pot-luck supper. Even if everyone else is breezing along with no problems, Peggy knows it will be helpful for her to be together with them.

The transition from the student nurse role to the working nurse role is a difficult one. The discomfort and difficulties of this role transition are made easier when you share them with others. More experienced nurses can help you solve problems. Clinical nurse specialists can help you hone your skills. Your nurse manager or staff-development representative can guide and reassure you. Family and friends can encourage you. Your peer group of other new nurses, however, can offer you a very unique kind of support. Because they share your experiences, your peer group understands you in a way that other members of your support system do not. New nurses empathize and validate the feelings that you experience as you move through this role transition. A unique and essential type of support and encouragement is gained from peer support groups. Help yourself through this difficult role transition by developing and using peer support groups.

How Can I Establish a Peer Support Group?

Develop a Formal or Informal Group

Talk with your staff development instructor to see if developing a new nurse support group is part of the orientation process. Work through the staff development department to form a support group, if at all possible. The formal, organizational support for such a group validates its significance. Developing a support group through staff development and the orientation program assures you that this group is perceived positively and constructively, rather than as a threat or as insignificant. If your organization chooses not to support the development of a new nurse support group, you can and should develop one independently. This independent group, however, must meet informally on personal time of its members.

Follow Group-Formation Guidelines

Whether your new nurse support group is formally sanctioned or is conducted independently, there are several guidelines you should follow in forming a group. First, find one or two other new nurses who agree on the need for a new nurse support group. Among yourselves, decide on the size you want the group to be. If there are many new nurses in your organization, you may want to develop several support groups. Group size and membership are determined by your preferences and goals. As a rule of thumb, groups dedicated to sharing feelings should be small, no more than a dozen members. Educational groups with minimal commitment to exploring feelings can be somewhat larger. When you decide on group size and membership, prepare a list of all the new nurses you want to include. Inform them of the purpose of the new nurse support group and the date, time, and place of the first meeting. A telephone call, personal introduction or brief letter are all effective ways to accomplish this task.

During the first meeting, a chairperson is helpful for keeping the group focused on some significant agenda items. Someone from the initial steering committee is a likely person to fulfill this role. The first meeting of a peer support group is spent on structuring the group. The chairperson leads a discussion of key structural issues listed below. Write responses to the discussion of these issues on newsprint to keep group discussion on track and to record the decisions of the group. Some important questions to be answered are as follows:

What is the purpose of this new nurse support group?

Will our meetings be structured with an agenda or unstructured?

Do we want speakers or presentations?

How frequently will this group get together and at what time of day?

How long will meetings last?

Where will meetings be held?

How do we plan to announce meetings—by mail, word of mouth, or phone?

Do we need some type of governing body or steering committee?

Do we need to feed back results of this group to the organization?

Do we need to notify anyone in the organization of the existence and purpose of this group?

If we have refreshments, what will they be and how shall we pay for them?

What shall we name this group?

It might take several sessions to answer these questions completely, but when you have, your group is structurally formed and ready to begin functioning as a peer support group. The structure of your group and the topics you discuss might evolve over time as the needs and interests of members change. Be flexible and be open to group evolution. Group change reflects the growth and development of the new nurses in the group.

Make the Most of Your Resources

Use the following guidelines to help you develop and make the most of your new nurse support group. First, identify clearly what you need from the group. As an adult, it is your responsibility to identify your needs. Don't depend on others to figure out your needs for you. Before approaching your peer support group, reflect on the type of support you need most. New nurse support groups frequently offer listening, emotional validation, clinical advice, interpersonal advice, and emotional release.

After you clarify the nature of your needs, follow the second guideline, which suggests that you ask others for what they have to give. Everyone has limits on what and how much they can give. If you need to let off steam, talk to people who are comfortable with frustration and anger. Avoid people who are not. If you need assistance in prioritizing your time, seek help from those who manage time well, not those who are as bad as or worse than you are in this respect. Asking others for what they don't have is like going to a dry well; you don't get anything to satisfy your needs. It increases rather than decreases your stress.

A third guideline for developing and using your peer support group is to diversify. This means using many different people for support. Broadening your support system is a self-protective mechanism. Relying on only one or two peers leaves you vulnerable; if they are absent from or decide to leave the group, you are left without support. To protect yourself, form relationships with many members of your peer group.

The last guideline for developing and using your peer support group is to take action on their recommendations. All of their advice is worthless unless you apply it to your life. While your peer group can offer many kinds of support, it is up to you to change your life by using it. Unless you follow through on the recommendations of your peer support group, the group will have no real impact on the success of your transition into nursing.

How Can I Work with a Preceptor?

Over Sunday brunch, Peggy and her school friend Liz share stories about their first few months as staff nurses. They laugh, groan, and speak with pride about their first exposure to "the real world." The high-tech, fast-paced world of the urban medical center has proved stimulating, but sometimes a bit too stimulating for Peggy. Her preceptor is the one person who has helped her learn to perform in this demanding environment.

As Peggy describes working in tandem with her preceptor, Liz feels a bit envious. Although the community hospital at which she works is smaller, she finds her job every bit as demanding as Peggy's. One difference is that she has no preceptor to help her ease into her role. Since the end of orientation, Liz is considered a full member of the staff, rotating shifts and taking as many patients as the more experienced nurses. At times, Liz feels overwhelmed by the responsibilities and details of the staff nurse role and finds other nurses too busy to help her work things out.

As you move into your first nursing position, you must begin to use your theoretical knowledge and clinical skills in the real world of health care. More is expected of a paid employee than of a student. You are expected to *do* patient care, not to be learning how to do patient care. As Peggy and Liz recognize, a conflict arises because the new nurse has much to learn about operating within the work world. There is a large learner component to the new nurse role, and this clashes with the expectations of professional performance.

Seek a Preceptor—Everyone Benefits

One way in which organizations attempt to address the learning needs of new nurses is to use experienced nurses as preceptors for inexperienced new professionals. To develop your clinical confidence and competence as quickly as possible, it is a good idea to work with a clinical preceptor. While some organizations have formal preceptor programs, others do not. If you work in an organization that has no formal preceptor program, seek out an experienced and effective nurse who will work closely with you in developing your capabilities. A preceptor, whether formally or informally chosen, is a clinical resource, role model, and teacher. A *preceptor* is a nurse who has proven clinical competence and is willing to form a student–teacher relationship with a new nurse.

Benefits of precepting are gained by the new nurse, the preceptor, and the organization in which they work. As Peggy discovered, the new nurse gains competence and confidence in performing clinical skills. The new nurse learns practical knowledge from clinical preceptors and is given close supervision and immediate feedback on performance. Socialization to the nursing role is facilitated and the impact of reality shock is eased when new nurses work with clinical preceptors.

The new nurse is not the only one to gain in the preceptor relationship. Although the preceptors expend a great deal of time and energy with the new nurses who work with them, preceptors are stimulated and challenged to grow. Preceptors refine their clinical as well as teaching skills. Organizations often provide tangible rewards for acting as preceptors. Intangible rewards, such as recognition and respect, are also associated with functioning as a preceptor. Finally, preceptors gain personal satisfaction from knowing that they have helped to train and ease the transition for new nurses.

Organizations also benefit from preceptor–new nurse relationships. Role transition problems are dealt with more expediently. New nurses become fully functioning members of a work group more quickly when they receive clinical coaching from preceptors. This helps the organization to function more productively, a priority for all of today's health care institutions.

Because so many people benefit from preceptorships, don't be afraid or embarrassed to ask your preceptor for help and guidance. You will grow, and your preceptor, organization, and patients will benefit if you use this relationship well. If you and your preceptor do not function well together, the benefits of the relationship are diminished. Try to work out your problems. If this fails, don't blame yourself or your preceptor. This wastes time and energy. Rather, go to your head nurse or staff development instructor to obtain a new preceptor with whom you can work.

Begin a Relationship

How to utilize your preceptor is clearly defined by Arlene Perish Grey in Stuart-Siddall and Haberlin's book *Preceptorships in Nursing Education.* Grey states that the phases used to establish a preceptor relationship are similar to those you use when establishing a therapeutic relationship with a patient. The three phases are:

1. The beginning or orientation phase when contact is established
2. The middle or working phase when contact is maintained
3. The end or termination phase when contact is evaluated and terminated

The objective of the *orientation* phase is to initiate contact between yourself and your preceptor. The purpose of the relationship is clearly defined during this phase. The roles, responsibilities, and privileges of both yourself and your preceptor are discussed. The standards for evaluating your learning are examined during the orientation phase. Often a skill checklist is used for this purpose. You and your preceptor should identify the skills you need to develop. The length of the relationship is designated during the orientation phase and is time limited. Finally, during this phase, it is important to start to establish a trusting relationship, with mutual understanding and respect. Sharing personal information, feelings or hopes for the relationship are some ways for you to begin to develop trust. Trust and respect between you and your preceptor evolve over time. They deepen as experiences are shared and as the relationship progresses into the next phase.

Work Together Closely

The middle or *working* phase of the preceptor relationship is focused on helping you to develop clinical confidence and competence. It is also dedicated to facilitating your assumption of the role of practicing nurse. During this second phase, your preceptor and you work closely together. You assume the role of student, and the preceptor acts as a teacher, resource person, and role model. You learn by doing, as well as by receiving feedback and guidance from your preceptor. As you gain in confidence and grow in capability, the preceptor steps back, allowing you to function ever more independently.

Evaluate and Terminate the Relationship

The final phase of the preceptor relationship is *termination*. The major objective of this phase is to evaluate the experience and the relationship in a mutually satisfying manner. As in a therapeutic relationship, you and your preceptor review the experience, each from your own perspective. You evaluate the outcomes on the basis of the objectives defined in the orientation phase of the relationship. To provide a sense of closure in the relationship, both you and your preceptor discuss what the experience meant to you, what you gained from the experience and what you would do differently if you had it to do over again. When preceptor relationships are part of a formal orientation program, results of this evaluation are fed back to the staff development department, which is responsible for new nurse orientation. Results are then analyzed in light of the evaluations of other new nurses and preceptors. As in the nursing process, the evaluations contribute to planning and developing preceptor relationships for future new nurses. When termination has occurred, you are no longer an orientee. You are now a full member of the staff and, with the help of the preceptor, you have mastered many of the challenges associated with the transition from student nurse to practicing nurse.

As you make the transition from student to practicing nurse, ease that transition by working with a preceptor. During employment interviews, ask the person who is conducting the interview to describe the orientation program. Ask specifically about the use of preceptors during orientation. Ask what the preceptor's credentials are, how preceptors are prepared for their role, how their effectiveness is evaluated. Ask for a description of how new nurses and preceptors work in this organization and how long the relationship lasts. If no formal preceptor program is included as part of the orientation, ask what informal arrangements can be made to assist you in assuming your new role.

How Can I Work with a Mentor?

Following the discussion with Liz, her former classmate, Peggy recognizes how fortunate she is to be working in an organization like ERMC. She recalls the difficulty with which she made that important career decision and is deeply grateful to have had her advisor's guidance. Peggy knows she never would have had the courage to risk moving and working at ERMC without the encouragement and support of her advisor.

Her advisor's years of experience in perioperative nursing proved to be an invaluable resource as Peggy evaluated her options. No question was ever too dumb to ask. Instead, Peggy's advisor was available, patient, and personally interested in helping her grow. In contrast, many of Peggy's classmates received little or no career advice from their advisors. Why her advisor showed such interest in her Peggy does not understand. Whatever the reason, Peggy feels very fortunate to have had the support and guidance of her advisor.

One final type of professional support is the mentor. A *mentor* is one who takes a deep personal interest in you and your career. Mentors are usually older, more experienced, and more skillful than the persons they guide. Like members of a professional network, mentors can play a significant role in your professional development and in the development of the nursing profession. A staff development instructor, clinical nurse specialist, experienced staff nurse, nurse manager, or nursing instructor can act as a mentor and help ease your transition from the student role to that of practicing nurse. By making a personal commitment to helping you develop your career, a mentor can teach, guide, support, and counsel you in this role transition. A mentor can protect you, stimulate you, and introduce you to valuable networking contacts. Table 5-1 presents a clear, concise description of the roles and characteristics of effective mentors. The role of the protegé complements that of mentor. To benefit from your mentor's greater experience, wisdom, and contacts, act as a student, a learner, a helper, and an active participant in the relationship.

Seek a Mentor—You Both Benefit

As in the preceptor relationship, both you and your mentor gain from working together. Peggy illustrates how you benefit by greater insight, knowledge, and connections. Your career grows more quickly and there is a greater likelihood of your becoming successful at a younger age. Finally, because of your mentor's support, the discomfort of role transition is eased. As a result, your move into nursing is more pleasant and less painful. Your mentor also gains from the relationship. Though Peggy doesn't realize it, the mentor has the pleasure of seeing her grow and achieve professional goals. The same concept applies to your mentor. Knowing that the mentor can help you reaffirms her or his experience, skills, and competence. Finally, a mentor experiences a broader professional satisfaction in knowing that supporting a protegé contributes to the development of the nursing profession.

Seeking out and developing a relationship with a mentor is based on the networking process. It is important to understand your professional capabilities and goals. This guides you in your choice of a mentor. Choose someone

166 Networking: Developing Professional Support Systems

Table 5-1　　　　**Mentor Characteristics**

1. Model	Someone you look up to, admire Someone you want to emulate
2. Envisioner	Someone who communicates an image, goal, or meaningful vision of the professional world
3. Energizer	Someone who stimulates you with a dynamic or enthusiastic approach to professional performance
4. Investor	Someone who manifests her or his belief in you by investing time and energy in your career and by actively helping you grow
5. Supporter	Someone who offers emotional encouragement and reassurance Someone who instills confidence and fosters risk taking
6. Standard prodder	Someone who pushes you to achieve excellence and high standards
7. Teacher–coach	Someone who teaches you or guides you in learning important technical, interpersonal, political, or professional skills
8. Feedback giver	Someone who offers both positive and negative feedback based on factual, observable data
9. Eye opener	Someone who broadens your perspective Someone who opens up new horizons, ideas, concepts, or possibilities
10. Door opener	Someone who willingly provides opportunities and professional experiences to help you grow
11. Idea bouncer	Someone who discusses ideas or opinions Someone who acts as a sounding board
12. Problem solver	Someone who effectively assists you in examining and solving problems
13. Career counselor	Someone who helps you clarify career interests, priorities, and long range plans
14. Challenger	Someone who stimulates you to think more critically or to explore issues more deeply

(Adapted from Darling LA: What do nurses want in a mentor? J Nurs Admin, October 1984)

who is knowledgeable in your area of interest and who can help you attain your career goals. Ideally, the person should also be confident, mature, capable, and willing to work with you in your growth. Take a proactive approach to developing a mentor–protegé relationship. Use your network to find and introduce you to the mentor you desire. Ask a potential mentor if she or he is willing to discuss certain of your areas of interest or topics of concern. Explain your commitment to professional growth and your recognition and admiration for her or his competence. Although initiating this contact may be uncomfortable, you may be surprised at the potential mentor's willingness to help you. The first step is often the most difficult. Initiating a mentor–protegé relationship usually is the responsibility of the protegé.

If you do not have a specific relationship with a mentor, don't worry about it. Although this is a very special type of supportive relationship, it is not essential to career success. You can obtain guidance and encouragement from many people in your professional network. It need not come from one mentor.

Assume Responsibility for Your Development

If you are fortunate enough to develop a relationship with a mentor, realize that this is no guarantee of professional growth or success. You must take responsibility for implementing the recommendations and using the support of your mentor. You are in charge because, no matter how helpful your mentor is, the developing career is yours. Your supporters, whether peers, preceptors, other professionals, or your mentor, can only support you. The responsibility for action and implementation always lies with you.

Mastering the transition from student nurse to practicing nurse is a tremendous challenge. To resolve problems that arise and learn all that you need to learn, the support of others is essential. Develop and use professional support systems to help you deal with the stress of this major life transition. It will help you to be a more effective nurse and a more satisfied person.

Bibliography

Darling L: The mentoring dimension series. J Nurs Admin October 1984–present

Harragan B: Games Mother Never Taught You. New York, Warner Books, 1977

Hennig M, Jardim A: The Managerial Woman. New York, Pocket Books, 1977

Kleiman C: Woman's Networks. New York, Lippincott/Crowell, 1980

Morrow K: Perceptorships in Nursing Staff Development. Rockville, MD, Aspens Systems, 1984

Nowak J, Grindel C: Career Planning in Nursing. Philadelphia, JB Lippincott, 1984

Persons CB, Wieck L: Networking: A power strategy. Nurs Economics, January–February 1985

Plasse N, Lederer J: Preceptors: A resource for new nurses. Supervisor Nurse, June 1981

Puetz B: Networking for Nurses. Rockville, MD, Aspen Systems, 1983

Stuart–Siddall S, Haberlin J: Preceptorships in Nursing Education. Rockville, MD, Aspen Systems, 1983

Welch M: Networking. New York, Harcourt Brace Jovanovich, 1980

Exercises

EXERCISE 5-1   YOUR SUPPORT SYSTEM

Directions.   Your support system is the group of people to whom you are linked, who provide you with resources necessary for living. Members of your support system provide instrumental support—the physical resources you need—or expressive support, which meets your psychosocial needs. Support systems are necessary for healthy living in both the personal and professional aspects of your life.

Use this exercise to identify who is a member of your support system—people in your life today or supporters from the past, people with whom you interact frequently or infrequently. Write your name in the circle on the following page. As you respond to the following statements, write the names inside circles that you draw on the paper as illustrated in the sample circle marked Sue. List members of your professional support system on the left side of the paper and personal supporters on the right side. Connect each circle to the one in the center of the page that has your name on it, as the sample circle illustrates. At the end of this exercise you will have a diagram of your personal and professional support system.

Write the names of people in your support system:

With whom you presently have the strongest, closest bonds

Who have given you strong support during past phases of your life

Who nurture you, reaffirming your goodness and uniqueness

Who challenge you to grow and develop as a person

With whom you relax, laugh, or have fun

Who would lend you money, a car, or some other instrumental resource you might need

Who let you vent anger, shed tears, or release other emotions

Who listen and give you constructive feedback

Who help you manage the details of daily living (e.g., child care, car or home maintenance)

Who help you solve problems

Who teach you or challenge you to grow as a nurse

Who affirm your professional capabilities and competence

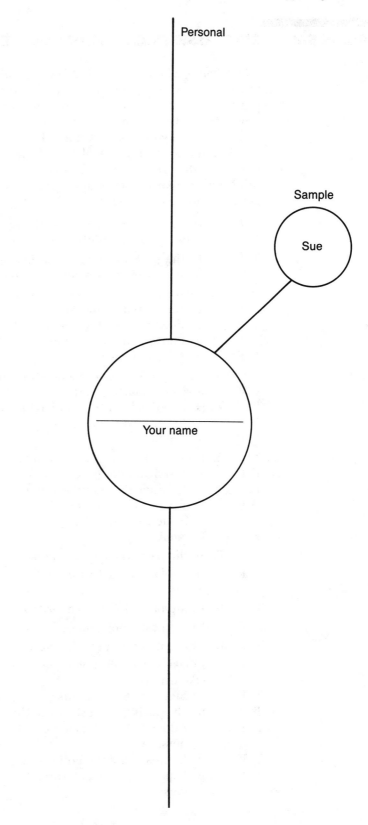

Professional

Personal

Sample

Sue

Your name

EXERCISE 5-2   SELF-ASSESSMENT: ARE YOU READY FOR NETWORKING?

Directions. There are several prerequisites to successful networking. You must have a positive self-concept and a desire to grow in your career. You also must be able to use others as resources for professional growth and allow others to use you in the same manner. Finally, you must be clear about what you need from your network and what you have to offer others.

Use the following list of true–false items to assess your attitudes and behaviors that prepare you for networking. True answers indicate that you think and act like a successful networker. Work to change false responses and get ready for networking.

T F 1. In the past week I have shared some of my knowledge, skill, or expertise with another professional person.

T F 2. In the past week I have asked for help, information, or feedback from another professional person.

3. I have at least two peers whom I can ask for:
T F a. Emotional support
T F b. Feedback on my behavior/decisions
T F c. Praise and recognition
T F d. A challenge

4. I have at least two peers who come to me for:
T F a. Emotional support
T F b. Feedback on their behavior/decisions
T F c. Praise and recognition
T F d. Challenge

5. I tend to live within the limits of my:
T F a. Physical energy resources
T F b. Emotional energy resources
T F c. Financial resources
T F d. Time resources
T F e. Knowledge

T F 6. In the past week I have done something just to please myself.

T F 7. In the last week I *proudly* told someone about one of my achievements.

T F 8. In the past year I have written a career plan.

T F 9. In the past week I have learned something new.

T F 10. I have met two new people in the past week.

11. I make it a general practice to nurture a positive self-concept and to take care of myself by:
T F a. Sleeping 6 to 8 hours per night
T F b. Exercising at least two to three times per week
T F c. Allowing myself to feel all of my emotions—anger, sadness, gladness, fear
T F d. Expressing my emotions honestly and directly
T F e. Separating the pressures of work from my home life and vice versa

T F   f. Socializing with others at least once a week

T F   g. Reading something other than work-related material

T F   h. Keeping abreast of current events

T F   i. Praying or meditating regularly

T F   j. Trusting in God or a "higher power"

T F   k. Validating myself as a good person

T F   l. Exposing myself to others who validate me as a good person.

EXERCISE 5-3 MINIGAME: THE GIVE AND TAKE OF NETWORKING

Directions. Networking relationships are a bit different from the helping relationships you develop with patients. Although assistance is given in both types of relationships, in networking, a "mutual-use" approach is used. That is, each networker approaches others from a position of strength, whether giving or taking. Networkers expect to get as well as to give. In contrast, the nurse–patient relationship is characterized by one giving to another and expecting little in return. Successful networking requires that you be comfortable in using others as resources and in turn, in allowing your network to use you.

Women and nurses are traditionally taught to be givers and helpers, but for many being a taker or user is quite uncomfortable. Use the following minigame in a group or classroom setting to practice and to assess your feelings about the give and take of networking.

Preliminary Steps

1. Give each person a 3 × 5 card and a straight pin. In large letters, print *Giver* on one side and print *Taker* on the other side of the card.
2. Divide the group into pairs.
3. Present the following situations to the pairs. Both people will act as a giver in one situation and as a taker in the other. Ask the pairs to decide between themselves who will be a giver and who will be a taker in situation A. They will switch roles for situation B. (You may choose to create your own situations, if you wish. When writing your own situations, make sure that one person needs assistance and the other person can offer suggestions or support.)

Situation A

Taker: A new nurse who is working the PM shift for only the third time finds organizing her time very difficult. It looks as if she will leave work late, once again. She is tired, frustrated, and unsure about how to organize her time more effectively.

Giver: An experienced nurse who has worked the PM shift for 2 years is taking a break before finishing up her work for the evening. The experienced nurse doesn't know the new nurse very well, but she recognizes ineffective organizational skills when she sees them.

Situation B

Taker: A senior nursing student is trying to decide where to work after graduation. The medical center is large, highly professional, and known for state-of-the-art medical care. The community hospital is smaller, more personal, and known for its patient- and family-centered care. Both seem challenging, and the student is unsure of which to choose.

Giver: A nurse who had 3 years of experience at the medical center before moving 2 years ago to the community hospital is willing to discuss the choice with the student. Though the student doesn't know the experienced nurse, she telephones her for some help with this career choice.

Action Steps

Situation A

1. In each pair, whoever plays the part of the new nurse pins the 3 × 5 card to her or his lapel, with *Taker* showing. The one playing the experienced nurse wears the *Giver* card.
2. Each person takes 5 minutes to plan how she or he will fulfill her or his taker or giver role.
3. Following the planning period, the pairs act out the scene, giving and taking assistance. Playing the scene should take between 5 and 10 minutes.

Situation B

1. Switch roles and lapel cards. The senior nursing student wears the *Taker* card; the experienced nurse wears the *Giver* card.
2. Each person takes 5 minutes to plan how they will fulfill her or his taker or giver role.
3. Following the planning period, the pairs act out the scene, giving and taking assistance. Playing the scene should take between 5 and 10 minutes.

Group Discussion

Discuss your observations and analyze your reactions to the game by answering the following questions.

1. What should you do to prepare to give in networking? To take?
2. What behaviors and communication skills helped you to effectively give in the networking situation? To take?
3. How did you feel as a giver in the networking situation? As a taker? Explain your reactions.
4. What could you do to perform more effectively or more comfortably as a giver in networking? As a taker?

EXERCISE 5-4 THE NETWORK YOU WILL NEED

Directions. Your broadest, most extensive professional support system is your network. Using your present network has helped you get to where you are today. To develop your career and to attain long-term goals, you must expand your current network, adding people with different skills, knowledge, or contacts.

Use this activity to remind yourself of who is in your present network. Then, focus on your career aspirations and begin to formulate the network you will need. Take action, contact new members of your network and ask for their assistance. Be sure that your questions are clear and well-defined. Limit the amount of help you request. You don't want to overload your network, especially new network members. Finally, thank people who assist you in any way, and offer yourself as a resource to them.

1. Who is in your current network?

Members of a current network:
  a. Co-workers or colleagues, past and present
  b. Teachers, school friends, and school acquaintances
  c. Parents and their contacts/networks
  d. Other relatives and their contacts/networks
  e. Acquaintances from communities, churches, or synagogues
  f. Acquaintances from clubs or professional organizations
  g. Anyone who is known and can readily be contacted, e.g., local journalists, elected officials, nursing leaders

My current network:

2. Who would you like to be in your future network?
Career aspirations:
   a. Major career goals

   b. The field in which I will work

   c. Related fields

Members of a future network:
   a. People who have attained my career goals
   b. People in the field in which I plan to work
   c. People in related fields
   d. People who will use my services in the future
   e. People with knowledge, skills, resources, contacts, or advice that will help me
   f. People who know others who will help me attain my goals

My future network:

How I will contact my future network

EXERCISE 5-5   **GUIDELINES FOR DEVELOPING A PEER SUPPORT GROUP**

Directions.   The transition from the student nurse role to the practicing nurse role is a difficult one. The difficulties and discomforts of this role transition are made easier when you share them with others. Your peer group of new nurses offers a special kind of support—empathy, sharing, understanding—that no one else can. Use this list of questions and suggestions as a guideline in developing and using a peer support group.

Seeking Out an Existing Group

1. Is there a formally organized new nurse support group within your organization? If so, how can you join the group?
2. Is there an informal group of new nurses within your place of employment who act as a support system for one another? If so, how can you join the group?
3. Is there an informal group of new nurses within a professional nursing organization who act as a support system for one another? If so, how can you join the group?

Forming a Peer Support Group

1. Who are two other new nurses who would like to form a support group?

    Along with these two people, work to initiate a peer support group by answering the following questions:
2. Do we want this to be an informal group or one operated formally, under the auspices of the organization?

3. What will be the goals of this group?

4. How large will this group be?

5. Who will be members of this group? Prepare a list of names.

6. How will potential group members be notified of the formation of this peer support group (e.g., phone, written invitation)?

7. What information will be included in the invitation to the group?

8. When will the first meeting be held?

9. How long will the first meeting last?

10. Where will the first meeting be held?

11. Who, if anyone, in the organization should be notified about the formation of the peer support group? How will they be notified?

Conducting the First Meeting

1. Create a circular seating arrangement so all participants can see and hear each other, in order to facilitate group communication.
2. Begin and end at the times designated in the invitation to communicate respect for members' other time commitments.
3. Consider providing refreshments to create a comfortable atmosphere and reinforce the nurturant nature of the group.
4. Begin the session with personal introductions to start developing relationships among group members.
5. The three initiators of the group should co-lead the meeting to provide leadership and help the group get organized. To help the group clarify its focus, ask members to discuss the following questions:
   a. What is the purpose of this group?
   b. Will our meetings be structured with an agenda?
   c. Do we want speakers or presentations at meetings?
   d. When (time of day/frequency) shall we meet?
   e. How long will meetings last?
   f. How shall we announce meetings?
   g. Where will meetings be held?
   h. Does this group need a governing body?
   i. Should we notify anyone in the organization of the existence and purpose of this group? If so, how?

j. Do we need to provide feedback to the organization? If so, how?

k. If we have refreshments, what will they be and how shall we pay for them?

l. What will we name this group?

Using Your Support Group

1. What specific kinds of help do you need?

2. Which members of your support group can best help you?

3. Are there people not currently in your support group who can help you? If so, how can you contact them?

4. Who in your support group needs your assistance? How can you help them?

5. How can you implement the useful suggestions of your support group?

EXERCISE 5-6 — WORKING WITH YOUR MENTOR

Directions. In her research, LuAnn Darling identified 14 characteristics that describe significant ways that nursing mentors guide professional development. Use this tool to assess the capabilities of a mentor. Use it in a second way to clarify your needs for yourself and for your mentor.

When you use this tool as a mentor assessment, circle the number for each characteristic that most accurately represents your mentor's qualities. High-quality mentoring is indicated by the following responses:

1. A score of at least 4 on one of the first three characteristics—model, envisioner, or energizer
2. A score of at least 4 on both investor and supporter
3. High ratings in several of the remaining characteristics

When assessing your own needs in Part 2, circle the number that most accurately represents how strongly you need this type of help from your mentor. Following the self-assessment, be sure to ask for this kind of help from your mentor or from other members of your professional support system.

Finally, compare the mentor assessment scores with your self-assessment scores. Where do the two scores overlap? Where do they differ? What do the scores say about your mentor/protegé relationship? Discuss your observations with your mentor.

Part 1: Mentor Assessment

Characteristics		Low				High
1. Model	Someone you look up to, admire Someone you want to emulate	1	2	3	4	5
2. Envisioner	Someone who communicates an image, goal, or meaningful vision of the professional world	1	2	3	4	5
3. Energizer	Someone who stimulates you with a dynamic or enthusiastic approach to professional performance	1	2	3	4	5
4. Investor	Someone who manifests her or his belief in you by investing time and energy in your career or by actively helping you grow	1	2	3	4	5
5. Supporter	Someone who offers emotional encouragement and reassurance	1	2	3	4	5

Characteristics		Low				High
6. Standard–prodder	Someone who pushes you to achieve excellence and high standards	1	2	3	4	5
7. Teacher-coach	Someone who teaches you or guides you in learning important technical, interpersonal, political, or professional skills	1	2	3	4	5
8. Feedback-giver	Someone who offers both positive and negative feedback based on factual, observable data	1	2	3	4	5
9. Eye-opener	Someone who broadens your perspective Someone who opens up new horizons, ideas, concepts, possibilities	1	2	3	4	5
10. Door-opener	Someone who willingly provides opportunities and professional experiences to help you grow	1	2	3	4	5
11. Idea-bouncer	Someone who discusses ideas and opinions Someone who acts as a sounding board	1	2	3	4	5
12. Problem solver	Someone who effectively assists you in examining and solving problems	1	2	3	4	5
13. Career counselor	Someone who helps you clarify career interests, priorities, and long-range plans	1	2	3	4	5
14. Challenger	Someone who stimulates you to think more critically or to explore issues more deeply	1	2	3	4	5

Part 2: Self-assessment

Characteristics		Low				High
1. Model	Someone you look up to, admire Someone you want to emulate	1	2	3	4	5
2. Envisioner	Someone who communicates an image, goal, or meaningful vision of the professional world	1	2	3	4	5
3. Energizer	Someone who stimulates you with a dynamic or enthusiastic approach to professional performance	1	2	3	4	5
4. Investor	Someone who manifests her or his beliefs in you by investing time and energy in your career or by actively helping you grow	1	2	3	4	5
5. Supporter	Someone who offers emotional encouragement and reassurance Someone who instills confidence and fosters risk taking	1	2	3	4	5
6. Standard-prodder	Someone who pushes you to achieve excellence and high standards	1	2	3	4	5
7. Teacher–coach	Someone who teaches you or guides you in learning important technical, interpersonal, political, or professional skills	1	2	3	4	5
8. Feedback giver	Someone who offers both positive and negative feedback based on factual, observable data	1	2	3	4	5
9. Eye opener	Someone who broadens your perspective Someone who opens up new horizons, ideas, concepts, possibilities	1	2	3	4	5

Characteristics		Low				High
10. Door opener	Someone who willingly provides opportunities and professional experiences to help you grow	1	2	3	4	5
11. Idea bouncer	Someone who discusses ideas and opinions Someone who acts as a sounding board	1	2	3	4	5
12. Problem solver	Someone who effectively assists you in examining and solving problems	1	2	3	4	5
13. Career counselor	Someone who helps you clarify career interests, priorities, and long-range plans	1	2	3	4	5
14. Challenger	Someone who stimulates you to think more critically or to explore issues more deeply	1	2	3	4	5

(Adapted from Darling LA: What do nurses want in a mentor? Nurs Admin, October 1984)

EXERCISE 5-7   **FOR YOUR CONSIDERATION . . . OR . . . FOR GROUP DISCUSSION**

Directions.   Use the following questions to reflect on key points covered in this chapter. Answer these questions individually or in a group discussion.

1. Which parts of the support system you had as a nursing student will/did you keep after moving into the work world? Which will/did you surrender?

   Retain:

   Surrender:

2. Why will/did your support system change when you move(d) from school to the work world?

3. In what situations do you find that nurses are supportive of one another? When do you find that nurses are not supportive of fellow professionals? What do you believe to be the cause of these differences?

   Supportive:

   Nonsupportive:

   Reasons why:

4. What barriers might you expect to encounter when forming a new nurse peer support group? What can you do to overcome these barriers?

Barriers	Ways to Overcome Barriers

5. What are some problems that arise in preceptor–new nurse relationships? What can be done to avoid or resolve problems in preceptor–new nurse relationships?

Problems	Solutions

6. What do new nurses have to offer to other members of a nursing network?

7. If you identify a potential nurse mentor, how could you best approach the person to discuss developing a mentor/protegé relationship?

8. What possible problems might arise in attempting to develop a mentor–protegé relationship? How might you handle those problems?

Problems	Solutions

6 Stress Management: Self-Care Skills for the New Nurse

While sitting in a traffic jam on the expressway for the third time this week, Beth Albertson is reflecting on her nursing career. When graduating from nursing school 6 months ago she was relieved, proud, and very excited. Getting through school at 37 years old, with two children, a husband, and a house to manage was no easy task. She and her family were happy to see that chapter in their lives come to a close. They were equally eager to move onto the next phase which promised income, more free time, and no more late nights studying.

Much to Beth's dismay, the late nights of studying have been replaced with late nights of working. Since completing 3 months of orientation to a 700-bed inner city medical center, she has been rotating between days and P.Ms on an antiquated, overcrowded 40-bed orthopedics unit. Most of the time, she is assigned to P.Ms. Not only is it difficult to be away from her family, but Beth is also finding it difficult to be with her patients after about 9:00 P.M. Being a morning person, Beth finds that her energy and her organizational and problem solving skills aren't their sharpest in the evening. The head nurse wants her to work on organizing so she can stop working overtime and stop leaving work for the increasingly disgruntled night shift nurses. Prioritizing and organizing are challenges, but Beth is embarrassed that she is having such difficulties. She wants to ask some of the more seasoned staff for help but doesn't yet know them well enough to seek their guidance.

Is Beth experiencing stress? If so, what is causing it? Should she try to do something to relieve the stress, and what should she do? Before you answer these questions, consider an even more basic question.

What Does "Stress" Really Mean?

If you were asked to define stress, what would you say? Many nurses describe it as tension, anxiety, fear, or too much to do during an 8-hour shift. They are correct, in that these feelings and pressures cause stress. However, these feelings and pressures cannot be equated with stress. Stated as simply as possible, stress is the way your body responds to the demands of life.

The idea of stress was initially articulated and studied in the 1930s by Hans Selye, a research physician. After several years of work in the laboratory, Selye began to notice a very interesting fact. No matter what type of experiment he conducted, the various physical responses of the laboratory animals always included three specific physiologic changes. Exposure to such diverse stimuli as caustic chemicals, pathogens, trauma, overcrowding, and physical restraint produced the same triad: adrenal hyperactivity, thymicolymphatic atrophy and peptic ulcers. Based on this observation, Selye began to believe that there is a link between all of these seemingly dissimilar situations, a "syndrome of just being sick." He turned his attention to the study of this syndrome, and the field of stress was born.

Since his early days in stress research, Selye has renamed the "syndrome of just being sick." It is now known as *stress* or, more formally, the *general adaptation syndrome*. Professionals from many disciplines have joined in developing the body of knowledge known as stress theory. Though various professions study and teach stress theory from different points of view, the definition of stress is shared by all. In Selye's words, stress is the nonspecific response of the body to any demand.

Three aspects of this definition are important if you are to grasp the concept of stress. First, stress is a *response of the body*. It is a real, physical process, not an abstract psychological theory. Everyone with a body experiences stress; no one is immune. Second, stress is a *nonspecific response*. There is no guaranteed, specific cause-and-effect relationship between a demand and your reaction. Your manifestations of stress are unique and are influenced by your internal and external conditioning. Third, stress is caused by *any demand*. Demands, called *stressors*, are both positive (graduation, moving, meeting new people) and negative (losing old friends, the anxiety of a new job, tight budgets). Whether exposed to positive or negative stressors, your body is required to adapt, and it adapts with a predictable, three-phase response known as the *stress syndrome*.

What Occurs during the Three Phases of Stress?

Encountering life's demands, or stressors, initiates the stress syndrome. Every stressor, no matter where it comes from or how you interpret it, is perceived on the tissue level of your body as a threat to your safety. Stress is a self-protective process; adaptation protects you and keeps you alive. The nature of your adaptation changes during each phase of the stress syndrome (Fig. 6-1). Consequently, your body provides different types of protection— fight or flight, resistance, and repair in phases one, two, and three, respectively.

To illustrate the stress syndrome, imagine Beth's situation the night she has to work her first 3–11 shift. The unit is short staffed. Her co-worker is off the unit for dinner when she enters a patient's room and finds that he has arrested. Her body responds in the general way in which anyone's body responds when encountering stressors.

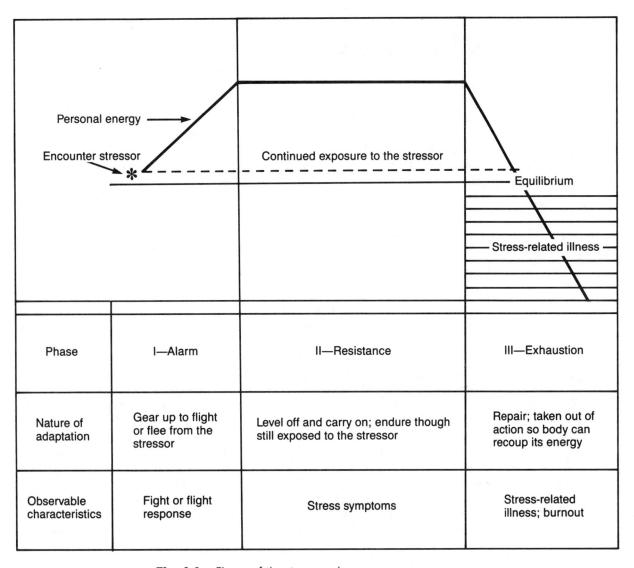

Fig. 6-1. Phases of the stress syndrome.

The arrest, the short staffing, the newness of her nursing role, and her being on the 3–11 shift for the first time are stressors in this situation. To adapt to them, her body sends messages (This is a code! I'd better get going fast!) from the cortex to the hypothalamus. To get her body to respond to this message (go call the code; begin CPR), the hypothalamus stimulates the autonomic nervous system and the endocrine system. The nerve impulses and hormones gear Beth up to handle the situation. In the early moments after discovering the code, Beth's body is in Phase I of stress, the *alarm* phase.

In this illustration, Beth manifests the classic signs of the fight or flight response. Her body experiences increases in respiration, pulse, blood pressure, and metabolism or oxygen consumption. Blood supply is diverted from the viscera to the heart and skeletal muscles. There is more sugar sent into the bloodstream. Beth's pupils dilate and she becomes diaphoretic. In a split second, all of these changes occur because her body knows that these responses will help her respond to the crisis.

Beth's body knows, however, that a new kind of response must supplant the intense activation of the alarm phase if she is to handle this code situation successfully. To help her "hang in there" while she and the other professionals try to resuscitate this patient, Beth's body uses adaptation energy to switch from fight or flight into Phase II of stress, *resistance*. Adaptation energy is the set of physical and mental functions her body uses to maintain her performance while still dealing with stressors. In the code situation Beth does such things as take a deep breath or remind herself of all the elements of the code procedure she learned in school. Physically and mentally Beth uses adaptation energy to level off, to counterbalance the intensity of the alarm phase.

Beth's supply of adaptation energy is finite. She cannot remain in the resistance phase for an indefinite period of time. Her ability to resist stressors is finite. When she continues to expose herself to life's stressors, her body manifests stress symptoms to warn her that she is consuming her finite supply of resistance or adaptation energy. As Beth nears the end of her supply, the symptoms increase in intensity. When all of her ability to resist is consumed, she is out of control. It is at this time that her body manifests stress-related illness.

Stress-related illnesses appear during Phase III of stress, *exhaustion*. These illnesses are a third way in which Beth's body adapts to stressors. In the alarm phase her body "gears up"; in the resistance phase it "levels off." In the exhaustion phase it "repairs"; Beth's body takes control out of her hands because she did not respond to the warning signals it sent in the form of stress symptoms. By becoming ill, Beth's body forces her to remove herself from contact with the stressors she did not voluntarily avoid. It is important to note, however, that stress-related illnesses are stressors, as well as a form of protection. Though stress-related illnesses take the body out of commission, the body must still cope with the demands of pain and discomfort. Consequently, it is important to avoid the exhaustion phase, if possible.

Returning one last time to the cardiac arrest illustration, Beth enters the exhaustion phase when the crisis is over, when she is no longer exposed to the major stressor. Beth does something to recoup her personal energy—she withdraws, cries, or talks with a peer. In this crisis situation, she experiences all three phases of the stress syndrome. But what about the other stressors mentioned—her other patients, the short staffing, Beth's insecurities at being a new nurse on the 3–11 shift for the first time? Beth is exposed to these stressors for longer periods of time. Failure to remove herself from these stressors could consume her finite supply of adaptation energy. This could lead Beth to experience stress-related illness.

In your life, as in the case of Beth, acute situations are superimposed on the day-to-day stress of adjusting to your job and on the lifelong stress of facing the challenges of life. You can think of stress in each of three time frames—crisis, short-term, or lifelong. In the very brief *crisis* time frame, you gear up to meet a challenge, deal with it, and then try to recover your balance after it is over. The entire stress syndrome is experienced within minutes or hours. In the *short-term* time frame, which lasts a few days to a few months, you follow the same process. The resistance phase is longer and consumes more of your adaptation energy than do crises. The repairing and recouping of energy is much more serious. In addition to the psychic level, repairing must occur on the physical level. Stress-related ills must be healed. Finally, on the *lifelong* level, you resist the debilitating effects of stressors on your body throughout your entire lifetime. Your ability to adapt to life's demands is finite. You can resist only as long as you have some adaptation energy available to you. When that is gone, you face the final exhaustion phase—death.

Because of this link between health, stress, and death, it is very important to learn how to handle stress effectively. You have only one body and one life to live. In addition to interfering with your health, mismanaged stress interferes with your personal and professional relationships. It can also diminish the quality of your professional performance. Using effective stress management techniques protects you from some of these negative effects of stress in both your personal and professional life.

How Can I Recognize Stress?

You can do nothing to improve your ability to cope with stress until you first determine that you are under stress. Recognizing stress in your life requires assessment of two key factors—the symptoms and the sources of stress. The first step in effectively managing stress and avoiding illness or burnout is identifying your personal and professional symptoms and stressors.

Read the following segments about personal and professional stress symptoms and about stressors. Think about yourself and create a list of your symptoms and stressors. When you have done this, you have completed the stress assessment and can then move on to developing a plan for stress management. But as in good nursing care, don't develop your plan until you have done a full assessment.

Personal Stress Symptoms

The symptoms of stress are a defensive early warning system. They are your body's way of signaling that you are endangering yourself by remaining in contact with stressors. Symptoms occur while you are in the resistance phase. They foreshadow the illnesses or professional burnout that occur during the exhaustion phase.

The personal symptoms of stress are grouped into five categories—physical, emotional, intellectual, social, and spiritual—based on the wholistic view of the person. Some common personal symptoms of stress are presented in Table 6-1. Use this table to identify the stress symptoms you experience.

Everyone manifests symptoms of stress in each of the five categories but not everyone has the same collection of symptoms. Because every human being is unique, each person presents a distinct constellation of symptoms. For example, you experience diarrhea, anxiety, indecisiveness, withdrawal, and self-doubt on the first day of work. Another orientee, however, experiences a headache, mistrust, diminished problem-solving ability, defensiveness, and self-doubt. You both experience stress symptoms in all five categories but have a different set of symptoms. It is important to be conscious of

Table 6-1   Personal Symptoms of Stress

Physical	Emotional	Intellectual	Social	Spiritual
Loss of appetite or anorexia	Frustration	Indecisiveness	Withdrawal from contact with others	Doubt of self-worth
Increased appetite	Complaining	Diminished ability to concentrate	Pressured need to be with others; inability to be alone	Perception of life as meaningless
Increased intake of "junk food"	Crying	Daydreaming		Inability to let go
Excessive alcohol consumption	Anger, hostility	Preoccupation		Ennui, deep boredom
Excessive smoking	Guilt	Forgetfulness	Sullenness	Purposelessness
Drug abuse	Irritability	Lack of attention to details	Defensiveness	Lack of commitment to values
Gulping meals	Use of defense mechanisms	Rigid or narrowed point of view	Blaming others ("They...")	
Indigestion	Panic	Loss of perspective	Quarreling	
Nausea/vomiting	Mistrust	Past-orientation rather than future orientation	Criticism of others	
Stomach ache	Mood swings		Lack of pleasure from enjoyable experiences	
Diarrhea	Disturbed affect—elation or depression	Lack of awareness of external stimuli		
Constipation	Apathy	Diminished creativity	Inability to relax during nonwork hours	
Frequent urination	Inability to express emotions	Diminished problem-solving ability	Worry about work during nonwork hours	
Dry mouth		Diminished fantasy life	Dominating conversations to the exclusion of others	
Cool, clammy skin		Boredom		
Sweaty palms		Confusion		
Hyperventilation				
Dilated pupils				
Blushing				
Trembling, tics, or twitches				
Tense muscles, muscle spasm				
Habitual teeth grinding				
Clenching jaws or fists				
Nail biting				
Disturbed motor skills				
Stooped posture				
Hyperactivity, restlessness				
Chronic fatigue				
Insomnia				
Nightmares				
Headache				
Pruritus				
Sneezing				
Impaired sexual function				

which physical, emotional, intellectual, social, and spiritual symptoms you manifest in response to stressors.

The personal symptoms of stress are seen in individuals at home and at work. When groups of people work together, stress symptoms are manifested in group, as well as individual, behavior. Table 6-2 lists common symptoms of stress in work groups. Use this table to identify which stress symptoms your work group manifests.

Table 6-2   **Symptoms of Stress in Work Groups**

Complaining, griping
Absenteeism
Tardiness
High turnover
Anger
Rigidity
Apathy
Resistance to change
Decreased motivation
Fatigue that is not relieved by normal rest
Increase in errors
Increased staff illnesses
Loss of self-esteem
Low morale
Decreased efficiency
Decreased productivity
Disorganization
Unwillingness to take risks
Conflict within work group
Conflict with other professionals or departments
Complaints from patients, families, other depart-
    ments or professionals
Disorganized, messy work area
Unkempt appearance of staff
Disparaging remarks
Gallows humor
Inability to laugh
Anxiety
Lack of trust among co-workers
Limited interests; turf guarding
Forgetfulness
Lack of concern for co-workers
Impaired judgment
Passive-aggressive behavior
Emotional outbursts
Schedules too full to allow breaks
Inability to "leave work at work"

Benefits of Recognizing Stress Symptoms

Developing your awareness of stress symptoms helps you in several ways. First, you are able to understand some of your experiences as warning signals to which you should respond. All too often, nurses focus on care of others but fail to practice self-care when experiencing stress. This leads to impairments in health, relationships, and professional performance. Understood in the context of stress, irritability and sullenness, for example, are not simply proof that you are a nasty person. The irritability and sullenness are signs that something is causing you stress. They provide motivation to address the "something" and to take care of yourself. They are no longer indictments of you as a person but are helpful signs that motivate you to take protective action.

The second way in which awareness of stress symptoms helps you is by improving your understanding of the behavior of others. The annoying behavior of a patient is no longer proof that she is a cranky old woman. It shows that she finds the prospect of surgery quite stressful, for example. Recognizing the disturbing behavior of others as stress symptoms helps you to be less judgmental, more accepting, and more constructive in responding to them. Ultimately, this reduces your stress because it decreases the interpersonal conflict in your life.

Finally, developing an awareness of your own stress symptoms helps you to develop your own stress management strategy. As in effective nursing care, appropriate interventions are based on thorough and accurate assessments. An effective stress management strategy is based on an assessment of symptoms, a recognition of stressors, and a plan of action that addresses both.

What Causes Stress?

In addition to recognizing personal and professional symptoms of stress, it is important to identify the stressors in your life. Stressors, the demands of life, initiate the stress process. There are many different types of stressors that can be categorized as either *internal* or *external*. Internal stressors are demands that come from inside you, which you place on yourself. Internal stressors fall into three broad categories—emotional, physical, or mental. External stressors are demands originating outside yourself, imposed on you by people or by physical aspects of nature. External stressors fall into two categories—interpersonal or environmental.

As a new nurse, there are many stressors with which you are dealing. Table 6-3 lists some that you might experience while making the transition into nursing. Use this table to reflect on yourself. Pick out your stressors from among those listed or identify some that are not found in the table. When the assessments of your symptoms and stressors is completed, proceed to the next portion of this chapter. It is designed to help you to develop a plan for effectively managing your stress.

How Can I Manage Stress in My Personal Life?

Identify, Plan, and Act

Managing stress is a three-step process. Identifying your stress symptoms and stressors is the important first step in successful stress management. The second step is developing plans for dealing with your symptoms and stressors. The third step is acting on your plans. Effective plans and actions flow from the first assessment step. Plans and interventions focus on either relieving

Table 6-3   **Sources of Stress for New Nurses**

Internal	External
Emotional	**Environmental**
Fear	Unattractive or disorganized work area
Anxiety; nervousness	Exposure to pain, suffering, and death
Self-doubt, insecurity	High noise level
Excitement	Interruptions
Loneliness	Foreign languages or heavy accents interfering with communication
Guilt over mistakes	Distasteful cafeteria food
Need to prove yourself	Hot or cold working conditions
Competitiveness	Touch/lack of touch
Isolation	Unpleasant odors
Peers expect tough, nonemotional response to crises	Overcrowded work area
	Inability to find supplies or information
Physical	Floating to a different unit
Fatigue, exhaustion	
Rotating shifts	**Interpersonal**
Sore muscles	Inflicting pain on patients
Lack of sleep	Patients' knowledge level
Working through breaks, mealtimes	Patients' manifestations of stress
Body not used to heavy workload or fast pace	Loss of a patient
Working against circadian rhythms	Large numbers of patients
Working when ill	New peer group, lack of trust
	New leadership role
Mental	Working short staffed
Worry about performance	Working overtime
Criticism of performance	Staff conflicts
Lack of knowledge of organizational policies and procedures	Working on holidays
Forgetting information learned in school	Expectations of nurse manager
Inadequate nursing education	Being evaluated
Expecting perfection of self	Lack of feedback regarding performance
Ancillary staff knows more about the patient than nurse knows	School standards vs. real-world standards
Unclear priorities	Pressure to document, paperwork
Lack of clear job description	Interdepartmental conflicts
	Problems with physicians
	Missing school friends
	Feeling critical of others' professional performance
	Interruptions
	Level of responsibility
	Feeling intimidated by co-workers' experience
	Lack of support or help from peers

stress symptoms, altering stressors you can control, or learning to live with stressors over which you have no control.

Developing effective stress management plans and behaviors is an individual process. There are many approaches to relieving symptoms and handling stressors. You must find the approach that is most effective and comfortable for you. Because you are an individual, with your own set of stressors and a unique constellation of symptoms, you need to develop your own stress management program. You are the best judge of what helps to relieve your stress.

The remaining sections of this chapter describe some effective approaches to stress management. Many approaches will prove useful to you; some will not work. Choose stress management strategies that help you relieve your symptoms, alter stressors you can control, or learn to live with stressors over which you have no control.

Implement Self-care Practices

Stress in your personal life can affect your professional performance. Similarly, stress at work can have an impact on your leisure time and your relationships outside of work. The personal and professional aspects of your life are interdependent. Consequently, as a new nurse developing effective stress management skills, it is important that you manage stress in your personal, as well as your professional, life.

Wholistic self-care practices are the most effective ways to manage stress in your personal life and are based on a wholistic philosophy. This philosophy states that human beings are made of five interrelated, interdependent parts. These are physical, emotional, intellectual, social, and spiritual. Symptoms of stress appear in any of the five parts. Because of the interdependent nature of the components of a person, symptoms are relieved by caring for any of those five aspects. Regular care of all of them helps in handling stressors and in avoiding the negative effects of stress. Lack of care of any of them weakens the whole being and diminishes resistance against the negative effects of stress.

Caring for all five of your parts is the way to practice wholistic self-care. Physical self-care includes anything you do to prevent illness and to maintain a healthy body. Emotional self-care practices consist of all you do to experience and express your feelings. Caring for the intellectual aspect of yourself involves challenging, broadening, or organizing your mind. Your social part is your interactive or playful part, and caring for it involves interpersonal, relaxing, or enjoyable pursuits. Finally, spiritual self-care comprises all you do to feel at peace with yourself and to link with the "Higher Power" that controls the flow of the universe.

How you actually carry out these five approaches to self-care is a very personal matter. *What* you choose to do is less important than that you do *something*. Action is the key to effective stress management. Thinking about self-care practices without implementing them is like thinking about dinner without eating it. The thought precedes the action, but thought alone does not nourish you. You must eat to retain vitality and health; the same applies to acting on stress management plans.

Table 6-4 presents a list of possible approaches to caring for all five of your components. You can use the table in several ways. First, use it to assess

Table 6-4   **Self-care Practices**

Physical

Exercise regularly
Rest
Eat a balanced diet
Limit "junk food"
Drink 8 glasses of water daily
Maintain weight in desired range
Limit alcohol consumption
Stop smoking
Visit your physician for regular
    check-ups
Use medications as prescribed
Practice the relaxation response
Control environmental stressors

Intellectual

Ask questions
Read
Attend seminars
Discuss controversial issues
Conduct experiments/research
Take risks
Daydream
Learn new skills, facts
Consider different viewpoints
Relabel unpleasant situations
Develop a life plan
Develop a career plan

Emotional

Allow yourself to feel and express
    emotions: anger, sadness, gladness,
    fear
Express emotions appropriately and
    respectfully
Resolve conflicts
Improve your self-awareness
Nurture yourself/treat yourself well
Don't take yourself too seriously
Work off anger with physical exercise
Say "no" when you want or need to
Ask directly for what you want
Cry
Laugh

Social

Develop and use support systems
Engage in hobbies
Talk with friends and family
Take time off/vacations
Rehabilitate or end a bad marriage
Rehabilitate or end unsatisfactory
    friendships
Limit amount of television viewing
    or watch television with others
Engage in creative pastimes
Enjoy intimacy or sex
Play with children
Seek enjoyable ways to work
Spend time alone
Go out to entertaining events

Spiritual

Pray
Meditate as a religious or nonreli-
    gious practice
"Let go" of unsolvable problems
Go to church or synagogue
Commune with nature
Read inspirational prose or poetry
"Flow" with the events of life
Appreciate the beauty of music, art
Do something for another person
Take one day at a time
Clarify your values and beliefs
Experience your self-worth

your current self-care practices. Remember, it is good to care for all five parts and to have a variety of different approaches in each area. Aspects that you seldom or never care for should receive the most attention. Aspects that you regularly address should receive continued attention, with some new approaches added to your repertoire.

The second use for Table 6-4 is as a guide for action. Identify listed self-care practices that sound reasonable, comfortable, and effective to you. Review your list of stress symptoms and stressors. Identify which self-care practices could help you to relieve symptoms or handle stressors. Some of your favorite approaches may not be listed in Table 6-4. If you think of any self-care practices that are effective but are not listed, write them in the book or begin an adjunct chart.

When you are experiencing stress in your life, return to Table 6-4, identify which self-care practices will help you to feel better, and then do them. Remember, all the stress assessments and plans in the world are worthless without action.

How Can I Manage Stress in My Professional Life?

New nurses experience some common stressors in making the transition from student to practicing nurse. In one way or another, all of the chapters in this book describe ways to deal with those stressors. Two additional sets of skills are important to highlight—outlook adjustment and self-management.* Though these are valuable in managing work-related stress, they are helpful in dealing with stress in your personal life as well.

Adjust Your Outlook

There are two ways that you can interpret stress. If life's demands seem bad or negative, this is called *distress*. If you perceive stressful situations to be positive, energizing, or motivating, this is *eustress*.

The difference between distress and eustress is strictly up to you. Your body responds only to *your* interpretations of life's demands; every person decides for herself or himself. Individual attitudes and values are what make situations negative or positive. Situations are not inherently sources of distress or eustress. For example, working in a long-term care facility may cause distress for you, but for other nurses it may be a positive work experience, generating eustress. Attitudes and values make this work situation good or bad.

It is important to recognize the distinction between distress and eustress for two reasons. First, eustress is much less debilitating to you and your body than is distress. You have a greater chance of becoming ill or breaking down when life's demands cause you distress. If given a choice, opt for a situation of eustress. Second, because your attitude helps to determine the nature of your

* The following techniques for dealing with stress were adapted from Tubesing DR: Kicking Your Stress Habits. Duluth, Whole Person Associates, 1981.

stress, you can control the amount of debilitating distress you experience by controlling your attitude. Attitude adjustment is a very powerful strategy for managing stress.

Adjusting your attitude involves using a variety of skills that help you perceive stressful situations a bit more positively. Altering your outlook helps you relieve stress symptoms and cope with stressors over which you have no control. Included among outlook adjustment skills are relabeling, surrender, whisper, and imagination skills.

Relabeling Skills: See Promise in Your Problems

If nurses on the preceding shift leave work for you to complete, you can be annoyed and upset about the situation. Using a different outlook, you could label it as:

An opportunity finally to raise the issue of work distribution with the previous shift's charge nurse

A challenge to see how well your shift can work together

A chance to get nurses from all three shifts involved in planning how to manage leftover tasks

In order to relabel problems, think and talk about them as growth producing, as opportunities, as chances or challenges. When you find yourself reacting negatively to one of life's demands, stop and try to find a more positive way to view or label the situation. If you have been given a basketful of lemons, why not make a lemon pie? Also, try to view your problems from the long-term perspective. Ask yourself how important this situation will be 5 or 10 years from now. Frequently, the major concerns of life today are forgotten or lose significance in the larger scope of life.

Surrender Skills: Learn to Let Go

After graduation, you take your first job in a small, rural hospital, about 100 miles away from your home. After several months, the thrill of living in a new place wears off and reality sets in. The standards of nursing practiced in the hospital lag far behind what you were taught to expect in school. You are very disillusioned and unhappy at work and feel terribly homesick for your family and friends. If you had the money, you would move back home in a minute, but school loans, the initial move, and setting up an apartment have put you deeply into debt. What will you do?

Avoid indulging in critical and judgmental attitudes. They increase your isolation and loneliness. Use surrender skills to help you "let go" of strict adherence to school standards and say "farewell" to the frequent contact with friends and family. When you let go, you don't give up. You accept the reality of your life and operate within your personal or situational limitations. You acknowledge that some elements of life are beyond your control. With surrender, all the energy tied up in holding onto the past is freed up for reinvestment in the present and future.

Practice surrender skills in several ways. First, recognize the feelings of fear, sadness, and loss that lie behind your dissatisfaction, loneliness, and judgmentalism. Tell someone about these feelings. Openly acknowledging your feelings and limitations helps you gain a better perspective on the situation and learn to surrender.

Use an imagining process to help you surrender. Close your eyes and imagine that you are holding in your hands the feelings, problems, or people you want to surrender. Talk to them. Tell them why you need to let them go. Then say good-bye and gently blow them away. As you watch them drift away, feel the sadness and sense of loss drift away too, and feel a sense of peace rise up within you.

Surrender can also be achieved through prayer and meditation. You can ask for help in handling your problems. Admit that you are not totally self-sufficient. Through faith, be open to the help available from others and from a "Higher Power." Ask for help in recognizing, accepting, and implementing the guidance you receive.

Finally, worry about problems when they present themselves. Don't worry ahead of time because that wastes your energy and diminishes your problem-solving ability. When the time comes to solve a problem, it may not even exist in the way you originally thought it would. If you cross the bridge before you get there, you'll have to pay the toll twice!

Whisper Skills: Send Yourself Positive Reinforcement

During your first 11–7 shift, you find one of the aides sleeping in the staff conference room. You know you must assertively confront this situation. Because this aide is 15 years older than you are and because she has such an aggressive manner, you fear the confrontation that will ensue. As you anticipate the encounter and throughout the discussion with the aide, you are involved in self-dialogue. You talk to yourself in your mind, whispering words that reflect your feelings in the situation. Your behavior will be anything but assertive if this self-talk includes such statements as, "I know I'm going to pay for this. She'll make my life miserable whenever I work with her. I'll never be able to handle it if she blows up at me. Maybe I should just forget it!"

Much of the time you engage in internal dialogue. There is a strong link between self-talk, self-belief, and behavior. You create much of your own distress and many stressful situations by telling yourself life will be bad. Conversely, you minimize distress or create eustress by whispering words of encouragement to yourself. Affirmative whispering helps you develop healthy attitudes about yourself and the situations you are in. Make a list of all the messages you regularly give yourself. If there are negative messages on the list, cross them out and replace them with positive ones. Whenever you feel distressed, whisper something positive to yourself. If you are involved in an activity and become aware of negative self-talk, consciously stop and replace it with positive messages.

When approaching the night-shift aide, whisper positive messages such as: "Relax. This will all work out fine. I can handle this. If she's angry, I can deal with it. I have a right and a responsibility to discuss this issue."

You can also practice whisper skills by using the creative visualization process. Creative visualization is the technique of using your thoughts and imagination to create what you want in your life—love, happiness, fulfillment, prosperity, health, rewarding work, peace. Creative visualization works with practice, over a period of time.

There are four steps for effective creative visualization. First, set your goal. Identify what you want to have, to work toward, to realize, or to create in your life. Second, create a clear idea or picture. Visualize a very specific mental picture of what you want and think of it in the present tense, already existing. Third, focus on it often. Bring it to mind in periods of quiet reflection and also casually, throughout the day. This helps what you want to become integrated into your life and to become more of a reality. Finally, give your visualization positive energy. Don't strive too hard or put an excessive amount of energy into visualization. Rather, use positive statements, affirmations that the goal exists, that it has come or is now coming to you. Work with this process until your goal is achieved or you no longer desire the goal. Your goals often change before they are realized.

If, as a new nurse, you are afraid of your first assignment to the night shift, visualize your competence and comfort in the situation. Use affirmations such as, "I have all that I need to work effectively on the night shift" or, "I am relaxed and centered; I have plenty of time to get all my work accomplished" or, "Every day I am growing more capable of handling the demands of working nights." As you whisper these affirmations, you change your outlook. Distress turns to eustress and the night shift becomes much less traumatic.

Imagination Skills: Let Yourself Laugh

You have been asked to organize and lead your first team conference. Though you are familiar with your primary patient's case, you have been anxious about the presentation for days. While standing in front of the group, you lean against one of the classroom tables and, with a loud crash, you and the table collapse on the floor. Is it awful or awfully funny? If you can see the irony and laugh, you are using imagination skills.

Laughter heals your pain and eases your tension. It helps you alter your attitude and assume a more positive perspective. It helps you to separate yourself from your problems and appreciate, rather than lament, life's incongruities. Develop your imagination skills by laughing at yourself. Don't take yourself too seriously. Asking yourself how terrible this situation will be a few years from now helps you gain a better perspective. Don't *try* to be funny. A sense of humor can't be developed by the direct approach. Rather, try to accept and enjoy the ironies and inconsistencies you encounter. Share them with others and, if you're smiling about them, others will too. Finally, stop complaining. Replace complaints with creative solutions or a comical retelling of the situation. Choosing a more positive focus helps you to transform a situation of distress into eustress, something you and your body can much more easily manage.

Adjust Your Behavior

Although outlook adjustment helps you when stressors are beyond your control, it is not the approach of choice in every situation. When stressors are within your control, that is, when some action on your part can ease your stress, you should take action. The specific skills to use when adjusting your behavior in an attempt to improve your situation are called self-management skills. Self-management skills help you to take charge of your life, to control the way you spend your energy, or to interact in a healthy manner with people and your environment. Included among the self-management skills are planning, time management, and nest-building skills.

Planning Skills: Set Goals and Work Toward Them

You want to become a surgical intensive care nurse, but the hospital policy requires that all staff members on that unit have at least 2 years of surgical nursing experience. You are nearing the end of your first year on a surgical floor and are feeling frustrated and bored. You don't believe you are learning anything on the unit and hate the idea of marking time for another year. Even worse, there are no guarantees that there will be a job in the surgical intensive care unit next year, when your 2 years on this awful unit are completed. What should you do?

Planning skills are helpful in this situation. The value of personal planning is twofold. First, planning helps you to focus your activity and to use your energy wisely. Second, planning helps to stimulate the energy and motivation necessary for achieving your goal. You become energized and motivated because each time you achieve a goal, you experience mastery. Mastery helps you feel that you can successfully handle the world and its challenges. It gives you a positive feeling about yourself that in turn reinforces your belief in your ability to handle other goals. If you believe you can achieve your goals, you will most likely take risks, using your energy and motivation to realize your plans.

Planning skills are soundly based on an awareness of your values.* Personally reflect on what makes your life worthwhile and, in this example, what makes your work meaningful. To accomplish this, focus on what makes you feel happy and energized or on where you spend most of your time. List these values on paper.

Effective choices and plans spring from the meaningful dimensions of your life. When faced with a major choice, list all the possible alternatives, no matter how far-fetched they seem. Then, for each alternative, identify positive and negative outcomes. Ask yourself, "What is the worst thing that could happen if I did this? What is the best? Which consequences could I most easily live with?" Compare the answers to these questions with your list of meaningful life dimensions to help you choose among alternatives.

When you choose an alternative and identify your goal, the planning process proceeds. The next step is defining specific steps that will help you to achieve your goal. The steps should be defined in observable, behavioral terms, that is, in terms of what you will actually do or not do to achieve your goal. Long-term goals should be broken down into small units, achievable in short periods of time. Accomplishing each small unit provides you with a mastery experience that encourages you to continue working toward your larger goal. Organize work on subgoals so that they build in a logical progression toward the larger goal. Assign a reasonable time limit for completing each subgoal.

As you try to decide what to do about your dissatisfaction with the surgical floor, start with a review of your personal and professional values. Identify

* For an in-depth discussion of values, read Chapter 2, Values Clarification: Making Choices.

all the optional courses of action you could take to resolve this stressful situation. Some options include struggling through on the surgical unit for another year, going to work at another hospital, taking surgical intensive care seminars during the year to learn and to keep up your spirits, and seeking a guarantee for a surgical intensive care position. Weigh these against the list of what you want to accomplish. Choose the one with the most attractive possible outcomes, the one that most effectively leads toward your goal. Then develop specific ways to work on the alternative you chose and set deadline dates for finishing each of the specific subgoals. Personal planning skills can help you face some distressing problems such as this. This planning process helps you take charge of your life and turn distressing situations to the eustress of a self-chosen challenge.

Time Management Skills: Spend Time Effectively

Where has the morning gone? It seems as if just a minute ago you were giving 9:00 A.M. meds. Now, it's 12:30 and time to go to lunch, but Mrs. Johnson's dressing hasn't been changed, two patient lights are on, and 1:00 P.M. meds have to be poured. You feel frustrated and frazzled. This is the third day in a row that you have begun the shift with plans that had to be scrapped by noon! You decide to skip lunch (again) in hopes of finishing the shift on time because the head nurse will explode if you work more overtime.

If this scenario sounds familiar, consider working to develop time management skills. Begin by identifying your time wasters, the people, the habits and situations that rob you of your time. Some time wasters are internal, creations of your own attitudes and behavior. Others are external, the result of people or circumstances beyond yourself. Evaluate which time wasters you can control or eliminate and which are the biggest drain on your time. Attack these first. Developing practical ways to set limits on these "bandits" adds hours and energy to your day.

Another important time management skill for new nurses is organizing. Developing organizational skills is a four-step process with each step building on the previous one. The four steps are valuing, prioritizing, sequencing, and acting. You must start to develop organization by first clarifying your values and those of the group with whom you work. To organize your time successfully, you must place your actions in harmony with those values. Harmony between values and behavior leads to motivation, energy, and job satisfaction. Disharmony between values and behavior leads to decreases in motivation and energy, to job dissatisfaction, and to distrust.

Many new nurses find the transition between school and work difficult because school-bred values frequently clash with those held by people in the work setting. Frustration and dissatisfaction are not only felt by new nurses. Co-workers and managers often are irritated by the idealism, judgmentalism, or seeming incompetence of the new nurse. Both parties are unhappy with each other because they don't understand or don't share the values of the other.

As a new nurse, it is important to clarify the values that govern your nursing care. In carrying out this *valuing* process, make a list of the aspects of your job you like and those you don't. Also, list the aspects of nursing care identified by your instructors as important signs of quality care. On the other side of the paper, list what your instructors identified as signs of poor nursing care. These lists give you a good idea of your set of values. But don't stop here. The values of your manager and co-workers also have a tremendous impact on your work. Ask them what they like and dislike about their work; what they consider signs of good- and poor-quality care. Comparing your lists may be an eye-opening experience. Be open to your co-workers' values; don't judge them too quickly or harshly. They may have learned some lessons in their experience that may help you. Be open to examining, and possibly altering, your values. Surrendering old values is not always a sign of weakness or of giving up. Sometimes shifting values reflects growth and maturity. For more on values, read Chapter 2, Values Clarification: Making Choices.

When you are clear about your values, continue developing organization by working on the second step of the organization process, *prioritizing*. Priorities are the bridge between values and the sequences that plan action. It is impossible to do everything you would like to do. Because of this, you must set priorities to help you sort out what you will and will not do. This applies in your professional as well as your personal life.

Take charge in prioritizing. It is your right, not someone else's, to set your own priorities. Stop fulfilling others' priorities and others' "You should" lists. Start developing your own priorities and "I want/I need" lists. To clarify the priorities of your job, write down all the tasks associated with your position. In reviewing these tasks, use the following questions list to help in identifying priorities of your job.

Will patients be jeopardized if this task is not done?

Is this task very important to you?

Do any time deadlines make this task a priority?

Is this task one of your manager's expectations regarding your performance?

Is this task one of the key elements of your job—one of the elements on which you will be evaluated?

Do any safety concerns make this task a priority?

Does the work of others depend on your completion of this task?

Do any legal or regulatory issues make this task a priority?

Will you face negative consequences if you fail to do this task?

Are you *really* the only one who can do this task?

Is this task irritating you and causing the quality of your work to suffer?

Will money be lost if this task is left undone?

If this task is postponed, will problems arise?

Is anyone depending on you to do this task?

Will this task take a small amount of your time and yield a large positive result?

When you answer "yes" to any of these questions you have a priority item. You have many priorities. Consequently, you need to rank your priorities and decide how to act on them.

Sequencing, the third step in the organizing process, helps you organize your priorities and decide what to do first. Before you begin work each day, write a "to do" list of the tasks you want or need to accomplish that day. Realistically, the list should not exceed 10 major items. Use a three-part scale to order your list of tasks. Anything that is urgent and important and will cause problems if left undone, should be ranked #1. Anything that is important but not urgent should be ranked #2. Anything that is of little importance or is simply interesting or enjoyable should be labeled #3.

The schedule for your day should be based on your "to do" list. A few key ideas will help you make the most of this planning tool. Items on your "to do" list should be specific, time-limited tasks. Large jobs, like A.M. care on all your primary patients, should be broken down into each aspect of A.M. care or into A.M. care for patients A, B, C, D, and E. Identify which tasks must be performed at or by a certain hour and mark those clearly on your list. Evaluate your biologic rhythms, identifying your high-energy and low-energy times during the day. Try to structure your daily activities with your energy levels in mind. Tackle tasks that demand precision or concentration at high-energy times. Do first things first; "to do" list items marked #1 should be accomplished before #2 items. Plan for crises, emergencies, or delays by reserving at least 30 minutes per workday as unscheduled time. This allows you to be flexible and helps you more effectively respond to unexpected situations. Don't let perfectionism paralyze you. Replace perfectionistic performance standards with more reasonable standards of "functional efficiency."

The final step in getting organized is *acting*. The previous valuing, prioritizing, and sequencing steps are meaningless without this fourth step. If you have difficulty managing and organizing your time, remind yourself that order is not an end in itself. Organizing is a way to make your personal and professional life more pleasant. It helps you flow more easily and function more effectively. Defiance of organization and time management can be self-destructive and, in clinical settings, it can have harmful effects on your patients. There is no one correct way to organize and manage your time. It is up to you to discover what works best for you. Developing effective time management skills is enormously helpful in increasing your comfort and competence as a nurse. So take action now. Isn't it time?

Nest-Building Skills: Create Liveable Environments

Look at this unit! There must be ten people crowded around the nurse's station, grabbing charts, complaining about illegible orders, answering phones or trying to get to the med cart. Beyond the desk, five medical students and an attending physician are conferring at the foot of Mrs. Solomon's bed. They are talking over the din in the unit and are obstructing Madeline, the new staff nurse, from changing the bed. The soiled linen is on the floor and the area smells quite unpleasant. Across the way a pastor is comforting Mrs. Adams as she tearfully watches the irregular cardiac monitor and hears her old mother struggling for her last breaths. In the next bed, Mrs. Morgan is moaning in pain. Her morphine must be wearing off.

As you look around your own work area, does the environment ever look, sound, or smell like this? Are you aware of it or are you oblivious to your environment? After a while, the sights, sounds, and smells of health care become so familiar that they lose their impact. Pain, death, and crises become so commonplace that they lose their shock value. Nurses become numb to environmental stimuli, partly because they are so familiar and also because they are so stressful.

When you next go to work, do a sensory check. What do you see? What do you hear? When eating, what do you taste? What do you feel—temperature, humidity, human closeness, equipment, exertion? What do you smell? All these stimuli are stressors, demands to which you body must respond. Do they generate distress or eustress? The interpretation is up to you, and so is your response.

If you find that many environmental stressors produce distress for you, use nest-building skills. *Nest building* includes all you do to beautify your environment at work or at home. Whenever possible, take positive action to control or eliminate negative environmental stimuli. Do your charting in a quiet corner of the staff room rather than seated by the telephone at the desk. Ask the attending physician and the five medical students to confer away from the foot of the bed. Develop a "let's organize the unit" committee to solve problems of disorder and disorganization. Do anything you can to make your environment look, sound, taste, feel, or smell better. These nest-building interventions help you handle stress.

Some negative environmental stimuli are beyond your control, and action to control or eliminate them is useless. Patients bleed, vomit, cry out in pain, and die. Instead of struggling to change something that is beyond your control, focus on what you can control and create a backdrop of peace. Making your workplace more pleasant or attractive neutralizes the impact of negative environmental stressors. Get organized by rearranging the utility room, by making supplies and laundry more accessible to all patient rooms or by instituting bedside charting. Beautify your environment by clearing the outdated memos from the bulletin board, by hanging an inspirational poster, or by bringing in flowers. Create a comfort zone by designating smoking and non-smoking areas at opposite ends of the lounge, by banning discussion of problems and patients during breaks, or by initiating quiet times in the lounge for breaks, charting, or reading. Finally, beautify and organize your home environment. A restful, peaceful haven at home helps you handle the environmental stressors of nursing.

There are many stressors in nursing. Being a new nurse, you experience some of them acutely and intensely. It is important for your health and professional development that you learn to manage the stressors in your life. Nursing stress does not cease when you complete your transition into the working world. Stress accompanies you throughout your life, at every phase of your career. Although the stressors change over time, the need for effective stress management strategies never changes. So start now. Learning to manage stress early in your nursing career helps you master the challenges before you and prepares you for those that lie ahead.

Bibliography

Bach G, Wyden P: The Intimate Enemy: How to Fight Fair in Love and Marriage. New York, Avon Books, 1968

Benson H: The Relaxation Response. New York, Avon Books, 1968

Bolles R: What Color Is Your Parachute? Berkeley, Ten Speed Press, 1984

Crystal JC, Boles RN: Where Do I Go from Here with My Life? Berkeley, Ten Speed Press, 1974

Garfield (ed): Stress and Survival: The Emotional Realities of Life-Threatening Illness. St Louis, CV Mosby, 1979

Gawain S: Creative Visualization. New York, Bantam Books, 1982

Lachman, V: Stress Management: A Manual for Nurses. New York, Grune & Stratton, 1984

Mackenzie RA: The Time Trap: How to Get More Done in Less Time. New York, JB Lippincott, 1976

Nowak JB, Grindel CG: Career Planning in Nursing. Philadelphia, JB Lippincott, 1984

Selye H: Stress without Distress. New York, JB Lippincott, 1974

Selye H: The Stress of Life. New York, McGraw-Hill, 1976

Sutterly D, Donnelly G (ed): Coping with Stress: A Nursing Perspective. Gaithersburg, MD, Aspen Systems, 1982

Tubesing D: Kicking Your Stress Habits. Duluth, Whole Person Associates, 1981

Winston S: Getting Organized. New York, Warner Books, 1979

Exercises

EXERCISE 6-1   SELF-ASSESSMENT: MY PERSONAL SYMPTOMS OF STRESS

Directions.   During the resistance phase of the stress syndrome, your body manifests symptoms of stress to warn you that you are experiencing stress. These early-warning signals are meant, also, to encourage you take care of yourself and to avoid the illnesses associated with the exhaustion phase.

Read the following lists of physical, emotional, intellectual, social, and spiritual symptoms of stress. Check the circle next to the symptoms you experience in your own life. If you experience any symptoms of stress that are not listed, write them in the space provided.

Physical	Emotional
○ Loss of appetite or anorexia	○ Frustration
○ Increased appetite	○ Complaining
○ Increased intake of "junk food"	○ Crying
○ Excessive alcohol consumption	○ Anger, hostility
○ Excessive smoking	○ Guilt
○ Drug abuse	○ Irritability
○ Gulping meals	○ Use of defense mechanisms
○ Indigestion	○ Panic
○ Nausea/vomiting	○ Mistrust
○ Stomach ache	○ Mood swings
○ Diarrhea	○ Disturbed affect—elation or
○ Constipation	depression
○ Frequent urination	○ Apathy
○ Dry mouth	○ Inability to express emotions
○ Cool, clammy skin	
○ Sweaty palms	○ _____
○ Hyperventilation	
○ Dilated pupils	○ _____
○ Blushing	
○ Trembling, tics, or twitches	
○ Tense muscles, muscle spasm	
○ Habitual teeth grinding	
○ Clenching jaws or fists	
○ Nail biting	
○ Disturbed motor skills	
○ Stooped posture	
○ Hyperactivity, restlessness	
○ Chronic fatigue	
○ Insomnia	
○ Nightmares	
○ Headache	
○ Pruritus	
○ Sneezing	
○ Impaired sexual function	
○ _____	
○ _____	

Intellectual	Social	Spiritual
○ Indecisiveness	○ Withdrawal from contact with others	○ Doubting self-worth
○ Diminished ability to concentrate	○ Pressured need to be with others; inability to be alone	○ Perception of life as meaningless
○ Daydreaming		○ Inability to let go
○ Preoccupation	○ Sullenness	○ Ennui, deep boredom
○ Forgetfulness	○ Defensiveness	○ Purposelessness
○ Lack of attention to details	○ Blaming others ("They....")	○ Lack of commitment to values
○ Rigid or narrowed point of view	○ Quarreling	
○ Loss of perspective	○ Criticism of others	○ _____
○ Past-orientation rather than future orientation	○ Lack of pleasure from enjoyable experiences	○ _____
○ Lack of awareness of external stimuli	○ Inability to relax during nonwork hours	○ _____
○ Diminished creativity	○ Worry about work during nonwork hours	
○ Diminished problem-solving ability	○ Dominating conversations to the exclusion of others	
○ Diminished fantasy life		
○ Boredom	○ _____	
○ Confusion	○ _____	
○ _____		
○ _____		

EXERCISE 6-2   SELF-ASSESSMENT: SOURCES OF STRESS IN MY PROFESSIONAL LIFE

Directions. The demands of life cause you to experience stress. Development of an effective approach to stress management requires that you recognize the stressors in your life. Read the following lists of internal and external stressors which new nurses might encounter. Check the circle next to those sources of stress which you experience. If some of your stressors are not listed, write them in the space provided.

Internal

Emotional
- ◯ Fear
- ◯ Anxiety; nervousness
- ◯ Self-doubt, insecurity
- ◯ Excitement
- ◯ Loneliness
- ◯ Guilt over mistakes
- ◯ Need to prove yourself
- ◯ Competitiveness
- ◯ Isolation
- ◯ Peers expect tough, nonemotional response to crises

- ◯ _____

- ◯ _____

Physical
- ◯ Fatigue, exhaustion
- ◯ Rotating shifts
- ◯ Sore muscles
- ◯ Lack of sleep
- ◯ Working through breaks, mealtimes
- ◯ Body not used to heavy workload or fast pace
- ◯ Working against circadian rhythms
- ◯ Working when ill

- ◯ _____

- ◯ _____

Mental
- ◯ Worry about performance
- ◯ Criticism of performance
- ◯ Lack of knowledge of organizational policies and procedures
- ◯ Forgetting information learned in school
- ◯ Inadequate nursing education
- ◯ Expecting perfection of yourself
- ◯ Ancillary staff knows more about the patient than nurse knows
- ◯ Unclear priorities
- ◯ Lack of clear job description

- ◯ _____

- ◯ _____

External

Environmental
○ Unattractive or disorganized work area
○ Pain, suffering, and death
○ High noise level
○ Many interruptions
○ Foreign languages or heavy accents interfering with communication
○ Distasteful cafeteria food
○ Hot or cold working conditions
○ Touch/lack of touch
○ Unpleasant odors
○ Overcrowded work area
○ Inability to find supplies or information
○ Floating to a different unit
○ Unpleasant odors

○ _____

○ _____

Interpersonal
○ Inflicting pain on patients
○ Patients' knowledge level
○ Patients' manifestations of stress
○ Loss of a patient
○ Large numbers of patients
○ New peer group, lack of trust
○ New leadership role for first time
○ Working short staffed
○ Working overtime
○ Staff conflicts
○ Working on holidays
○ Expectations of management
○ Being evaluated
○ Lack of feedback regarding performance
○ School standards vs. real-world standards
○ Pressure to document, paperwork
○ Interdepartmental conflicts
○ Problems with physicians
○ Missing school friends
○ Feeling critical of others' professional performance
○ Interruptions
○ Level of responsibility
○ Feeling intimidated by co-workers' experience
○ Lack of support or help from peers

○ _____

○ _____

ACTION PLAN: PERSONAL STRATEGIES FOR MANAGING STRESS

Part 1: Assessment

Directions. Effective stress management is based on the regular practice of self-care. Symptoms of stress appear in all aspects of your life. Similarly, care of all aspects of yourself helps relieve your stress and protect you from developing stress-related illnesses.

Reflect on your own self-care practices. List anything that you do to care for your body or physical appearance in the box labeled *Physical*. Anything that you do to learn or expand your mind should be listed under *Intellectual*. What do you do for fun, to play, or to interact with other people? List these in the box marked *Social*. List the things you do to experience, express, or calm your emotions in the *Emotional* box. Finally, identify what helps you feel at peace with yourself or in harmony with a Higher Power. List these in the box marked *Spiritual*.

	Physical
Physical Spiritual Intellectual Emotional Social	
Intellectual	Social
Emotional	Spiritual

Part 2: Action

Listed below are some effective strategies for managing personal stress. Identify at least one strategy in each box that you do not presently practice but that would be helpful to you. Check the circle next to those strategies and commit yourself to practicing them within the next 2 weeks. Continue using your familiar self-care practices listed on the preceding page. Expand your repertoire of self-care practices and expand your ability to cope with stress.

Physical

○ Exercise regularly
○ Rest
○ Eat a balanced diet
○ Limit "junk food"
○ Drink 8 glasses of water daily
○ Maintain weight in desired range
○ Limit alcohol consumption
○ Stop smoking
○ Visit your physician for regular check-ups
○ Use medications as prescribed
○ Practice the relaxation response
○ Control environmental stressors

Intellectual

○ Ask questions
○ Read
○ Attend seminars
○ Discuss controversial issues
○ Conduct experiments/research
○ Take risks
○ Daydream
○ Learn new skills, facts
○ Consider different viewpoints
○ Relabel unpleasant situations
○ Develop a life plan
○ Develop a career plan

Social

○ Develop and use support systems
○ Engage in hobbies
○ Talk with friends and family
○ Take time off/vacations
○ Rehabilitate or end a bad marriage
○ Rehabilitate or end unsatisfactory friendships
○ Limit amount of television viewing or watch television with others
○ Engage in creative pastimes
○ Enjoy intimacy or sex
○ Play with children
○ Seek enjoyable ways to work
○ Spend time alone
○ Go out to entertaining events

Emotional

○ Allow yourself to feel and express emotions: anger, sadness, gladness, fear
○ Express emotions appropriately and respectfully
○ Resolve conflicts
○ Improve your self-awareness
○ Nurture yourself/treat yourself well
○ Don't take yourself too seriously
○ Work off anger with physical exercise
○ Say "no" when you want or need to
○ Ask directly for what you want
○ Cry
○ Laugh

Spiritual

○ Pray
○ Meditate as a religious or nonreligious practice
○ "Let go" of unsolvable problems
○ Go to church or synagogue
○ Commune with nature
○ Read inspirational prose or poetry
○ "Flow" with the events of life
○ Appreciate the beauty of music, art
○ Do something for another person
○ Take one day at a time
○ Clarify your values and beliefs
○ Experience your self-worth

EXERCISE 6-4   MINIGAME: TIME MANAGEMENT: PRIORITIZING AND GETTING ORGANIZED

Objective.   To provide a simulated experience in setting priorities and getting organized.

Problem.   You are a new staff nurse 5 months out of school. You work on a 40-bed general medical–surgical unit that uses principles of primary nursing when staffing is sufficient, which is not very often these days! It is 2:45 P.M., nearing the end of the 7–3:30 shift. Your head nurse approaches you to ask if you will work a double shift. Two of the P.M. shift nurses have called in sick, and she is desperate to cover 3–11:30. Without you, there will only be two RNs and one aide. You reluctantly agree to stay and begin to wonder how you will handle another 8 hours.

Procedure.   Read, evaluate, and assign priority numbers to each of the following items. Decide which problem to handle first, second, third, etc. Mark each item with the number that indicates where it ranks on your list of ten. Take no more than 5 minutes to complete the ranking.

Priority List.

_____ Complete admission paperwork on a patient scheduled for cholecystectomy the day after tomorrow. Including calls to schedule lab and x-ray time for work to be done tomorrow, this will take 20 minutes.

_____ Return to Mr. Williams' room to discuss with him and his wife diet restrictions for ulcer patients. They expected you at 2:30 and planned to spend 30 minutes with you.

_____ Answer the telephone an arms length away, which is ringing. The ward clerk is in the back room—15 feet away—putting away supplies.

_____ Find the head nurse and negotiate with her to be sure you will be assigned to work with the same patients you had during the day shift. Anticipated time: 10 minutes.

_____ Report to P.M. shift nurses and aide coming on duty at 3:00 P.M. This will take 15 minutes.

_____ Answer your postoperative patient's call light for the seventh time today! Remind Mrs. Wilson that Meperidine HCl (Demerol) cannot be given again until 4:00 P.M. This will take 15 minutes.

_____ Go to the cafeteria for a quick snack. Because you missed lunch, your energy is very low. Anticipated time: 30 minutes.

_____ Assess which aspects of your P.M. patients' care can be delegated to the aide and plan your time for the P.M. shift. Anticipated time: 15 minutes.

_____ Help Mr. Normand (4 days post-MI) back to bed. He's been up since lunch time and will need to use the bathroom before you and the orderly get him settled. Anticipated time: 20 minutes.

_____ Return the car mechanic's phone message to hear how he diagnoses your car's strange noise and to find out when you can go to the corner gas station to pick up your car. Anticipated time: 5 minutes.

Postgame Discussion.   Place the following chart on a blackboard or newsprint. When participants have finished prioritizing the 10 items, each should mark their rankings on the chart, placing hatch marks in the box numbered with their priority ranking for each action.

Priority Ranking ⟶

Nursing Action	1	2	3	4	5	6	7	8	9	10
Complete admission										
Discuss ulcer diet										
Answer telephone										
Negotiate P.M. assignment										
Report to P.M. staff										
Answer early medication request										
Go to eat										
Plan time and delegation for P.M. shift										
MI patient to bathroom and bed										
Phone auto mechanic										

1. Why did you choose the priorities that you chose?

2. Why did you mark certain items as low priorities?

3. What might be some ways of saving time with this list?

4. What are some guidelines for prioritizing that might be helpful for new nurses to remember?

EXERCISE 6-5   PLANNING AND SETTING PRIORITIES

Directions.   Many new nurses find it difficult to plan and prioritize the use of their time. Use the following four-step process to help develop your skills in planning and setting priorities for your time at work.

I. To Do List

Write down all the specific tasks you need to accomplish while you are at work today.

☐ _____ ○

☐ _____ ○

☐ _____ ○

☐ _____ ○

☐ _____ ○

☐ _____ ○

☐ _____ ○

☐ _____ ○

☐ _____ ○

☐ _____ ○

☐ _____ ○

☐ _____ ○

☐ _____ ○

☐ _____ ○

☐ _____ ○

☐ _____ ○

☐ _____ ○

☐ _____ ○

☐ _____ ○

☐ _____ ○

II. Ranking

Identify the relative importance of each item on your to do list by labeling it with the number, 1, 2, or 3. (Refer to text for questions that help in prioritizing.)

1 = Urgent and very important; serious consequences if not accomplished.

2 = Important but not urgent; no serious consequences if delayed.

3 = Not important but interesting; enjoyable or a good idea.

Go back and write the number 1, 2, or 3 in the *circle* next to each item on your to do list above.

III. Sequencing

Identify the most reasonable order or sequence to follow in accomplishing the items on your to do list. Consider ranking; do #1 items first, #2 items second, and #3 items last. Also, consider deadlines; do tasks that must be completed at a certain time (e.g., medications or a meeting scheduled for 10:00 A.M.) when they should be done, regardless of their ranking. Go back and write "A" in the *box* next to the to do list item you should do first. Write "B" in the box next to the item you should do second. Write "C" in the box next to the item you should do third, and so on, until all to do list items are sequenced.

IV. Acting

Use the ranked and sequenced to do list as a guide for action during your day at work. When you are interrupted, think about how much of your to do list is as yet incomplete and think of the consequences of allowing this interruption to hinder you from accomplishing the plans and priorities you have set for yourself.

Expect that crises will arise and plan for them. Remember, crisis situations are essentially situations with new priorities. Before responding impulsively to a crisis, stop and think. Ask yourself "What are the items that this change or crisis has added to my to do list? What are the appropriate rankings for the remaining items on my to do list? What is the appropriate sequence for the remaining items on my to do list?" After answering these questions, you will have a guideline for action. The more you practice this model the easier it will become and, over time, your work priorities will become quite clear.

EXERCISE 6-6   **TIME MANAGEMENT: CONTROLLING TIME WASTERS**

Directions.   When you waste time, you do something that has less value than others tasks or that keeps you from accomplishing a more important task. As a concept, "wasting time" is all relative. No action is inherently wasteful. It all depends on the values and priorities in your life.

Handling time wasters is a three-step process-identify, assess, and act. Answer the following questions to begin work on controlling you time wasters.

I. Identify

What are my internal time wasters? (my own attitudes/behaviors/habits)

What are my external time wasters? (environmental factors/circumstances, other people's behavior)

II. Assess

Which time wasters can I control, minimize, or eliminate?

Which time wasters are the biggest drains on my time?

III. Act

What are some practical approachs I could institute to address the time wasters listed above?

When will I take action?

EXERCISE 6-7   **FOR YOUR CONSIDERATION . . . OR . . . FOR GROUP DISCUSSION**

Directions.   Use the following questions to reflect on key points covered in this chapter. Answer these questions individually or in a group discussion.

1. What are the stressors in your professional life?

2. What are the symptoms of stress that you observe in individual nurses at work?

3. What are the symptoms of stress that you observe in groups of nurses at work?

4. What impact does stress in your personal life have on your professional life?

5. What impact does stress in your professional life have on your personal life?

6. How are stress and burnout related?

7. What has been successful in handling stress in your personal life?

8. What has been successful in handling stress in your professional life?

9. What impact does stress in patients and their families have on nurses?

10. What are the stressful aspects of making the transition from student to practicing nurse with which you need some help?

7 Acting Assertively: Practical Solutions to Problem Situations

As Maria Gonzales enters the classroom, she feels a mixture of excitement and apprehension. This is Maria's first continuing education class since being hired as a medical–surgical staff nurse 5 months ago. Having the hospital pay the tuition is a treat, but the real excitement comes from finally attending an assertiveness course. There is some apprehension, however, in knowing how much there is to learn and in wondering if she can learn to be assertive.

During her first months as a staff nurse, Maria has grown increasingly comfortable with her patient care skills. She has come to realize that her skills for interacting with some other professionals, however, are inadequate and need to be developed. Fortunately, Maria handles patients and nursing assistants with relative ease. She's able to communicate expectations, say "no," and voice dissatisfaction when it is appropriate. People in authority are another story. Maria cannot say "no" when the head nurse asks her to work a double shift. When the preceding shift's charge nurse asks Maria to complete one of her staff's unfinished procedures Maria always agrees to help. But, when the charge nurse on the following shift yells about an incomplete task, Maria says nothing and stays late to finish her work. Finally, despite the hospital policy requiring physicians to write all orders, Maria often bends this rule to keep the doctors happy.

In attempting to please those around her, Maria is becoming dissatisfied with her professional relationships. She is annoyed with the head nurse for her frequent overtime requests. Maria is impatient with nurses who don't do their jobs and with those who won't help a busy colleague. She is frustrated with physicians who work the system to their advantage, never considering the needs of others. Mostly, Maria is mad at herself for her nonassertive responses to these people.

As Maria enters the classroom she recalls that pain is a great motivator. Although her professional relationships are painful, they have motivated her to attend this assertiveness class. Facing herself and the prospect of change is another source of pain, but Maria is hopeful that with some work, she will gain the skill and confidence to change her behavior and start acting assertively.

Maria knows she acts nonassertively with authority figures. Sometimes, however, it is difficult to know the difference between acting nonassertively, aggressively, and assertively. Think of situations in your own life. What is really happening when you are feeling proud of yourself for acting assertively and your head nurse counsels you about your aggressiveness? When you fail to support a peer in a staff meeting and later she accuses you of passive–aggressiveness, weren't you actually acting nonassertively? By answering three straightforward "diagnostic" questions, you can resolve these and other doubts about whether or not you are acting assertively. But learning to "diagnose" is only part of developing your assertiveness. The other key component is developing your ability to use three types of assertiveness skills in problem situations. The three diagnostic questions and the three categories of assertiveness skills are discussed at length in this chapter.

What Are the Differences Among Acting Nonassertively, Aggressively, and Assertively?

Assertiveness is distinguished from nonassertivenes and aggressiveness on the basis of three factors. Answering questions about each of these three factors helps you diagnose behavior and understand whether it is nonassertive, aggressive, or assertive. Table 7-1 presents the three factors and related questions that help determine the nature of behavior.

When you act *nonassertively*, your rights are violated and another person's rights take precedence. This occurs as a result of the way you choose to communicate or behave. There is a cause-and-effect relationship between how you communicate and what happens to your rights. When you fail to

Table 7-1   **Characteristics of Nonassertive, Aggressive, and Assertive Behavior**

Three Factors	Three Questions	Three Behavioral Answers		
		Nonassertive	*Aggressive*	*Assertive*
My rights/needs	What is happening to my rights/needs?	Violated Receive less attention Denied	Take Precedence Receive more attention Acknowledged	Balanced with other's Acknowledged
Other's rights/ needs	What is happening to the other's rights/ needs?	Take precedence Receive more attention Acknowledged	Violated Receive less attention Denied	Balanced with mine Acknowledged
Communication/ behavior	How am I expressing my thoughts/feelings/beliefs?	Fail to express or express passively or powerlessly	Overtly or covertly hostile Disrespectful	Honestly, openly, directly Harmony between verbal and non-verbal, respectfully, responsibly

express yourself or do so in a passive, powerless manner, your rights are violated. Maria's inability to say "no" to her head nurse clearly illustrates this point.

When you act *aggressively*, the balance shifts and your own rights take precedence while the other's rights are violated. Again, this is the result of the way you choose to communicate or behave. When you express thoughts, feelings, or beliefs in a disrespectful or hostile manner, you violate the rights of the other person. In Maria's case the physicians who disregard the policy requiring orders to be written act aggressively. They put their needs above those of other professional colleagues.

When acting *assertively* you seek a balance between your rights and those of the other person. Though this balance is not always obtained, you attempt to respect the other's rights, as you stand up for your own rights. You responsibly "own" and have an awareness of your thoughts, feelings, and beliefs. You communicate them as honestly, openly, and directly as possible. The nonverbal messages you send mesh with your words and accurately reflect the meaning of your message. Maria's ability to say "no" and communicate expectations to subordinates demonstrates that she has some ability to act assertively.

It is important to recognize that acting assertively in a professional context sometimes differs from assertiveness in a nonprofessional context. In the nurse–patient relationship, the balance of rights is uneven, with more emphasis placed on patients' rights and less on the rights of the nurse. It is appropriate that, at times, the needs of patients take precedence over yours. The patient role usually includes some degree of dependence. Patients look to you to meet needs they are incapable of meeting on their own. The patient looks to you to protect and advocate for his or her rights. Nurses often fail to realize that this special set of expectations applies only to the nurse–patient relationship, not to relationships with other health professionals. You "nurse" patients, not nurses, physicians, or other health care workers. Learn from Maria's mistakes. Do not fall into the trap of thinking that as a nurse you are responsible for putting others' needs or rights before your own. Except in the case of patients, your rights deserve the same respect and attention as anyone else's. Remembering this helps you handle interpersonal problems assertively.

Will It Really Make a Difference if I Act Assertively?

For you, as for Maria, there is no guarantee of getting your way when acting assertively. Sometimes you get the results you want; sometimes you don't. Many times, you need to compromise. Often your honest, responsible, respectful approach disarms other persons, opens them up or turns them around to your point of view. Sometimes it happens while you are talking with them. At other times, it happens afterward, when they have a chance to reflect on their discussions with you. Occasionally, no matter how assertively you behave, you do not get what you want. Even in this situation, though, you benefit from having handled the exchange honestly and respectfully.

Understand clearly, assertiveness is not designed to make someone fulfill your wishes. All you can be sure of when acting assertively is that:

You feel good about standing up for your rights in an acceptable manner

You treat others as they deserve to be treated, with respect

You avoid the alienation and hostility of aggressiveness

You avoid the self-renunciation of nonassertiveness

You have a greater chance of getting what you want than if you choose nonassertiveness or aggressiveness.

What if I Don't Know How to Act Assertively?

Even if you tend to act nonassertively or aggressively in most problem situations, there is cause for hope. Assertiveness is a learned behavior and, with practice, you can develop the skills of assertiveness.

You are not genetically predisposed to either assertiveness, nonassertiveness, or aggressiveness. No one is! As you grow up, you learn these behaviors as ways to stand up for yourself and solve "people problems." In her childhood, Maria Gonzales was taught that being nice, respecting elders, and pleasing others are ways to build functional relationships. In her present life, these people skills are often dysfunctional. She is attending an assertiveness class to learn new interpersonal skills. You too can learn new ways to handle problems and replace dysfunctional aggressive or nonassertive behavior with functional assertiveness.

What Functional Skills Are Used in Acting Assertively?

There are three categories of assertiveness skills that build from general to specific. Table 7-2 lists the three categories of assertiveness skills and the specific skills that fit into each category.

The challenge of learning assertiveness involves knowing not only what assertiveness skills are, but also when to use them. You need only consider acting assertively if there are problems between people, that is, if someone's rights have been violated or if someone's needs are not being met. The preparatory, core, and accessory skills of acting assertively help you handle these situations, because they all have different purposes and characteristics.

Purposes of Different Assertiveness Skills

The purpose of the preparatory skills is to prepare you to face situations that demand assertive behavior. Preparatory skills reinforce the value of your individuality and serve as the springboard for assertive action. Without these, you are incapable of acting assertively. The core skills build on the preparatory skills, and their purpose is to provide general guidelines for all assertive

Table 7-2   **The Skills of Acting Assertively**

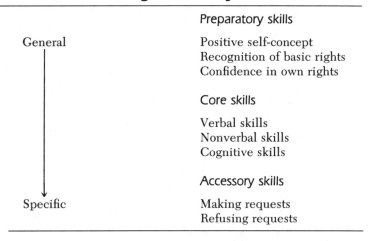

	Preparatory skills
General	Positive self-concept
	Recognition of basic rights
	Confidence in own rights
	Core skills
	Verbal skills
	Nonverbal skills
	Cognitive skills
	Accessory skills
Specific	Making requests
	Refusing requests

action. Core skills are the heart and soul of acting assertively. If you grasp the core skills, you can apply them in designing assertive responses to any problem. Finally, the accessory skills apply the generic core skills to particular problems. The purpose of the accessory skills is to define specific guidelines for assertive action in situations such as making or refusing requests. Developing an understanding of, and a facility in, the use of preparatory, core, and accessory skills helps you act more assertively in both professional and personal situations.

How Do I Develop Preparatory Skills?

As presented in Table 7-2, the preparatory skills include a positive self-concept, awareness of basic human rights, and confidence in your own rights. It is the first set of skills that Maria Gonzales must develop if she is to become assertive with authority figures. It is imperative that you also develop these skills in order to support your use of the core and accessory skills. Preparatory skills provide the self-assurance and confidence you need to handle problems in an assertive manner. Without the self-assurance and confidence derived from the preparatory skills, your attempts at assertiveness dissolve into aggressive or nonassertive behavior.

Develop A Positive Self-concept

You develop a positive self-concept by regularly practicing four behaviors. First, accept and respect your own individuality. There is no other person exactly like you in the world. Though in trying times you might doubt it, you are special, and the world needs your distinct strengths and talents. Don't expect your thoughts, feelings, beliefs, or problem-solving approaches to be exactly like those of another person. Don't try to make yourself be like someone else. That is denying your own personhood, and self-denial undermines your self-respect. Try to discover the qualities that make you unique. Focus your energies on developing the ones that are functional in your life. Curtail any judgmental or harsh criticism of your limitations. These limits also make you who you are. If some of your personal qualities are dysfunctional in your life, take positive steps to change them.

Second, affirm yourself and seek affirmative relationships. Tell yourself that you accept yourself unconditionally, that even when you make mistakes you are still a lovable person. The more you affirm yourself in this manner, the more you believe in yourself. Effective assertive action is based on self-belief. It is also very important that you seek out people who affirm you in this way. Negative messages from those around you undermine your positive self-concept. If you have such relationships with other people, ask them to stop criticizing and judging you, and instead to accept and affirm you. If they cannot do this, limit or totally eliminate contact with them.

Third, put yourself in situations in which you experience mastery. Mastery is the positive, "I-can-do-it" feeling that you experience after successfully meeting a challenge or reaching a goal. Mastery experiences are exhilarating, motivating moments that feed your self-esteem. They encourage you to take more risks, expand your limits, build confidence. Avoid taking on projects with a high probability of failure. Put yourself in mastery situations by trying new experiences, accepting manageable challenges, and setting attainable goals. Be sure to identify several reasonable, short-term objectives for each goal or challenge, so you experience a sense of accomplishment more frequently and receive the encouragement of mastery. These provide motivation during the interim between goal setting and goal completion. Each time you successfully complete a short-term objective, you experience mastery and renewed motivation for the longer journey toward your major challenge.

The fourth and final suggestion for enhancing your self-concept is take care of yourself. Take care of all parts of yourself.* As a wholistic being you are composed of five interrelated, interdependent parts—physical, emotional, intellectual, social, and spiritual. Feeding any part of you nourishes your whole being. Identify your favorite ways to care for all five parts of yourself and practice them regularly. Make being good to yourself your *modus operandi*. It is not selfish. Self-care is a healthy and growth-producing way of life. Nurturing yourself is primarily your responsibility; you take that responsibility from your parents when you leave childhood. Fulfilling this self-care responsibility enhances your self-worth. Only when you feel good about yourself are you able to act assertively.

When you treat yourself well, you teach others that you are worthy of respect and that you expect them to treat you that way. So, developing self-respect is in part a preventive measure: warning others against taking advantage of you. It also provides an inner source of personal security. It diminishes your need for defensiveness in problem situations and opens you up to acting assertively.

Recognize Your Rights

You need to act assertively in order to protect your rights from violation or to stand up for your rights when they are violated. Assertive action demands that

* For an in-depth discussion of self-care, read Chapter 6, Stress Management: Self-Care Skills for the New Nurse.

you recognize a few facts about human rights. First, every person has rights, by virtue of the mere fact that they are human beings. Specific human rights are presented in Table 7-6. Become familiar with these rights. Awareness of basic rights helps you when it comes time to formulate an assertive message. Second, all human rights are worthy of respect. Third, violation of rights leads to interpersonal problems. Fourth, respect for one another's rights leads to respect among people.

Finally, as a nurse, you possess a special set of rights that enables you to fulfill professional responsibilities. Ignorance of your professional rights diminishes the quality of your work performance and leads you to act aggressively or nonassertively.

Nurses have the right to:

Be treated with respect

Function as a full member of the health care team

Have and express thoughts, feelings, and beliefs in a way that does not violate the rights of others

Practice nursing within the parameters of their state's nurse practice act

Make decisions about the nursing needs of their patients/clients

Function as a patient advocate and encourage patients to assert their own rights

Provide health teaching

Be informed about what is expected at work

Expect a fair distribution of the workload and work responsibilities

Have access to information that affects nursing care

Question, challenge, or request information

Promote personal, work group, and system change

Change their minds

Make or refuse requests

Be imperfect and human; make mistakes

Choose not to act assertively

Act to get their own needs met

Expect accountability and high-quality performance from those to whom tasks have been delegated

Become familiar with your nursing rights. These are helpful when you are facing problems in nursing.

Have Confidence in Your Rights

Confidence flows from awareness of your personal and professional rights. At times, it takes a concerted effort to acknowledge and believe in your rights. Confidence in your rights bolsters flagging courage and provides you with the strength to handle difficult situations in an assertive manner.

Develop this confidence by telling yourself over and over again, "I do have a right . . . ." Discuss personal and professional rights with other people. Listen to their opinions and state yours about your rights. Remember that possessing your own rights does not diminish those of others. Finally, pay attention to your feelings. When someone respects your rights, compare your feelings to those you experience when your rights are violated. The positive feelings you experience when your rights are respected feeds your self-esteem. Other people feel similar emotions when they are treated with respect. Remember this the next time you need to act assertively. Realizing that assertiveness helps people feel good is the source of some of the confidence you need to stand up for your rights. Use this fact, along with the three preparatory skills—positive self-concept, awareness of rights, and confidence in rights—to ready yourself for acting assertively.

How Do I Decide Which Core Skills to Use?

As identified in Table 7-2, the core skills of acting assertively are verbal, nonverbal, and cognitive. These are the things you actually say, do, and believe that allow you to stand up for your rights, while not violating the rights of others. These skills are called into play in any situation demanding assertive action. Which of the verbal, nonverbal, or core skills you decide to use depends first on identifying the problem and second on who owns the problem.

Ask Three Diagnostic Questions

Identifying the problem and who owns the problem is achieved by answering three diagnostic questions. All subsequent assertive action flows from your answers to these questions. Answering these questions allows you to choose the appropriate assertive action.

Question 1 is, "What right is being violated or what need is not being met?" Your answer determines whether it is your right or need or that of the other person. When answering this question, name the specific right or need that is being violated or is not receiving proper attention. This is the first and most important diagnostic question. Answer this before proceeding to questions two and three. The problem, the essential reason for acting assertively, lies in the fact that rights are violated or needs are not met. It is this problem that you address in acting assertively.

In Maria's interaction with the yelling charge nurse, Maria's right to be treated respectfully is being violated. It is possible that her right to a reasonable workload is also being violated. The charge nurse's right to expect other professionals to do their work is being violated. In this case, both people have violated rights.

Question 2 is, "Who has stirred-up feelings?" The answer to this question helps you identify who owns the problem and, therefore, what type of action you should take. Whoever has violated rights or unmet needs experiences stirred-up emotions. He or she is angry, frustrated, annoyed, or upset. Violated rights and emotional turmoil go hand in hand and are often the first clue that a situation demands assertive action. The charge nurse in the case clearly has stirred-up feelings. She is yelling. Maria does, as well, because her rights are being violated by the yelling and by the workload.

There is one caution to keep in mind regarding your answer to Question 2. Sometimes the feelings of nurses and others in a care-giver role get stirred up when another person's rights are violated. As a nurse, you are educated to be empathetic and concerned with the needs of others. Problems arise when you sympathize with the feelings of others, take their feelings on as your own, and make their problems yours.

Assuming responsibility for problems that are not truly yours has three negative results. First, you waste your problem-solving energy on an issue that is not yours to solve. Second, when problems arise that are yours, some of your energy has been spent, and therefore you are less able to handle your problems. Third, you communicate a belief that the other person is unable to handle his or her own problems. This message can undermine the other person's self-esteem and also undermine the relationship you share with him or her. It is a good rule of thumb to solve your own problems and let others assume responsibility for solving theirs.

The third and final diagnostic question is, "Who owns the problem?" You answer this in one of three ways. These three responses prescribe how to act assertively in any given situation. The person who owns the problem is the one whose rights have been violated or whose needs are unmet, who has stirred-up feelings, and who needs to act assertively. Table 7-3 identifies how to link the core skills with your assessment of problem ownership. As is often true, both people in the situation described at the beginning of this chapter own the problem. Note, however, that the charge nurse's problem is different from Maria's because each has different rights that are being violated. Maria owns her problem, the charge nurse owns hers. Both need to act assertively, using the following skills.

Choose Your Approach on the Basis of Problem Ownership

If you own the problem, use the leveling type of "I" message and send out strong, but not hostile or threatening, nonverbal cues. If the other person owns the problem, use the skills of active listening. This involves verbal skills such as door openers, feedback, and paralingual cues, as well as nonverbal skills such as attentive silence, nodding, and maintaining eye contact.

Table 7-3   How to Use Core Assertiveness Skills

Who Owns the Problem?	What Core Skills Should be Used?		
	Verbal	Nonverbal	Cognitive
My problem	Leveling "I" message	Erect posture Quiet body Good eye contact Use of space	Remove blocks Assertive belief system
Other problem	Door openers Feedback Paralingual cues	Attentive silence Erect posture Quiet body Good eye contact Use of space Encouraging gestures	Remove blocks Assertive belief system
Shared problem	All of the above	All of the above	As above

As in the case of Maria and the charge nurse, if both you and the other person have violated rights and stirred-up feelings, you share the problem. When dealing with a shared problem, use all of the verbal and nonverbal core skills. Level with the other person about your part of the problem and actively listen to the other's perspective on his or her part. No matter who owns the problem, the same cognitive skills are used.

How Do I Act Assertively if I Own the Problem?

"I" messages are used when you own the problem. An "I" message is a simple, direct, and respectful way of telling the other person what you think and feel. The implication in an "I" message is that you take responsibility for your position. You are not foisting it off on the other person, projecting, or blaming the other person for your feelings or problems. "I" messages generate openness and a willingness to solve problems. They can be used with anyone.

A *leveling* type of "I" message reveals your feelings about a problem in a direct, honest, and respectful manner. There are three parts to every leveling message:

1. "I feel *(describe your own stirred-up emotions)*
2. about *(describe the other's specific, observable behavior)*
3. because *(describe your own violated right or unmet need.")*

When leveling, you begin by telling the person how you feel about the problem. Expect to feel some anger or hurt when your rights have been violated.

If you have difficulty identifying or expressing your feelings, remember that most emotions fall into one of four categories—anger, sadness, gladness, or fear. Each of these categories exists on a spectrum ranging from minimum to maximum intensity. The English language is very rich and has a variety of words that reflect the different levels of intensity of each of these four emotions. For example, "anger" ranges in intensity from the minimal level of feeling annoyed, ticked-off, peeved, or frustrated to the more intense level of feeling livid, furious, enraged, or homicidal. The words you use depend on how aware you are of what you feel, how intensely the problem affects you, how comfortable you are discussing your feelings and what words you normally use to express yourself. Choose the words that feel comfortable to you and reflect the actual intensity of emotion you feel.

Finally, because you are a complex being, it is not uncommon to feel more than one emotion at a time. Don't be surprised if, in addition to anger, you also feel fear or sadness or gladness. If you experience several emotions simultaneously, formulate a leveling message about each. Examples of leveling messages Maria might send simultaneously to the charge nurse are:

"I feel *scared*
about *receiving a negative reaction to what I have to say*
because *I need to be able to work closely with you."*

and

> "I feel *angry*
> about *being yelled at in front of other staff members*
> because *I have a right to be addressed respectfully.*"

Being clear in leveling helps the other person understand your position and increases the likelihood that he or she will work with you to resolve the problem situation.

In the second part of the leveling message, tell the person about his or her specific observable behavior that is disturbing to you. Avoid use of the word *you*. Whenever possible, describe only the behavior. Tell the person actually what he or she said or did not say, did or did not do. This includes nonverbal behavior as well as actual words that were said. Avoid sweeping generalizations (you doctors are all the same!), gross overstatements (always, never), and nebulous accusations (you have a bad attitude). These, along with use of the word *you*, generate defensiveness and hinder your attempts to solve the problem because they are perceived as attempts to place ownership of your problem on the other person.

By focusing on behavior rather than attitude or personality factors, you are acting within your rights. You have a right to ask another to alter behavior if that behavior violates your (or your patient's) rights. You do not have a right to ask another person to change his or her attitudes, values, or personality. In addition, when you focus on specific behavior, the scope of your request is reasonable. The request for a change in behavior is usually manageable for the other person. This specifically minimizes the other's need to be defensive and maximizes the probability that he or she will respond to your request.

The last part of the leveling type of "I" message is very important but unfortunately often deleted. The "because . . ." portion of the message helps you engage the other person in solving the problem. Tell him or her why you are disturbed about his or her behavior by identifying which of your (or your patient's) rights were violated or which need was left unmet by the other person's behavior. The value and power of the "because" portion of a leveling message lies in linking behavior and violated rights. Most people do not really want to cause hurt or anger. Most people do not see themselves as stomping on the rights of others. That goes against a positive self-image. When you show the other person that his or her behavior has violated another's rights, you introduce the most compelling reason for behavior change. You suggest that the person change behavior, not for you, but to retain his or her self-respect.

How Do I Act Assertively if the Other Person Owns the Problem?

If the other person has stirred-up feelings because of violated rights or unmet needs, he or she owns the problem. Consequently, this person is the one who needs to act assertively. In this case, the approach you use is called *active listening*. You probably recall learning active listening skills in your nursing education. It is taught as one of the communication skills to use when interacting with patients. It is also an invaluable tool for communicating assertively with anyone who is upset about a problem.

Active listening is a collection of skills that allows you to be actively involved in hearing what another person thinks or feels about a situation. In Maria's case, she can use these to help her arrive at a clear understanding of the charge nurse's feelings and thoughts about Maria's incomplete procedures. These skills help Maria shift focus from her view on the problem to the charge nurses's view. Only when this shift in focus takes place is it possible to solve the problem—Maria's or yours. In active listening you empathize with the person's position and support him or her in problem solving but you *never assume the responsibility of solving the other person's problems*. Active listening involves both verbal and nonverbal behavior. The four skills of active listening are:

1. Attentive silence
2. Nonverbal and paralingual cues
3. Door openers
4. Feedback

Offer Attentive Silence

Attentive silence means exactly what these two words say. When the other person speaks, you stop talking and give that person your complete attention. Often, when you are silent you are thinking of what to say next or of how to counter the other's argument. If you engage in strategizing while you should be listening, you often miss the true meaning of what is being said. You also communicate a lack of true concern for the other's position. Use of attentive silence helps to remove these blocks and to facilitate assertive problem solving.

Send Out Nonverbal and Paralingual Cues

Nonverbal cues are the messages you send with your body, your face, and the space around your body. *Paralingual cues* are the messages you send with your voice that are not expressed by words. Certain nonverbal and paralingual cues tell the other person you are actively listening, that you are involved with what he or she is saying and are not going to interrupt or take over the conversation. Table 7-4 lists nonverbal and paralingual cues that are integral components of assertive communication.

When you are involved in active listening, effective cues to send include good eye contact, erect posture, and quiet body, which means no fidgeting or nervous movements. To communicate openness, directly face the person with no desk or table between you. Uncross your arms and legs and lean slightly toward the other person. Nod your head and use paralingual cues like "mm-hmm." This encourages communication, in addition to transmitting your openness, interest, and attentiveness.

To communicate a balance of power, position yourself so that you are at the same eye level as the other person. Place yourself neither too close nor too far from the person. Finding the proper distance between you is tricky. The best distance varies according to each person's preferences. If you are unsure

Table 7-4 **Nonverbal and Paralingual Cues**

Nonverbal Cues	Paralingual Cues
Eye contact	"Mm-hmm"
Posture	"Oh!"
Body position relative to the other	"Tsk" (clicking sound with tongue)
Position of arms and legs	Sighs
Hand gestures	Tone of voice
Use of space	Volume of voice
Facial expression	Emphasis on words
Nervous body movements	Speed when speaking
Relative eye levels of both people	Fluidity of speech

about how close to get to the other person, first, use your own level of comfort as a guide and, second, observe the other person. If he or she is backing away, leaning back in the chair, turning away from you, or folding arms or legs, you are most likely being told nonverbally that you are invading the person's territory. Back off and yield more space.

Provide Door Openers

Door openers are questions or statements that invite the other person to expound on his or her views or feelings. Some examples of door openers are listed below:

Statements

"I'd like to hear more about that."

"I wonder if you could expand on that idea."

"Please tell me what happened next."

"Go on."

"Tell me more."

Questions

"Who was involved in the argument?"

"What is your perception of the problem?"

"When did that happen?"

"Where did you last see her?"

"How long has this been going on?"

Door opener statements are direct encouragements to continue talking or direct requests for more information. Door opener questions are open-ended questions, i.e., questions that cannot be answered with a simple yes or no. Questions beginning with the words *who, what, when, where,* and *how* encourage others to describe their perceptions.

Questions beginning with *do* or *did* are closed ended, that is, they tend to close off communication. Avoid closed-ended questions. Also, avoid asking "why" if you are discussing a threatening topic. "Why" questions ask for a level of self-analysis that often is beyond the capabilities or the comfort level of the other person. In either of these cases, "why" questions generate defensiveness and hinder communication.

Give Feedback

Feedback is the last of the active listening skills. It is often incorrectly equated with judgments or evaluations. By definition, feedback is sharing your perceptions of another's behavior. "Sharing your perceptions" implies that you are revealing something of yourself, not analyzing or critiquing the other person. Like leveling, feedback is an "I" message. Feedback is also similar to leveling in that both allow you to state your position respectfully in an honest and direct manner. While leveling messages reveal your feelings, feedback differs in that it describes your perceptions of the other's behavior. When you use feedback, you open up the communication and decrease the need for defensiveness on the part of the other.

Feedback is an essential element of active listening for two reasons. First, it is the quality assurance mechanism whereby the accuracy of the communication is checked. Because communication is intangible, it is difficult to ensure its accuracy. After words are said, all that remains is your perception of what was said. Feedback allows you to verify that your perception of the message you receive is accurate. In other words, when using feedback you check that the message the other person intended to send is actually the one you received. Use of this feedback process is a key component of active listening because you can't work with another person to solve a problem if you're working on two different problems.

The second reason why feedback is such an important part of active listening is that it allows you to be actively rather than passively involved in the problem-solving process. As you listen to the other person describe his or her problem or feelings about it, you react emotionally, attempt to understand the message, analyze the information, and often formulate opinions about what you hear. The other person wants and needs your reactions to help resolve the problem. He or she needs to hear your ideas voiced constructively. You are being invited to react and to be involved without being critical or taking over. Feedback is the most effective way for you to accomplish this.

How Do I Act Assertively if We Both Own the Problem?

When you find yourself in a situation in which both you and the other person have stirred-up feelings, because you each perceive that your rights have been violated or your needs have not been met, you have a *shared problem*. This is also called a *conflict*. Some conflicts are intense and acute, others are low key or long term. Don't expect all conflicts to be heated shouting matches. Some are quite subdued, but are conflicts nonetheless. The skills necessary for resolving conflict of any kind are a combination of leveling and active listening skills. You level about your part of the conflict and actively listen to the other's part.

It is important to recognize that when you are in conflict with another person, you are dealing with two different although interlocking problems. Expect to have different complaints, definitions of the problem, and proposed solutions. As Maria and the charge nurse clearly illustrate, both people in a conflict have different rights that have been violated, and both have feelings that are upset. Maria is upset about being yelled at and being asked to work overtime. The charge nurse is upset about being asked to do a task that was another person's assignment. Maria and the charge nurse have different complaints. To resolve their conflict, they must find a solution that satisfies these different but intertwined problems. When you encounter conflict you must come to a resolution of two separate but intertwined issues—your problem and the other person's problem.

Try to understand the other person's feelings and the problem as that person sees it; ask yourself, "Which right of hers does she think has been violated?" You must address this issue for the conflict to be resolved. Similarly, it is imperative that you clearly communicate your own feelings, violated rights, or unmet needs. When doing this, be sure to use "I" messages, avoiding accusatory "you" messages. Do not attempt to consider alternative solutions to the problem until you first use active listening and leveling. Always deal with the emotional aspects of conflict before attempting to define reasonable solutions.

An equitable, mutually acceptable solution is often difficult to arrive at. Recognizing that a conflict is really a pair of problems is most helpful in the search for an effective and satisfying solution. It is also important to remember that there is never just one solution to a problem. Finally, be willing to compromise. (Further information on conflict is found in Chapter 4, Working Together: Building Effective Work Groups.)

How Do Cognitive Skills Help Me Act Assertively?

In addition to verbal and nonverbal skills, acting assertively requires some cognitive skills. *Cognitive skills* are beliefs that support assertive action. Assertiveness involves not only what you say and do, but also what you believe. It is partly a mental process. In order to handle a situation assertively, you don't just blurt out your feelings or ideas without first thinking them through. Assertiveness requires some thought, planning, and preparation. The cognitive skills support your verbal and nonverbal core skills. There are two cognitive skills: recognizing blocks to acting assertively and developing an assertive belief system. These are both used in any situation that calls for assertive action, no matter who owns the problem.

Recognize Blocks to Acting Assertively

Do you find you can tell the nurse's aide that you believe her behavior is unprofessional, but you could never say that to a raving physician? Why? Are you able to say "no" to the head nurse's request that you work a double shift, but unable to refuse a peer's third request to switch weekends? Why?

By handling some situations assertively, you prove that you possess the skills required for assertive action. After you learn assertiveness skills, the reason you fail to use them in certain situations is that something is blocking you. Blocks keep you from using your assertive skills in situations that call for them. Blocks are either cognitive or emotional—ideas or feelings. These ideas or feelings convince you that it is unwise to act assertively, so you choose to act nonassertively or aggressively. Table 7-5 lists some commonly held cognitive and emotional blocks.

Everyone has some cognitive and some emotional blocks that hinder assertive action. To develop your capacity for acting assertively, it is important for you to become familiar with the particular blocks in your life. You have some in both categories and frequently must face at least one of them in situations that demand assertive action. Your blocks vary according to the situation and the people in the situation. Sometimes you feel them intensely, and at other times they seem insignificant. Recognizing your blocks is a major part of acting assertively, so work on developing an awareness of your blocks.

Overcoming your blocks to assertiveness flows directly from this awareness. Allowing yourself to act in spite of the blocks is the most effective way to

Table 7-5   Cognitive and Emotional Blocks to Assertiveness

Cognitive blocks

The notions that:
Assertiveness should not threaten others.
If you don't have anything nice to say, don't say anything at all.
Nurses/women/students should not act assertively.
If you feel uncomfortable while presenting your position, you are nonassertive.
Assertiveness comes spontaneously.
Norms of the organization in which you work don't support assertive behavior.
There is not much difference between assertiveness and aggressiveness.
Assertiveness won't change the situation much, so why bother?
Some people are just aggressive (or nonassertive) and not much can be done about it.
You should think of others first; don't be selfish.
You should be modest and humble; don't act superior.
You should be understanding and accepting; don't complain.
You should be sensitive to other's feelings; don't hurt others.

Emotional Blocks

Fear of:
Being punished; retaliation
Dead-end conflicts
Being too aggressive
Rejection; feeling alienated
Being unfeminine
Losing control
Learning the truth (or revealing the truth) about yourself
Alienating another
Making the situation worse
Making a mistake, being wrong, or looking foolish
Guilt ("It wouldn't be right.")
Rage or very intense anger
Being in love
Intense joy or happiness
Intense sadness, grief, or depression

overcome them. It is all right to be afraid or nervous when you are leveling or giving feedback. It is acceptable for you to doubt that an assertive response has as much impact as an aggressive outburst. Being afraid, nervous, or doubtful does not necessarily mean you are nonassertive or aggressive. You are assertive if you choose to speak or act assertively, in spite of the presence of the block. Make the choice consciously. Say to yourself, "Although my feelings or thoughts suggest that I should not act assertively, I will act assertively. I will use this situation as an experiment to see if assertiveness works." Acting assertively in spite of your fear or nervousness, acting assertively in spite of your thought that an aggressive outburst would have a greater impact—this is what makes you assertive. Acting in spite of your blocks helps you to overcome them in a particular situation and, over time, to completely conquer these blocks.

Table 7-6   **Basic Assertive Beliefs**

A. Assertion—rather than manipulation, submission, or hostility—enriches life and ultimately leads to more satisfying personal relationships.
   1. By standing up for ourselves and letting ourselves be known to others, we gain self-respect and respect from other people.
   2. By trying to live our lives in such a way that we never hurt anyone under any circumstances, we end up hurting ourselves and other people.
   3. When we stand up for ourselves and express our honest feelings and thoughts in direct and appropriate ways, everyone involved usually benefits in the process.
   4. By sacrificing our integrity and denying our personal feelings, relationships are usually damaged or prevented from developing. Likewise, personal relationships are hurt when we try to control others through hostility, intimidation, or guilt.
   5. Personal relationships become more authentic and satisfying when we share our honest reactions with other people and do not block others' sharing their reactions with us.
   6. Not letting others know what we think and feel is just as selfish as not attending to other people's thoughts and feelings.
   7. When we frequently sacrifice our rights, we teach other people to take advantage of us.
   8. By being assertive and telling other people how their behavior affects us, we are giving them an opportunity to change their behavior, and we are showing respect for their right to know where they stand with us.

B. Everyone is entitled to act assertively and to express honest thoughts, feelings, and beliefs. More specifically, this involves beliefs such as:
   1. We all have the right to respect from other people.
   2. We all have the right to have needs and to have these needs be as important as other people's needs. Moreover, we have the right to ask (not demand) that other people respond to our needs and to decide whether we will take care of other people's needs.
   3. We all have the right to have feelings—and to express these feelings in ways that do not violate the dignity of other people (e.g., the right to feel tired, happy, depressed, sexy, angry, lonesome, silly).
   4. We all have the right to decide whether we will meet other people's expectations or whether we will act in ways that suit us, as long as we act in ways which do not violate other people's rights.
   5. We all have the right to form our own opinions and to express these opinions.

(Adapted from Lange J, Jakubowski P: Responsible Assertive Behavior, p 55–56. Champaign, IL, Research Press, 1978)

Develop an Assertive Belief System

The second cognitive skill requires developing an assertive belief system, a set of beliefs that support the risk-taking involved in assertive behavior. Developing an assertive belief system is another valuable approach for overcoming the blocks to acting assertively. There are two major elements to an assertive belief system. First, believe that assertion enriches life and leads to more satisfying interpersonal relationships. Second, believe that everyone is entitled to act assertively. Both of these beliefs are supported by several correlated beliefs, and all of these are presented in Table 7-6.

To develop these beliefs within yourself, read this table over and over until you feel comfortable with all of these ideas. Give yourself permission to believe them and to allow these concepts to guide your behavior. Observe yourself and the people around you for evidence of the truth of these ideas. Discuss them with others. In a situation that calls for assertiveness, think these thoughts before you act. An assertive belief system is a core skill in acting assertively. What you believe is just as important as what you say or do. Use these beliefs to support you in your attempts to handle problems in an assertive manner.

How Do Accessory Skills Help Me Act Assertively?

In addition to the preparatory and core skills, there is a final group of assertiveness skills called accessory skills. Accessory skills build on the preparatory skills and apply the three core skills to particular problems, prescribing what to say, do, and think about in specific situations.

Two important accessory skills are described in the guidelines for making and refusing requests, presented in Table 7-7. Before you say a word, identify any thoughts or feelings that keep you from assertively asking for what you want or from saying no to someone else's request. These are your cognitive and emotional blocks. Review in your mind the assertive beliefs that support making or refusing a request. It is imperative that you recall your rights and those of the other person. Knowing your rights encourages you to act in your own best interest, in spite of some emotional or cognitive blocks you have. Finally, clarify your desires or needs. Identify specifically what you want before making a request. This helps you avoid dependently or manipulatively expecting the other person to guess your needs. Before refusing or granting the other person's request, think about how each of those responses affects you. Be sure your response is not simply designed to please or placate the other. Be sure you are pleasing yourself or doing what is right for you when granting or refusing a request.

When analyzing Maria's relationships with authority figures, it is clear that she has problems refusing requests. She cannot refuse when asked to work a double shift, to complete a procedure for a peer or to bend hospital rules for physicians. She is blocked both cognitively and emotionally. She thinks of others' needs before considering her own. She believes she should be understanding and should not complain. In addition to these cognitive blocks, Maria's fear is an emotional block to saying no. In order to refuse the

Table 7-7   **Accessory Skills: Making and Refusing Requests**

	Making Requests	Refusing Requests
Related core skills		
Cognitive skills	Identify cognitive and emotional blocks. Recognize your right to have needs. Recognize the other person's right to say no. Clarify your desires or needs.	Identify cognitive and emotional blocks. Recognize your right to decide whether or not to meet the other person's needs. Affirm your right to say no. Recognize the other person's right to express herself or himself assertively. Clarify your desires or needs.
Nonverbal skills	Transmit the following cues: Firm, respectful presentation Good eye contact Erect posture Quiet body Controlled vocal volume No whining or pleading	Transmit the following cues: Firm, respectful presentation Good eye contact Erect posture Quiet body Controlled vocal volume No harsh vocal tone
Verbal skills	Use "I" messages. Avoid apologies or justifications. Give choices and recognition.	Say *no* directly to the other; own your refusal. Avoid apologies or justifications. Use the broken record technique.

request of authority figures, Maria must overcome her blocks, just as you must overcome your blocks if you are to act assertively.

When making and refusing requests, make certain that the nonverbal and paralingual cues you send out are firm but respectful. These unspoken messages communicate more strongly than the words you speak. In fact, if nonverbal and paralingual cues are not assertive, they cancel out the impact of any assertive words you say. The other person responds first to nonverbal messages, so pay close attention to these when making or refusing requests.

Look the other person straight in the eye when you speak. Stand or sit with erect posture. Stand still, avoiding nervous gestures. As you speak, be aware of the quality of your voice. Control the volume. When you speak too loudly you seem hostile or aggressive, and when you speak too softly you seem powerless or nonassertive. Voice tone is also important. Avoid a whining or pleading tone, which sounds dependent and childlike. Also, harsh or critical tones are often perceived as judgmental or uncaring. Although at opposite ends of the spectrum, these two vocal tones have a similar effect on assertiveness—they undermine it.

In both making and refusing requests, using a direct verbal style is most important. It communicates confidence in your position; it is a responsible and respectful approach in which you are accountable for, and clearly state, your desires. Because a direct verbal style is matter-of-fact and nonthreatening, it diminishes the other person's need to be resistant. It also increases the chances of your wishes being fulfilled. So, when you verbalize a request, begin with an "I" message by stating, "I want," "I need," or "I would like." When refusing a request say, "No," "No, thank you," "I do not want," or "I cannot."

In both making and refusing requests, avoid apologies and justifications. They weaken your message. There is no need to apologize because you have a right to say "no" or to ask that your needs be met. Justifications are attempts to prove you have a right to make or refuse a request. There is no need to justify because the existence of human rights is an assumption in our society. In the United States, everybody's rights are supported by our constitution. In trying to convince another person of your rights, you open yourself up to manipulation. You never have to justify your rights to another or apologize for assertively exercising your rights.

There are two very effective ways that you can strengthen your position when making and refusing requests. First, provide choices to the other party. Allowing the other person to select *how* to carry out your request increases the likelihood that they will carry it out at all. Freedom of choice gives the other person a sense of self-control, which reduces his or her need to resist your request. There are times when you refuse a stated request, but are willing to say yes to an alternative. Presenting that choice to the other person allows the needs of both parties to be satisfied. When this is possible, it allows for the most gratifying of all possible solutions, a win–win solution.

The second method of strengthening your position when making and refusing requests is to recognize the other person's feelings, preferences, or efforts on your behalf. Acknowledging his or her disappointment or annoyance with your "no" communicates your awareness of that person's feelings and needs. You express concern for the other person when you recognize the validity and importance of his or her preferences. Thanking the other party for granting your request or for considering your needs sends back some of the consideration that that person may have shown you. Honest recognition is a way of opening up communication and extending yourself to the other person. It is a very helpful tool in the often delicate situations of making and refusing requests.

To illustrate the use of these two strategies for strengthening your position when making and refusing requests, think of Maria. She maintains her refusal and minimizes the other's resistance when she offers options to her "no" and recognition of the other's position. Some examples of how Maria can give choices and recognition are:

"I cannot work this double but I'm willing to work tomorrow."

"I won't finish the procedure but I will take these orders off for you."

"I understand how busy you are but here is the chart for you to write the orders."

"I appreciate how difficult it is to get coverage on short notice but no, I won't work the double shift."

The choices and recognition are not required. Offering them insincerely diminishes the assertiveness of requests or refusals. Offer choices or recognition when it honestly reflects your feelings, to support you when making or refusing requests.

One final verbal skill is useful when you encounter a person who refuses to accept your "no." If someone pushes you to change your mind, try using the broken record technique. This is the practice of repeating the same response over and over again, no matter what the other person says. It helps you to stand your ground in the face of coercion and manipulation because it prevents you from arguing, justifying, or altering your position. You accomplish this by firmly, matter-of-factly repeating, "No, I will not" or "No, I cannot" in a broken-record fashion. Do this every time the other person repeats the request. After several exchanges, the manipulative nature of the person's behavior becomes quite clear. He or she stops asking and you have succeeded in saying "no" assertively.

How Do I Begin to Apply All This Information about Acting Assertively?

This is a fitting final question because changing your behavior involves use of these skills in real-life situations. Only you can do that, but here are some helpful suggestions.

The most important thing you must do is practice acting assertively regularly. Rehearse your behavior before you attempt to handle difficult situations. Practicing helps to decrease anxiety and to improve your ability to apply assertiveness skills. Practice role-playing situations with a trusted friend. Practice with a tape recorder, playing back interactions to hear your voice. Practice in front of a mirror to see your body language. Write out your leveling messages on paper and practice them mentally. It doesn't matter how you do it, just practice! This is the best way to change behavior from aggressive or nonassertive to assertive.

Another aid in developing your expertise in using assertiveness skills is starting with small, less threatening situations and moving to more complex problems later. Whenever you handle these small situations successfully, you feel mastery. That gives you energy and confidence to handle the larger problems successfully. Start small, with minor problems or minimally emotional situations. This approach improves the likelihood of success.

Finally, get a partner to work with you in developing assertiveness skills. She or he gives feedback, suggestions for more effective solutions, and moral support and will act as a role-play partner and motivator. Changing behavior is no easy task. At times, it is tiring and confusing. Having a partner lessens the load and makes celebrating your successes much more fun.

Bibliography

Alberti RE, Emmons ML: Your Perfect Right. San Luis Obispo, CA, Impact Press, 1974

Alberti RE, Emmons ML: Stand Up, Speak Out, Talk Back! New York, Pocket Books, 1975

Bakdash DP: Becoming an assertive nurse. Am J Nurs, October 1978, pp 1710–1712

Chenevert M: Special Techniques in Assertiveness Training for Women in the Health Professions. St Louis, CV Mosby, 1978

Clark CC: Assertive Skills for Nurses. Wakefield, MA, Contemporary Publishing, 1978

Donnelly GF: RN's assertiveness workbook. Various articles. RN, November 1978–May 1979

Herman SJ: Becoming Assertive: A Guide for Nurses. New York, Van Nostrand, 1978

Kelly C: Assertion Training: A Facilitator's Guide. La Jolla, CA, University Associates, 1979

Lange AJ, Jakubowski P: The Assertive Option: Your Rights and Responsibilities. Champaign. IL, Research Press, 1978

Smith M: When I Say No, I Feel Guilty. New York, Bantam Books, 1975

Exercises

EXERCISE 7-1   ACTING ASSERTIVELY: SELF-ASSESSMENT

Directions. Acting assertively requires that you recognize and use assertive communication skills in problem situations. The more effectively and comfortably you use these skills, the more assertively you behave.

Evaluate your effectiveness and comfort in being assertive by responding to the following situations. Use the scale below to assess yourself.

VU—Very uncomfortable

U—Uncomfortable

C—Comfortable

VC—Very Comfortable

	VU	U	C	VC
With Superiors in the Work Setting				
1. My supervisor observes me interacting with patients/clients just prior to my evaluation.				
2. The hours I am scheduled to work conflict with a personal commitment, and I seek to change the hours.				
3. I differ with a physician I respect and speak up for my point of view.				
4. I have been expected to take responsibility not designated in my job description, and I ask my supervisor for clarification.				
5. My contribution to the organization is not acknowledged, and I explore ways to have my needs met.				
With Co-workers				
6. A co-worker has borrowed a textbook, and I ask to have it returned.				
7. The person I usually work with uses obscenities when angry. I confront the person about the nonprofessional behavior.				
8. I request another department to deliver equipment that was promised, but not received.				
9. I maintain eye contact, keep my head upright, and lean forward when criticized by a co-worker.				
10. My co-worker compliments me on my nursing judgment and intervention.				
With Subordinates				
11. When I direct others to do specific tasks, I maintain eye contact with the person.				
12. A patient makes sexual advances.				
13. I give praise for more work done than expected.				
14. I have a personal problem that is consuming my time and energy, so I direct those beneath me to do some of my job.				
15. I direct subordinates to do tasks I know they dislike doing.				

	VU	U	C	VC

With Myself

16. I refuse to do a favor for a friend.
17. I describe myself positively to others.
18. I refrain from saying, "I'm sorry" when I do not really mean it.
19. In a new situation I introduce myself and start a conversation.
20. I say, "No" when I realize that is the unexpected response.

EXERCISE 7-2   **PRACTICE LEVELING WITH SAMPLE "I" MESSAGES**

Directions. When you are upset because your rights have been violated or your needs are not being met, you need to act assertively. The leveling type of "I" message is an effective assertive response in such a situation. It is a simple, direct, and respectful way of telling the other person what you think or feel. It is one of the core skills of acting assertively. To develop your skills in acting assertively when you own the problem, practice leveling with the following sample "I" messages. Read the description of each scenario and fill in the blanks with an assertive message. Return to the text for assistance if you have difficulty formulating a leveling message.

Scenario 1

After a hectic P.M. shift, your relief nurse comes to work 45 minutes late. She did not call in to advise you of her delay and offers no explanation when she arrives. When you sit down to give your report, you say:

"I feel _____

about _____

because _____."

Scenario 2

In your 6-month evaluation your nurse manager offers criticism that you think is unfair. Although you have had some difficulty with time management, it is not true that you are depending on other staff nurses to do your work. In response to your manager's comment, you say:

"I feel _____

about _____

because _____."

Scenario 3

While performing a procedure on your primary patient, the resident says to you, "Can you help me with this, honey?" and "Thanks for the hand, doll." You feel annoyed and insulted with such nonprofessional references to you. After you leave the patient's room, you say:

"I feel _____

about _____

because _____."

Scenario 4

Earlier this evening, an 84-year-old patient fell out of bed because the aide neglected to put up the side rails, as had been ordered. After X-rays, you know that the patient has not been seriously injured, but you are still upset. In the privacy of the head nurse's office, you tell the aide:

"I feel _____

about _____

because _____."

EXERCISE 7-3   USING THE CORE ASSERTIVENESS SKILLS

Directions.   Applying abstract concepts to real-life situations is often difficult. Old habits are deeply ingrained, and new approaches are easily forgotten
under the pressure of actual problem situations. Without cues, reminders, and
encouragement, what is learned from a book or in a classroom often stays
there.

   Use the following guidelines to help you use the core skills in an actual
situation. Choose an interaction that will occur in the near future. Follow the
steps of this guide to assess the problem and to plan what you will say. When
you are actually in the situation, some of this plan will come to mind and help
you act assertively. Do not worry if you forget some of the plan. You are
learning to use the core skills, and learners are never perfectly proficient. In
addition, human interaction is dynamic, and dynamic processes are unpredictable. Be open to altering your approach in response to the other person's
communications.

Step 1: Identify the Problem

A. Briefly describe the people involved and the key components of the situation.

_____

_____

_____

_____

_____

B. Define the problem. (One or both parties may be involved.)

My feelings _____

My rights that are violated or needs that are not being met.

_____

_____

Other's feelings _____

Other's rights that are violated or needs that are not being met

_____

_____

C. Identify who owns the problem and therefore who needs to act assertively. (Circle one.)

My problem   Other's problem   Shared problem

Step 2: Plan Assertive Action

A. Cognitive skills: List beliefs that will support assertive action in this situation. List cognitive or emotional blocks that might hinder assertive action.

Supportive Assertive Beliefs	Cognitive or Emotional Blocks

B. Nonverbal skills: Identify nonverbal cues that will strengthen and support the assertive nature of the interaction.

_____

_____

_____

_____

_____

C. Verbal skills: Prepare some leveling messages to use if you own all or part of the problem.

I feel _____

about _____

because _____

or/and

I feel _____

about _____

because _____

or/and

I feel _____

about _____

because _____

D. Verbal and Nonverbal skills: Prepare some specific ways to use the active listening skills if the other person owns all or part of the problem.

1. The points in the conversation at which I will use attentive silence.

_____

_____

_____

2. The nonverbal and paralingual cues that will communicate attentiveness.

_____

_____

_____

3. The door openers that will encourage the other to describe their problem (e.g., who, what, when, where, how, can, I wonder, I'd like to know).

_____

_____

_____

4. The feedback statements that will help me share my reactions in a positive manner and that will help avoid misunderstandings (e.g., I hear you saying, Am I correct in understanding that, What you're telling me is)

_____

_____

_____

_____

EXERCISE 7-4   THE BLOCKS TO ACTING ASSERTIVELY

Directions.   Everyone has some cognitive and emotional blocks that hinder assertive action. To develop your capacity for acting assertively, it is important for you to become familiar with the particular blocks in your life. Develop an awareness of which blocks affect you by reading the following list. For those which apply to you, name a time when that belief or feeling kept you from acting assertively. Return to the text and review the assertive belief system for some assistance in overcoming the blocks to acting assertively.

Part 1: Cognitive Blocks

Assertiveness should not threaten others.
Example:

If I don't have anything nice to say, I should not say anything at all.
Example:

Nurses/women/students _____ should not act assertively.
Example:

If I feel uncomfortable when presenting my position, I am nonassertive.
Example:

Assertiveness comes spontaneously.
Example:

Norms of the organization in which I work do not support assertive behavior.
Example:

There is not much difference between assertiveness and aggressiveness.
Example:

Assertiveness won't change the situation much, so why bother?
Example:

Some people are just aggressive (or nonassertive), and not much can be done about it.
Example:

Think of others first; don't be selfish.
Example:

Be modest and humble; don't act superior.
Example:

Be understanding and accepting; don't complain.
Example:

Be sensitive to others' feelings; don't hurt others.
Example:

Part 2: Emotional Blocks

Fear of being punished; fear of retaliation
Example:

Fear of dead-end conflicts
Example:

Fear of being too aggressive
Example:

Fear of rejection or alienation
Example:

Fear of being unfeminine
Example:

Fear of losing control
Example:

Fear of learning the truth (or of revealing the truth) about myself
Example:

Fear of alienating another
Example:

Fear of making the situation worse
Example:

Fear of making a mistake, being wrong, or looking foolish
Example:

Guilt ("It wouldn't be right . . .")
Example:

Rage or intense anger
Example:

Being in love
Example:

Intense joy or happiness
Example:

Intense sadness, grief, or depression
Example:

EXERCISE 7-5   ASSERTION REHEARSAL GUIDE

Directions.   Research on assertiveness documents that behavior rehearsal is the most effective tool for changing nonassertive or aggressive behavior into assertive behavior. Use this assertion rehearsal guide to assist you when practicing acting assertively. Also, use it to evaluate your behavior following actual attempts at acting assertively. Use this tool individually or to guide feedback and discussion with someone who observes your assertive behavior. Answer each of the questions listed below. Record observations or comments that suggest ways to improve assertion skills.

1. Before initiating the interaction, did you define the components of the problem (feelings, rights, needs) and who owns the problem?

2. Did you stand up for your rights without violating the rights of the other person?

    A. What were those rights?

    B. What behavior did you use to assert those rights?

    C. What elements of your assertive belief system supported your assertion?

    D. What active listening skills did you use when the other person spoke?

3. Did you feel confident about your skills and your right to act assertively?

4. Did your nonverbal and paralingual cues communicate assertiveness? Identify the cues.

5. Did you tell yourself positive things as you were acting assertively?

6. Did you experience any cognitive or emotional blocks?

    A. What were those blocks?

    B. How did you deal with them?

7. Now that the interaction is complete, what steps would you like to take about this situation?

EXERCISE 7-6   **FOR YOUR CONSIDERATION . . . OR . . . FOR GROUP DISCUSSION**

Directions.   Use the following questions to reflect on key points covered in this chapter. Answer these questions individually or in a group discussion.

1. What are the situations in which you find it difficult to act assertively? Which cognitive or emotional blocks hinder your acting assertively in these situations?

Difficult Situations	Cognitive or Emotional Blocks

2. Who are the people with whom you find it difficult to act assertively? Which cognitive or emotional blocks hinder your acting assertively with these people?

People	Cognitive or Emotional Blocks

3. Why is it important that new nurses act assertively?

4. What makes it difficult for new nurses to act assertively?

5. In what situations or with what people is it important that new nurses act assertively? Explain.

Situations or People	Rationale

6. What experiences in your nursing education reinforced nonassertiveness? Aggressiveness? Assertiveness? What impact do these have on your attempts to act assertively as a new nurse?

Reinforced Nonassertiveness	Impact Today

Reinforced Aggressiveness	Impact Today

Reinforced Assertiveness	Impact Today

7. What are some effective ways of overcoming your blocks to acting assertively in your new nursing role?

8. If you could, how would you alter the nursing education or nursing practice systems to encourage assertive action?

Education	Practice

8

Dual Commitments: Meeting the Demands of Career and Family

When Nancy finished her first year of nursing school and Tom graduated from college, the two were married. Tom began his career as a computer analyst, and Nancy worked part-time as a nursing assistant on an orthopedic unit while she finished her education. When Nancy graduated from nursing school, she was 2 months pregnant. Within a short time, her two goals would be reached: she was a nurse and was going to be a mother. She enjoys the anticipation of her baby and the excitement of her first position as a staff nurse on the hospital unit where she had been working.

As Nancy wrote her request for a leave of absence, the implications of her dual commitment began to surface. If she took longer than a 6-week leave, her position would not be guaranteed. She had been fortunate to get the position, as the hospital near her home had only hired three new graduates. The head nurse valued Nancy's enthusiasm. She confided in Nancy that she would be able to send two nurses to an out-of-town, week-long orthopedic conference, and hoped Nancy would be one of the delegates. How was Nancy going to leave her new baby? There was also a possibility she would be considered for the orthopedic resource team in the hospital. Would she be able to spend the extra hours required at work?

Finding a desirable child care arrangement is becoming another concern for Nancy. She wonders how she and Tom are going to manage getting a baby ready in the morning, when they can hardly get themselves to work on time. Who is going to stay home from work to take care of the baby if he is sick?

When will there be time for herself? Will Nancy have time and energy to continue in her exercise class twice a week? When will Nancy and Tom have time just for each other? How will they be able to make some of the improvements in the home they are planning to buy?

Reflecting on these questions, Nancy becomes aware of the challenges and responsibilities accompanying the dual commitments to career and family. She wonders how she will meet the demand.

Through personal growth and self-awareness, women want to feel whole, to love and be loved, and to be productive. A growing number of women are recognizing that their personal wholeness requires commitments to both a professional career *and* a family. In the past, there were women who sought full-time professional careers and remained childless. Many women who had a family considered nursing a job, not a career. Since the 1960s women have expressed their desire and willingness to have both a career and a family. In some cases, however, there are still limited support, understanding, and confidence in choosing to have dual commitments.

When making a commitment to motherhood and to a career, the art of balancing the demands of each causes some nurses to have self-doubts. They wonder what the long-term effects of their decision will be on their children, their careers, their relationships, and themselves. They feel guilty for wanting both roles. They question whether the rewards are worthwhile or really important compared to the costs of always being tired and having limited time and energy for themselves and their partner.

The questions, "Should I be a full-time mother only? Should I focus full time on my career only? Should I balance being a mother with a career commitment?" have an individual answer for each person. There are no right answers, except the one that is right for you. The premise is that being committed to both brings you the joys of two exciting worlds. However, meeting the demands of both is not without struggles. We hope that this chapter will be helpful in working through the process of successfully balancing dual commitments in your life.

Specifically, this chapter focuses on the dual commitment to a nursing career and to being the mother of a family. A nursing career means more than a job in the workplace; it is a life-long commitment to practice your profession. Being committed to a nursing career is manifested when nursing is part of your identity and is what you do. Having a family indicates a commitment to having both the privileges and responsibilities of raising children. For many there is also a commitment to an intimate relationship with your partner. How these two strong commitments to career and family are put into practice is still significantly influenced by the attitudes and values of the past.

What Traditional Views Influence Commitments?

For many nurses, balancing commitments to a family and a career is difficult because they are influenced by many of the traditional roles and social expectations of women. Although the trend toward women having both a family and a career began 20 years ago, many women in the 1980s still see themselves primarily as mothers. Society still expects a woman to be the primary parent, even if she has a career. With the rising cost of living, it is difficult for many families to be supported by one income, so the mother's career is considered insurance for a desirable life-style. Sometimes a woman makes a commitment to her career and begins setting her goals in nursing, but feels she must exclude a role as mother in order to meet her goals. Probably the biggest influences on a woman are the roles and expectations of her mother. Many nurses find traditional factors have a stronger impact on how they feel about their dual commitments than their present values, beliefs, and desires.

The first traditional influence is the social expectation that a woman should give her family first priority. You may think of a neighbor, family member, or friend who is the topic of behind-the-scene conversation about the way she focuses on her career development. She is criticized when she leaves her children to be cared for by others or to care for by themselves. Perhaps you have a classmate or co-worker who is absent frequently or who requests schedule changes because she is involved with all of her children's activities. In both of these situations the point of view is that a woman is first a mother, and everything else should be secondary to the responsibilities of motherhood. Because many of your mothering role models did not have career responsibilities, their activities were guided by the needs and interests of their children. Some women with a career still feel they must make the family their primary responsibility 100% of the time, and job responsibilities have a lower priority. The perception that a mother is expected to be totally involved in her children's lives and activities indicates that little time and energy should be allowed for herself or her career.

A second traditional influence is that the woman's income is not a primary source of family support. The traditional role of the man is to earn the living and financially support the family while the woman takes care of the children, the domesticities, and the community affairs. If the man loses his job or the financial need otherwise arises, it is "nice" if the women can seek some kind of employment. Traditionally, a woman pursued an education to help her find a husband, or to give her something to do until she found her knight on a white horse. Then her career was considered insurance for reentering the job market at a later date if the family needed it. In the 1980s, it is often difficult for a beginning family to survive on one income, let alone purchase a house, buy furniture, and be able to take vacations. During the initial stages of a couple's becoming a family, the incomes of both partners are used to establish a home and life-style. As these initial goals are reached, and the husband's career and income climb to a more adequate level, even in 1986 we often see a return to the roles of mother or grandmother. As children come into the family, nursing is viewed as a career to be put aside and returned to if or when needed in the future.

A third traditional influence is the expectation for women with a career to defer having a family. In either your family or community, is there a woman who is quite successful in her career? When you think of a person you could use as a model for the way she progressed in her career and accomplished her professional goals, is she single? Does she have children? In all probability, the person who comes to your mind in each of these situations is a single person. Are your friends who are making plans to continue their education and setting goals for moving up the career ladder also talking about how they will do this *and* have children? Images and fantasies of career success are very much influenced by the past, when career women were single and single women had careers. Although there are role models of women who have successfully integrated dual roles, the old stereotypes persist. Your fantasies of career accomplishments and family responsibilities are visualized on two separate screens. You have on the one hand a nurse working in her profession, on the other hand a mother rearing her children. How does a woman practice nursing and also raise a family?

A fourth traditional influence is your mother. What your mother did or does in terms of raising children and having a career is a strong message for what you are expected to do. If your mother worked in the home and always greeted you at the front door when you came home from school, you probably expect yourself to meet your children. If your mother worked outside the home and expected you to be independent and self-reliant as a child, you may have the same expectations of your family members. Your expectations of yourself probably are similar to what your mother expected of herself, even though your interests, ambitions, strengths, limitations, and goals may be very different.

If your mother was a full-time homemaker, you may find yourself staying up late at night baking so the cookie jar is filled with homemade chocolate chip cookies. Or you rush home from work to prepare a hot dinner every night for the family. These activities may not be enjoyable to you or your children, but they were important to your mother. You may be laundering your children's clothes although they are capable of doing it themselves, because your mother did all family members' laundry. If your mother worked outside the home and would have preferred not to, her negative attitude, words, and behaviors may have sent strong messages to you. If your mother had both a career commitment and a family commitment and was extremely successful in both areas, you may expect yourself to do equally well. You may not have been aware of your mother's struggles, although you experience them yourself. Your expectations of yourself as a mother and career woman, and your attitudes, are influenced in part by those of your mother.

A look into the past is a reminder that, while there have always been nurses who had career and family commitments, a significant number placed the family as a priority while their career was a job with less significance. They viewed their career as insurance, or chose not to have children if they focused on a career. Many women are influenced more strongly by the roles and rules of their mothers than their own values and beliefs. Recognition of the impact of traditional influences is helpful in understanding some of the conflicts women experience. At the beginning of this chapter, the traditional roles of Nancy's family did not provide her with role models and personal experience to prepare her for her own dual commitments to a career and family. For this reason the guidance and support from her parents may be quite limited. Especially if they are in disagreement with her decision, their response and behavior may even enhance the conflict and confusion she feels in making her decision.

What Are the Rewards of Dual Commitments?

In much of what we do in life, we make trade-offs. With the sweet there is often a sour part, with the gains are losses, and in the worst storms are rays of sunshine. So it is when a woman makes family and career commitments. There are liabilities, but also rewards. It is helpful to gain perspective by listing the advantages of having both a career and family.

What are the advantages you think of first? Perhaps you value the self-fulfillment and growth you experience as a mother and a nurse. As a new nurse, with tuition loans lurking in your budget and a home to establish, do you place special importance on the financial resources gained from employment? Maybe you like the balance that is created by family and career activities. Housework and daily child care may not be your forte, so a career may be an impetus for sharing those responsibilities with others. The gratification you receive from both your work and supporting your child's (children's) development is satisfying. It is important to identify the reasons career and family commitments are important for you, so that when you question yourself you have an answer.

Self-fulfillment and Growth

From both family and career commitments you experience self-fulfillment and personal growth. However, the sources are different. Those on a personal level come from having children and those on a professional level come from working.

Because you are a whole person made up of more than one part, the inclination to have children may come from more than one source. Socially, there may be a desire to contribute to the family and community membership and meet the expectations to procreate. Physically, there may be a desire to experience your body's ability to create and nurture another person. Intellectually, there may be a desire to be a parent and to pass on knowledge and understanding. Emotionally, there may be a desire to feel the full range of emotional responses birthing and parenting can precipitate, from immense joy to intense frustration. Spiritually, there may be a desire to encounter one of life's awesome realities. The need to satisfy your wholeness and seek completeness can be met in a number of ways, and having children is one way.

Love is exemplified by being concerned for, feeling responsible for, having respect for, and truly knowing another person as he or she is. Love comes from an intimate relationship with another person. Out of that special kind of relationship comes an opportunity also to learn who you are. In a relationship of trust and acceptance you can peel off your protective layers and acknowledge who you are. The "I" you find may have parts you like and parts you would like to change. In a supportive relationship you are more confident of your ability to make the changes to become the person you want to be in order to achieve personal growth. This is a life-long process and occurs best in the loving relationship that results from a family commitment.

No matter how fulfilling and growth-producing Nancy's relationship is with Tom, or how eagerly she anticipates her baby, she is also aware of how much satisfaction and growth she experiences in her work. In Nancy's position as a staff nurse, her creativity is continually challenged as she seeks ways to meet the wholistic needs of long-term orthopedic patients. It is not easy to find combinations of treatments to relieve bone pain. It is difficult to find ways to help long-term depressed patients. The more Nancy learns, the more effective she becomes in identifying the best approach to the problems patients have.

Nancy also enjoys developing policies and guidelines by working on committees with her peers. As her co-workers share their thoughts and ideas, she finds herself recalling ideas she learned in nursing school. It is thrilling to find new applications for old ideas and to have her knowledge and understanding of nursing practice grow.

On days when she is in charge, Nancy is a little overwhelmed by the responsibility, but pleased with the way she is learning to coordinate the activities on the unit. At the end of the shift, she is very tired, but is also aware of how her management skills are expanding. On days when things go smoothly, she feels confident about her ability to manage a home and a baby along with her career. She recognizes that she has the ability to manage effectively. Being organized and able to solve problems and setting priorities are helpful both in the work setting and at home.

Expanded Resources

When a couple chooses traditional roles, it usually means the family is supported by one income. When a mother works in the home, her main contacts are with family members. A focus on a career without a family limits your involvement. However, having a family and a career provides opportunities to expand the numbers and kinds of resources you have available.

Additional income is a desirable result of working. Being the sole provider for a family is a heavy burden. How a couple shares in the wealth and financial obligations is a personal matter, but two paychecks increase your options. Money means different things for different people. If money contributes to your personal sense of worth and esteem, having two sources for the family income can contribute to a psychological as well as physical sense of well-being.

Human contact is a well-documented need. Although a partner may be attentive, and a child stimulating, the social value of your co-workers is tremendous. When you need someone to listen to a painful experience, want to know the name of a good mechanic, or are looking for ideas for a dinner menu, a co-worker is often a wonderful resource. In many work groups, familiarity with each person and his or her family and friends grows as if it were an extended family. The esprit de corps provides a wonderful resource for sharing questions, joys, or sorrows. Nurses are excellent friends who know how to be empathic, to be good listeners, and to solve problems. Just as they respond to patients, nurses also respond to each other.

Have you ever noticed how much perception, sensitivity, and perspective a co-worker develops after she becomes pregnant and has a child? Being a parent has an interesting way of helping you to develop breadth and depth in your appreciation and understanding of others and of life itself. The words to use in describing the change are not always clear, but there is a discernible difference brought on by motherhood. The response to others reflects more insight and objectivity and expanded internal resources.

Although more of your resources are needed when you have both a career and a family, having dual commitments also expands your resources. The family income is augmented by both partners contributing. Having a community of friends at work as well as in the neighborhood expands your support system. Being in the work world broadens your perspective at home, and having a family enhances your objectivity about co-workers and the work environment.

Balance

A positive result of family and career commitments is the sense of balance they create. A family validates the nurturing, passive, emotional self, while a career validates the aggressive, active, intellectual self. If you have strong androgynous (feminine and masculine) characteristics, there is a completeness you recognize when both sides are stimulated and expressed.

The feminine characteristic of being nurturing, supportive, and giving is frequently manifested by the desire to have a child. Some women say that when they smell a baby, it makes them want to have one themselves. The drive to create and nurture can be very strong. Being pregnant and giving birth to a baby is the most feminine experience a woman can have. For a woman, childbearing is encountered somewhere on a continuum ranging from the most painful to the most pleasurable of events. However, it is a uniquely female experience. The emotional responses to pregnancy, birthing, and parenting a child range from the highest high to the deepest low. A sleeping baby can cause you to forget you haven't been to bed for 24 hours. Hearing "Mommy, I love you" can erase all questions of self-worth. Seeing family characteristics in your offspring gives you a sense of utter amazement. Being overwhelmed by the responsibility of parenthood can lead to frustration and helplessness. Sometimes the words that describe the nurturing feelings babies stir seem not to exist.

Beginning with labor, a woman learns to let go of a need to be in charge. Labor is a powerful force that is best dealt with by flowing with the contractions and letting the body breathe and work with the energy generated from within. Although a very active process, labor is a time for a woman to have a passive response and forget about being in control. This is difficult to do, especially for nurses who are educated and expected to be in charge and in control. Labor is the other side of hanging on; it is a passive response to an active process.

Parents are most successful when they remain responsible, but let go of a need to control and dominate their children. They foster and support the development of the child to become the person he or she is meant to be, not who or what they want. It is important to nurture the child's potential, but to let go of imposed expectations. Having children often involves a decision to let go and foster what will be, which is the opposite of what is expected in your nursing career.

In contrast, nursing provides an active opportunity to be "in charge." The work world demands goals and objectives, with plans for getting things done. With more leadership skills, the level of responsibility grows and expands. Each day a nurse systematically assesses, diagnoses, plans, implements, and evaluates. The best course of action is directed with the intellect, not the emotions. A nurse must be in control. A nurse knows the destination and the course for getting there. A laissez-faire style is not rewarded by accomplishments.

In managing assignments or the activities of a unit, creativity is an asset. Rather than sustaining what is, the art of nursing involves imagination. Whatever kinds of problems need to be solved, there are avenues for being inventive, visionary, and intellectual in a nursing role.

In practice, a nurse uses knowledge from every course she has ever taken. Whether it is a scientific principle, a sociologic theory, or a skill from a physical education class, the intellectual resources are called into play as she provides health care. Knowledge is helpful for an efficient homemaker and effective parent, but a nursing career demands the utmost intelligence. The capacity to acquire and apply knowledge and to use the faculty of thought and reason is satisfied and stimulated in nursing practice.

Some people have strongly feminine inclinations toward the nurturing passive emotional experience of being a mother, and others have strongly masculine inclinations satisfied in a work setting. Then there are some who, though female, express their identity best by being androgynous. Having both a family and a career results in a balance of the feminine and masculine characteristics.

Shared Responsibility

Few people can honestly say they find household and child care responsibilities continually exciting and rewarding. For many, doing the shopping, preparing meals, cleaning the house, doing the laundry, and cutting the grass are simply chores to be done. Changing diapers, entertaining an active child, and comforting a fussy baby can become laborious even for the most tolerant parent. When both parents work outside the home, there is an opportunity for these duties to be shared.

Sometimes it is helpful for both partners to begin sharing by making a list of the tasks that need to be done and which ones each dislikes and doesn't mind doing. From the four lists, each parent then identifies the chores she or he will do. If the lists of likes and dislikes are similar, the tasks are negotiated. However, it is surprising how complementary the interests and dislikes of a couple often are.

A word of caution is important here. Don't get hooked by traditional role expectations. If you have never before seen a man iron clothes, you may have difficulty keeping your mouth closed and your fingers in your pockets. If none of the women in your neighborhood cut the grass, you may consider the task inappropriate for you. You may have some tasks you are not particularly skilled at doing, but wouldn't mind learning. Allow each other to learn. Learn to let go of some role expectations. Don't impose your standards. Let your partner do tasks in his own way. Trying to interfere and tell another how to do a job is intrusive and disrespectful, and generates resentment. Be supportive, encouraging, and accepting of yourself and your partner. If a job is not done perfectly, how important is it really, in the larger scope of life?

Another word of caution. Sometimes the Wonder Woman syndrome causes problems. As a nurse you are especially vulnerable to this phenomenon, because you are educated to be all things to all people. Don't expect yourself to have a full-time job, be a full-time homemaker, be a full-time parent, and then start feeling guilty or inadequate when you aren't filling all of those roles. Your full-time job, as for your partner, does not allow time and energy to do everything else. The "everything else" can be shared.

By sharing the domestic and child care responsibilities, there develops shared power in the home. The home is not the man's palace or the woman's domain, but rather the retreat for each at the end of a busy day. Both the privileges and the responsibilities belong to each of you. Decisions are more likely to be mutually agreed upon when tasks and chores are done by both of you. Not having a boss in the house, but a partnership, generates a happier and more cooperative spirit.

What Are the Liabilities of Dual Commitments?

As if you didn't already know, there are some disadvantages to family and career commitments. No matter how self-fulfilled, balanced, or insightful the combined commitments make you, there is the other side. The undesirable aspects include time demands, continual change in priorities, going against the norm, and guilt.

Excessive Time Demands

When you take two full-time jobs like motherhood and a career, and put them both into 24 hours, the day often ends before the jobs are done. At the end of the day, after giving to others in your job and being attentive to the needs of your children, you find there is no time left for yourself. Doing twice as much places double demands on your time.

A new mother will tell you her day is filled with feeding the baby and trying to get some sleep. A daily shower becomes a rare occurrence. It is hard to imagine how much time can be consumed by one infant, toddler, pre-schooler, or any combination thereof. Direct child care and the indirect tasks of meal preparation, laundry, and housekeeping fill many a mother's day.

Although a nurse is scheduled to work an 8-hour shift, the expectations of the position frequently require 9 or 10 hours a day. After a demanding day, your thoughts continue to race and replay the events. At other times, it is hard to find enough energy to get a weary, tired body home. After getting home, there may be a patient care plan to write, a meeting to document, or a disease to look up. A nursing career is rarely fulfilled in a 40-hour work week.

With children and a job, there is frequently little time left for personal interests or private time. With both a family and a career making demands on your time, an exercise program, reading, and hobbies quickly phase out of the picture. Personal enjoyment and leisure activities become rare or cease to exist. A woman will say how much she longs for one morning to sleep until she is ready to wake up, for a quiet hour at home with no expectations, or for a shopping trip without a list.

A woman with a family and a career is a busy person. An ongoing complaint of working mothers is not having enough time to get everything done. Even the most organized and efficient nurse finds herself wishing for a few more hours in the day.

Continually Changing Priorities

In nursing, you are taught to establish priorities. After assessing a patient's status, you determine which problem is an immediate priority to resolve. An effective nurse makes plans that allow for crises and changing circumstances. In time management, you learn to designate A tasks, B tasks, and C tasks in making decisions about how to spend your time. Even with this kind of preparation, a major difficulty with family and career responsibilities is the ever-changing priorities.

You get up a little early so that you can stop at the bakery on the way to work to pick up donuts for a co-worker's birthday. It is your husband's day to take the baby to the day-care center, although it is your turn to dress and feed the baby. Everything seems to be going along smoothly until you notice the baby feels warm and has a temperature of 102°F. Getting donuts becomes a forgotten matter, as you begin to decide both what the problem with the baby is and what you are going to do about it. Your child quickly becomes your first priority.

One of the nurses scheduled to work the next shift calls and says she will be late. You agree to cover until she arrives, although you had planned to pick up your child from the day-care center and go to the park. Having the unit staffed and staying to give a complete report takes precedence over playing in the park.

Along with changing priorities are the conflicting needs of family and job. Your family depends on you. You are counted on and expected to meet job commitments. How do you respond when meeting the needs of your family conflicts with meeting the needs of your job? Your reaction will depend on two factors: your evaluation of the situation at the time and your values. What you choose to do on one day may be different from what you would decide a week later. At a given time you weigh the risks and the negative and positive consequences of your alternatives. Then you trust and accept the choice you make. You may suggest that your employer modify the job expectations. Or you may ask your partner to expand his responsibilities for the family. The scale does not always clearly tilt toward either the job or the family. Then you rely on your ability to do what intuitively seems best. What your intuition directs you to do is to reflect on your values. As discussed in Chapter 2, Values Clarification: Making Choices, your values also change. If you're just starting on the career ladder, your job may be less valued than it will be when you have achieved a charge position. You may have a stronger value for parenting when your child is an adolescent than when he or she is an infant. Being clear about your values and how they change makes the decision process less anxiety producing. When both your job and your family want your all, be ready to make a choice. Then trust yourself to make the best decision you can at the time. Finally, accept the reality that there may be undesirable consequences from the options. However, there are frequently tradeoffs in life, and having both a family and a career will provide you with an abundance of opportunities to develop comfort in this reality.

Breaking Traditional Role Expectations

In the 1980s, unlike 20 years ago, there are numerous nurses who are committed to both careers and families. In the past 10 years the number of child care facilities has grown. Some employers provide day care as a resource or benefit. Professional organizations and churches sponsor opportunities for career women with children to meet together. Nurses themselves seek support from one another in their dual responsibilities. However, even in the 1980s you may still feel you are rowing against the current of social norms and extended family expectations. Having resources and support is a help, but you continue to experience the stresses and strains of having two major commitments.

While pregnant, you may begin to get questions that sound more like decrees: "You will be quitting work when the baby gets here?" Or, "Has your replacement been hired?" Your firmly made decision to continue with your career begins to shake a bit. You go back and forth across your options like a shuttle on a loom. You evaluate the pros and cons and reevaluate yourself. In subtle and not so subtle ways you begin to feel like a pioneer, determined and a little scared about an unpredictable future. You look at your stay-at-home friends with their babies and wish you could be as content. You look at the dedicated nurses without children and wonder how they cannot experience the maternal desires you feel so strongly. Although you know there are devoted mothers who are also devoted nurses, you feel alone in your conquests of two loves.

If you and your partner reverse traditional roles or share responsibilities different from those of your extended family members and friends, the result may be a reduction in their support and understanding. They may not be available to provide emergency child care. Their interest in and appreciation of your professional accomplishments may arise from a superficial level rather than genuine enthusiasm and acceptance. The result may be a lack of feeling connected with family and friends. You experience isolation and a sense of being alone.

You vacillate between being hard-shelled and thin-skinned and forge the rapids and ride the waves of nursing and motherhood. Sometimes you feel invincible and at other times as vulnerable as if you were an infant yourself. The journey of dual commitments has been made by many before you, and many more will follow, but for you this is a virgin voyage. Often you feel you are a crew of one, making progress against a strong gale of opposition.

Guilt

Your biggest enemy in meeting the challenges of family and career responsibilities is your own sense of guilt. The head of the guilt monster seems to appear more often than you would like and when you have the least amount of energy available to resist. You blame yourself for not having an energy reserve after giving 100% to your family and 100% to your job. Remorseful feelings about not being satisfied with either commitment alone lurk into your consciousness. Snapping at your partner for no valid reason except that you are short on sleep and long on exhaustion cause you to wonder if you have undertaken some reprehensible act. Guilt keeps you from restful sleep through the night and from productive work during the day.

Of all the consequences of a mother working, the most persistent seems to be a woman's guilt either about her career or about her child. While this seems unfortunate, the favorable aspect is that guilt is something you have control over and can do something about. What can you do about your feelings of guilt?

First, acknowledge that the guilt monster exists for you. Say, "I feel guilty because I do not want to stay home from work and be a full-time mother." Or,

"When I am playing with the children I feel guilty because I am not working on a project for my job." Or, "While I am at work I feel guilty because someone else is caring for my child's needs." Being aware of guilt is painful. Sometimes it seems easier to deny guilt than to experience the sadness and frustration that also surface. However, before you can confront the beast, you must be aware of its presence.

Second, plan a strategy for getting the guilt feelings into perspective and under your control. Guilt will not go away. But you can put it in a cage. Determine when and why guilt occurs for you. Is it when you are tired and exhausted? Do you respond with guilt when you are confronted by certain people? Is feeling guilty about career and family commitments your usual response to having what you desire? Become acquainted with when and why guilt exists for you. Then when it occurs, greet it with familiarity and with less fear and anxiety. Part of being tired may mean having feelings of guilt. Knowing that specific people touch your sensitive buttons, avoid them if possible or contrive to minimize their impact. Start accepting that you are a deserving person. Find a way to put guilt within your control.

Last, accept the feeling of guilt. People have both strengths and limitations, and guilt may be one of your limitations. That does not make you a bad person; rather it is part of who you are. At a time when you decide guilt is something you would rather be without, consider changing. The chapter on values clarification can help you with the process. But until you have the time and energy available to do one more thing, such as changing a part of who you are, keep the guilt monster in its place. Allow guilt to have a minimum of your resources, which can more pleasantly be spent with your family, job, or self.

How Can I Successfully Handle Dual Commitments?

Decide What Success Means to You

What is success? How would you measure success as a nurse and as a mother? The answer is complex and is different for each person. It includes both external and internal criteria.

The external standards come to mind readily. As a nurse, you may list such things as position, salary, recognition, and responsibility as reflections of success. As a mother, you may determine that a supportive family unit, happy children who do well in school, and a solid relationship with your spouse as evidence of success.

Internal proof of success is more difficult to determine, because it involves taking an honest look at yourself. Your internal criteria will be as individual as you are. The questions to explore include: What do I find satisfying about my family? What do I find satisfying about my job? Do I really want both family and career responsibilities? Are the trade-offs worth trading off? Are my decisions consistent with my values? And, is what I am doing each day what I want to be doing? These questions evaluate your measuring sticks and indicators of personal success.

Refer back to the beginning of this chapter. It is important for Nancy, as she is on the precipice of her dual roles, to decide what success means for her.

It is too easy to get caught up in using other people's measuring sticks. If Nancy judges what she does according to someone else's ruler, the result could be a sense of failure. Even when she loses sight of her own indicators of success, she may get into the "I'm a failure" mode. Being successful in dual commitments begins by knowing why you want both a career and family and accepting the responsibilities that come with the privileges of this combined role.

After deciding that you want both a career and a family, and accepting those responsibilities, what else can you do to make your dual roles compatible? You need to reinforce a positive self-concept, communicate effectively with your partner, and negotiate and compromise. In successfully handling work commitments, you need to develop supportive friendships, consider work arrangements, and explore child care options.

Reinforce Your Positive Self-concept

A healthy attitude includes accepting who you are by acknowledging your strengths and having insight into limitations by sharing responsibility and being prepared for criticism. A positive self-concept is reflected in these thoughts: "This is me. I have strengths and limitations. There are parts of me I like a whole lot, parts that are okay, and parts I wish were different. The parts I wish were different probably will be some day. I am resourceful and also can share responsibility. I am open to criticism, will take from it what is useful and let the rest float away."

Acknowledge what you like about yourself and what you do well. Recognize your goodness. As a nurse, admit that you are skilled in diagnosing a patient's status and knowing the right plan of action. Recognize that you have a marvelous ability to listen to a patient and hear the meaning behind the spoken words. When you are in charge, acknowledge when you are able to organize what needs to be done in a calm, efficient manner. As a mother, give yourself praise for your ability to be up all night with a sleepless child and still be able to say "I love you," when that same child spreads cereal across the kitchen. Treasure your sense of humor when you are able to laugh at running out the door for work without taking off your bedroom slippers. Value your thoughtfulness in sending flowers to a friend who feels forgotten. Recognize and remember your strengths and your goodness. Another part of acknowledging your goodness is making your own reward system. You work hard and give to a lot of other people. Also give to yourself. If a facial and manicure is satisfying to you, make an appointment. If having a bubble bath is a treat, take one. If reading a novel gives you pleasure, set aside a day to indulge in a favorite book. Waiting to be rewarded for your efforts could be futile. Determine a way to give yourself rewards on a regular basis.

Develop insights into what you may not be too proud of, but can accept as being part of your wholeness. In discovering your limitations, dig deep into those well-protected zones of yourself. Acknowledge that you may feel hurt when you are not given recognition. Know you lose interest unless you are in a leadership role. Be aware that you expect yourself to be a perfect nurse, perfect wife, and perfect mother, all wrapped up and tied with a perfect bow. These insights are valuable pieces of information to use in evaluating how they relate to the real world and in helping you decide whether you want to change them. Having limitations is part of being human; it does not make you a bad person, but simply human. By learning to live with your limitations, you spend less time trying to defend or hide them. In accepting your limitations, you become aware of the fallacy of the Wonder Woman syndrome. For awhile and at certain times, it is amazing what you can accomplish. However, continually expecting yourself to prepare three meals a day, have a picture-perfect house, attend every activity of your child, work at your job 8 or 9 hours a day, and play a vigorous game of tennis every Saturday is ridiculous. By expecting yourself to be a superperson you end up beating upon yourself when you can't do everything. Don't let the cycle be perpetuated. Accept you are a wonderful person, but have limitations. The roots of guilt lie in unfulfilled "shoulds," either your own or those of others. Be honest with yourself and identify what your limitations are. You can accomplish a lot, but there is much you can delegate.

Sharing responsibility is another way of saying delegate. When you let go of trying to be all things to all people and stop attempting to accomplish the impossible, you open up the opportunity to distribute responsibility and work. The willingness to share is one of the keys to successfully meeting your dual commitments. Beginning at home, share the tasks that need to be done with your spouse and children. Avoid traditional role expectations and an authoritarian approach. Learn to let the planning and doing be mutual activities. A spirit of playfulness and fun can make unpleasant tasks more tolerable. When possible, hire someone else to do the laborious projects. Remember one of the steps of delegating is to relinquish control and trust the other person to do the best job possible. Try to be accepting of a different standard of performance. Be patient. Remember it takes time to learn, too. In the work setting it is also important to delegate tasks and not place unrealistic expectations on yourself. Having an attitude of working together and teamwork is more positive than considering yourself the only one who can get the job done.

Being prepared for criticism is another part of a positive self-concept. What is right for you and the way you choose to live your life may be different from those of your friends, family, and co-workers. Be prepared for their criticism. Be aware of your vulnerabilities and acknowledge that your choices are sometimes difficult to fulfill. Accept that you are capable of many things but some things are hard to achieve. Acknowledge that your qualities may distinguish you from other nurses or mothers, but you are who you are. When you receive criticism, use it as a piece of information. Sift through what is said, pick out what has value to you and let the rest disappear.

Having a positive self-concept involves accepting who you are with strengths as well as limitations. It includes a willingness to share responsibility both at home and at work. Anticipate your vulnerability to criticism as you develop a life-style that may be unlike that of others, but is right for you.

Communicate Effectively with Your Partner

In order to maintain connectedness with your partner, it is important to communicate effectively. Since communication is so important and such a broad topic, a brief review of communication is presented below. The act of verbal communication involves five steps, as illustrated in Figure 8-1.

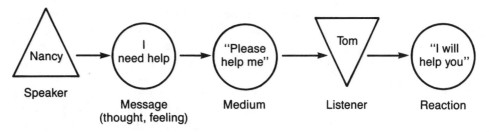

Fig. 8-1. Steps in verbal communication.

1. The sender (speaker) senses his or her desires to share thoughts and feelings with another person and to achieve a desired response.
2. The sender (speaker) symbolizes mentally his or her thoughts and feelings and formulates a message. (This is sometimes called encoding.)
3. The sender (speaker) sends his or her symbolized message through the medium (words/gestures) he or she chooses.
4. The receiver (listener) receives the speaker's message and resymbolizes or decodes it in terms of his or her past experience.
5. The receiver (listener) responds mentally and emotionally to his or her interpretation of the symbolized message and may return a verbal and/or visual reaction to the speaker. This feedback may, in turn, motivate the sender to modify his or her message.

There are two major roles in the communication process: speaker and listener. Although an interaction with another person involves both roles, as a rule *you don't do both at the same time.* A responsibility to your partner is to *speak* when you have something that needs to be communicated, and *listen* when your partner is talking. Both roles make communication possible. If you have something you want to say, but no one is listening, the thought goes by uncommunicated. At times, conflict begins because no one listens, and then no one speaks. Both partners want to be heard and both want to talk about what is important to them. Probably both you and your partner want to hear what the other has to say, but the messages sent by each of you do not facilitate communication. The conflict is magnified by the lack of communication. Conversely, conflicts can be avoided through honest, open, ongoing, meaningful listening and speaking. Talking about what is occurring keeps both partners in reality, and aware of what the other is thinking. Listening to your partner indicates your respect and appreciation for the thoughts and ideas. However, conflict does occur. Dealing with conflict is discussed in detail in the chapter on assertiveness. Here the steps of conflict resolution are briefly applied to conflict resolution with your partner.

When conflict occurs, there are two communication tools you can use: "I" messages and active listening. To decide which tool will be most effective, first diagnose who owns the problem. Are *you* having a problem? Does your *partner* have a problem? If you own the problem, the communication tool you use is an "I message." An "I" message is a statement that begins with, "I feel *frustrated . . . .*" The feeling should be an honest expression of what you are truly feeling (anger, sadness, gladness, fear, or whatever). The next part of the statement identifies what caused the strong feeling: "I feel frustrated *about being responsible for preparing dinner every night. . . .*" Then the last part of the sentence identifies the effect the behavior has on you: "I feel frustrated about being responsible for preparing dinner every night *because I feel used.*" This statement communicates to your partner what you feel is going on. Don't assume or expect your partner to know what you feel unless you state it. Also remember *not* to fill your "I" message with "you's—an easy trap to fall into when tension is high. It is easy to blame your problems on someone else, especially a vulnerable partner.

When your partner owns the problem, the communication tool to use is active listening. Be silent and listen. To indicate your concern you can say what you observe: "You seem rather quiet today." or, "I am wondering what is going on with you." As your partner relates what the problem is, you listen and use the cues discussed in Chapter 7, Acting Assertively: Practical Solutions to Problem Situations. Remember, the problem belongs to your partner. Don't try to take over solving the problem, or personalize what he or she says.

Ideally, having a set time at the end of each day for the two of you to talk with and listen to each other keeps communication open. However, in the real world of parents who also work, there is not time in every day. Perhaps what is more realistic for you is a set time every week, or at least every month, where you and your partner are alone. If you don't have a set time together, problems often develop and walls begin to build. Have a special time for the two of you when minor irritations and needs can be explored, before they become emotionally charged issues.

A premise in interpersonal relationship is that the two people really care about each other and do not mean to cause hurt or unhappiness. People do say or do things that cause others to feel hurt. However, when each person knows the effect his or her behavior has on the other, the action will probably not be repeated. It is scary to tell someone how you feel; you may feel bad when your partner tells you he or she is hurt or sad. By sharing your thoughts, feelings, and ideas you come to know each other better. Knowing each other leads to respect, acceptance, and appreciation for who you each are. Open communication strengthens a relationship and decreases conflict.

Negotiate and Compromise

When your emotions are stretched and your time is limited, new conflicts arise with your partner. Situations may arise with your partner in which you both have strong feelings and conflicting needs. In these situations an agreement or resolution requires compromise. To settle your differences each of you needs to make concessions. The goal is to reach a win–win solution whereby each gives up something but also gets something in return. After becoming aware there is a problem, the following steps help you to sort out the feelings, clarify the issue, and reach a win–win solution.

There are four steps you can follow when resolving conflict. The steps are sequential but all four do not need to occur in one time frame. The process of negotiation takes thought. Reaching a compromise may occur over a period of hours or days. The quality of the solution is more important than the speed.

Step I. Define the conflict. When problems occur, discussion usually begins with identification of the signs and symptoms. Remember to focus on the issue and not personalize what is said. Determine what rights you think have been violated. After each person has listed his or her perceptions and listened to the partner's perceptions, state what the conflict is. Put the problem into words you both agree on and are willing to take responsibility for resolving.

Step II. Explore your alternatives. Begin to explore your options by individually outlining what you wish for when the conflict is resolved. Develop a continuum ranging from the most you would like to achieve to your minimum needs. Determine potential trade-offs. Together, share your lists. Consider what is important to your partner. Let your partner know what is important to you.

Step III. Design a strategy. Timing is a key element when you begin to negotiate. Avoid times when you or your partner is tired, has another important commitment, has had a negative experience, or doesn't have sufficient energy. In designing a strategy, look for options that provide both of you with as many of your wants as possible. Respect each others' bottom lines. Determine what you are each willing to give up. Generate a plan together. This involves give and take. As you did when you defined the problem, put the strategy into writing. Be sure you both agree on the plan and are willing to put it into action.

Step IV. Implement the solution. When you initiate the action plan, be prepared to change your behavior. There is probably something you did or did not do that now needs to be different. Be sensitive to emotional responses such as anger, feelings of loss, depression, and uncertainty that change creates. It is helpful to use humor as you adapt to new ways of behaving or as you accept different responsibilities. It also helps to keep a positive attitude and stay focused on resolving the conflict. Give yourselves praise as you follow through on your agreement. Negotiating results involves each person getting something that is important, but not everything. When you both gain something you have reached a win–win solution.

When the members of a couple begin to parent together and pursue careers, conflicts frequently occur. By developing a process for dealing with differences, the relationship is strengthened. Learning to compromise and negotiate is a way to acknowledge each other's needs and find win–win solutions to the conflicts.

Develop Meaningful Friendships

In addition to developing intimacy with your partner, it is also important to reach out to other nurses. Find a nurse whose professional skills you admire and who also has a family. If the nurse is in your work setting, have lunch together. If it is someone you don't see every day, meet the person for breakfast or after work. Ask for suggestions for dealing with the problem you encounter as a working parent. Determine how other people respond to the demands of both a career and family. Offer your support to your co-workers and accept theirs. Sometimes knowing and talking with someone who shares similar responsibilities makes carrying them out more tolerable. You learn from each other, but even more, you know you are not alone. Expand your group to include other women who have your dual interests. In many work settings, there are often nurses who have children of various ages. These co-workers are excellent resources. One of them might become a role model for you.

Having a role model you can watch, listen to, and question is a precious gift. Putting together your life, with one part dedicated to your family, one part to your career, and a third part to yourself, is a complex puzzle. Often you feel you are the only one who has attempted such a difficult feat. At moments when you feel overwhelmed, tired, and uncertain, it is an inspiration to know someone else has met similar expectations.

In addition to friendships with nurses, there is value in relationships with nonnurses. Establish rapport with people who share your nonprofessional interests. Perhaps you will find women who have careers other than nursing but who also balance their work with a family. A special-interest group or class in your community is another possible source of friends. An individual or group that focuses on a hobby, subject, or activity that is important to you validates your individuality and helps meet those needs.

You may recall high school, college, or neighborhood friends who also have dual commitments. Not only do their mutual commitments lend support to you, but they also may have an interest in sharing child care responsibilities. Having play groups for children gives you time to spend with your children and their friends. It also gives you time for yourself when another mother is "in charge." For a child, playing with other children at home or in a friend's home is often a welcome change from the routine of a regular babysitter or day care center. Providing an opportunity for your children to enjoy themselves with their friends helps you feel good about yourself. If it is difficult for you to allow time for yourself, trading the child care responsibilities with a friend is a possible option.

Consider Alternative Work Arrangements

It is a challenge to find a nursing position that satisfies your professional needs and is also compatible with family constraints. Career goals may need to be compromised for a while. However, be as creative as you can in searching for opportunities. An exciting reality is that nursing practice is expanding in such a way that positions you are not aware of today will be possibilities in the future. Some new roles are in containing health care cost for industry, maintaining quality assurance in community agencies, and providing wellness programs to senior citizens. Look for a setting in which to both treat illness and maintain health. In order to find available jobs, read local newspaper ads, review positions listed in professional journals, contact a professional placement agency. Consider marketing your skills and services by preparing a brochure and distributing it to prospective employers.

What alternatives can Nancy explore? As a new graduate, she began practicing nursing on an orthopedic unit in a hospital. Most often she works the day shift, with one or two evening shifts a week. Because there are no straight day positions available, a consideration for Nancy after the baby arrives is to change to a straight 3:00–11:30 shift. This would provide predictability in her schedule. Because Tom works 8:00–5:00, fewer hours of child care would be needed. A hospital is not the only setting for an orthopedic nurse. A freestanding emergency center or occupational health center would be other considerations for Nancy to explore for potential positions. These options may offer more flexibility in hours.

Although Nancy enjoys the involvement and continuity of a full-time position, another option is to work part time. Her initial decision to work full or part time does not necessarily need to be the one she sticks with when circumstances change. The financial rewards from full-time employment may not be worth the cost of being perpetually tired and frustrated with too much time away from the child.

In her present work setting, there are opportunities for Nancy to be a member of an orthopedic resource team. Perhaps some of the work for that project could be done at home. Writing policies, preparing procedures, and gathering resource materials are tasks Nancy could be involved with independently and then meet with the group members from time to time to discuss. Often it is possible to be more productive away from the usual work setting. Although doing work in her home, Nancy should make sure she is paid for her time and effort.

Explore Child Care Options

While at work, you need to provide care for your child. Start exploring your options and resources at least 3 months before they will be needed; it takes time. Explore all possibilities when arranging care for your child. Is there a grandparent available who would enjoy watching your child? Do you have a neighbor who would like to watch an additional child? Some questions to answer when considering a babysitter or day-care center include:

1. Is the environment safe?
2. Do you feel confident about the caregivers?
3. What is the staff-to-child ratio?
4. Will your child be content with the arrangement?
5. Are the services and hours compatible with your needs?
6. Is the location convenient to your home or work?

Consider options within your own home. Perhaps a live-in housekeeper would care for your child as well as do household tasks. If you are not interested in having someone living in your home, have someone come to your house during the hours needed. A college student is a possibility for either living in your home or part-time babysitting.

One woman found that having someone else care for her child while she worked relieved her of the nitty-gritty tasks such as toilet-training and daily discipline. Time with her child was a prime opportunity for reading stories, playing, and letting the child know he was loved. She was happy to have someone else be attentive to the routine tasks for much of the day, allowing her opportunities for happy one-on-one interactions.

The alternatives that you need to examine to help meet family obligations will change as your children grow and develop. When you have an infant, you need custodial care. Toddlers require opportunities to play and explore. When children go to school, you share responsibilities with a teacher and may need to arrange before- and after-school guidance. When you have older children, they can help care for younger siblings. Prepare yourself for the changing needs. The plan you have for this year may require alteration next year or in 3 months. The positive aspect of change is knowing difficult times will go away. Children grow up, their dependence on you will be different, and your ways of responding to your children's needs will change.

Having dual commitments to a career and a family means you have two jobs. Society seems to expect you to do both well, and you expect it of yourself. Perhaps some of the traditional expectations, irrelevant standards of excellence, and conventional ways of fulfilling career and family responsibilities need to change. Be ready to define for yourself the realistic expectations, the standards you want to achieve, and the approach you will use to meet family and career responsibilities. Don't expect meeting your commitments to be easy. But what you gain from a career and family is satisfying.

In aspiring toward your career and family goals, it is important to seek the rewards that are along the way. Find pleasure in what you contribute in your job each day. Rejoice with each stage of the growth and development of your family. Take time to enjoy your life, not just survive it.

For many nurses, having a family is a natural response to who they are. Their career is a life-long commitment, and children add the necessary balance. The rightness of the decision to take on these dual commitments is certain. How to juggle time, energy, and conflicting demands is an ongoing struggle.

The norm for an increasing number of career-oriented nurses is to have a family also. Having children and continuing to develop professionally is no longer the style of a trendy minority. When you are feeling overwhelmed with the dual responsibilities or excluded and isolated with what you have undertaken, reach out to your partner, your peers, and your friends. You are not alone.

Bibliography

Curtis J: A Guide for Working Mothers. New York, Simon & Schuster, 1975

Freeman L: What Do Women Want? New York, Human Sciences Press, 1978

Harbeson G: Choice and Challenge for the American Woman. Cambridge, MA, Schenkman, 1967

Harris B: Beyond Her Sphere: Women and the Professions in American History. Westport, CN, Greenwood Press, 1978

Holmes K: Working wife and house husband: When roles are reversed. Parents, February 1981, pp 47–51

Klett S: Women at work: The benefit implications. Business and Health, March 1985, pp 25–29

Kundsin R: Women and Success: The Anatomy of Achievement. New York, William Morrow & Co, 1974

Lamb K: Freedom for our sisters, freedom for ourselves: nursing confronts social change. Nursing Forum, 12(4):328–352 1973

Levine K: Mother vs. mother. Parents, June 1985, pp 63–66

Roland A, Harris B: Career and Motherhood. New York, Human Sciences Press, 1979

Tripp M: Woman in the Year 2000. New York, Arbor House, 1974

Woolery K, Barkley N: Enhancing couple relationships during prenatal and postnatal classes. Matern Child Nurs, May/June 1981, pp 184–188

Exercises

EXERCISE 8-1   REWARDS AND LIMITATIONS OF DUAL COMMITMENTS

Directions. Dual commitments to a family and a career have both rewards and liabilities. Recognizing both of these aspects helps you to have a perspective and a sense of balance. In this exercise you will determine what you experience as rewards and liabilities. Under the appropriate headings write your lists.

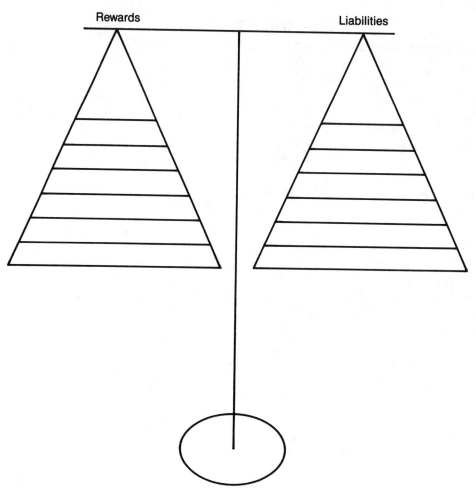

Explore your answers to the following questions:

How does the scale tip with your lists of rewards and liabilities?

How do your lists manifest themselves in your personal life?

How do your lists manifest themselves in your professional role?

What can you change in order to shorten the list of liabilities and lengthen the list of rewards?

Ask your partner to list the rewards and liabilities of dual commitments. Are your lists similar?

EXERCISE 8-2   SHARING RESPONSIBILITY

Directions.   When both you and your partner share career and family responsibilities, it is also helpful to share the household and child care tasks. Complete this exercise with your partner.

First, make a general list of the child care tasks and household chores that need to be done regularly.

Second, in the space below, write which of the tasks you each like and dislike doing.

You   Partner

Likes   *Dislikes*   *Likes*   *Dislikes*

_____   _____   _____   _____

_____   _____   _____   _____

_____   _____   _____   _____

_____   _____   _____   _____

_____   _____   _____   _____

_____   _____   _____   _____

_____   _____   _____   _____

_____   _____   _____   _____

_____   _____   _____   _____

_____   _____   _____   _____

_____   _____   _____   _____

Third, if you have the same items in your dislike lists, negotiate with each other. (Refer to the section on negotiation in Chapter 4, Working Together: Building Effective Work Groups.) The mutually disliked activities can also be shared by each of you doing the task for a specific length of time on a rotating basis. Be sensitive to your own needs and those of your partner when negotiating.

Fourth, Reevaluate. From time to time, as children grow, job responsibilities vary and resources change; the tasks and chores are different. Depending on your situation, it may be necessary to generate a new list every month, every 6 months, or every year and to redefine what needs to be done. Sharing responsibilities includes adapting to change. Utilizing the content on communication presented in this chapter will be helpful in compromising and reaching agreement with your partner.

EXERCISE 8-3   HELPING YOURSELF FEEL GOOD

Directions.

Part 1

You need to feel good about yourself in order to be effective in meeting your responsibilities as a nurse, a parent and a spouse. To help yourself maintain enthusiasm and balance, identify activities you like to do in each of your roles. List five things you like to do for yourself:

1. _____
2. _____
3. _____
4. _____
5. _____

List five things you like to do as a couple:

1. _____
2. _____
3. _____
4. _____
5. _____

List five things you like to do as a family:

1. _____
2. _____
3. _____
4. _____
5. _____

List five ways you enjoy nurturing your child(ren):

1. _____
2. _____
3. _____
4. _____
5. _____

List the five most important activities you like in your career:

1. _____
2. _____
3. _____
4. _____
5. _____

Part 2

Put an X beside the activities in your lists you have not done in the past 6 months.

Part 3

Remove the obstacle(s) that has (have) prevented you from doing those activities marked with an X, and plan a time to incorporate them into your life during the next month.

How to Incorporate	When
Self	
Couple	
Family	
Children	
Career	

EXERCISE 8-4   GETTING RID OF GUILT

Directions. Given the wide range of mothering styles that you have observed at one time or another, you know there is no one right way to mother. What is important is to genuinely be happy about the choices you have made and to rid yourself of guilt feelings. This exercise helps determine when and why guilt occurs for you, and how you can put it under your control. Answer each of the questions in the boxes below. When each box is filled, think of the guilt feelings being under your control in the boxes.

1. What do you feel guilty about?	3. Why do you feel guilty?
2. When does the guilt occur?	4. How can you change the guilty feelings?

EXERCISE 8-5   RECEIVING AND GIVING SUPPORT

Directions.   Your peers, who also share dual commitments to a family and a career, are valuable sources for support and guidance. This exercise is to be done with a group of friends. Each person makes out a list of what she would like to receive as support or encouragement in her dual commitments. Be both specific and realistic with your ideas. Your list may include such things as: meet once a week to talk about frustration, schedule a time to exchange taking care of the group's children, develop a plan to present to our employer for sharing full-time work responsibilities on a part-time flexible schedule.

Share your list with your friends in a group situation and listen to the lists presented by your friends. The ideas expressed may stimulate additional thoughts. After listening to each other's lists, determine which requests you want to meet. Make sure each person receives something from her list and has an opportunity to give to someone else.

On an ongoing basis, continue to develop your list. On a regular basis, weekly or monthly, continue to meet as a group and share your lists. Don't end a meeting time without each person both receiving something and planning to give to someone.

The Support or Encouragement I Would Like to Receive

_____

_____

_____

_____

_____

_____

_____

_____

_____

_____

_____

_____

_____

_____

_____

_____

_____

EXERCISE 8-6   **FOR YOUR CONSIDERATION . . . OR . . . FOR GROUP DISCUSSION**

Directions.   Use the following questions to reflect on key points covered in this chapter. Answer these questions individually or in a group discussion.

1. Which of the traditional roles and social expectations have the greatest influence on your career and family commitments?

2. What are the advantages you experience as a result of dual commitments?

3. What are the disadvantages you experience as a result of dual commitments?

4. When you feel out of balance with career and family responsibilities, what are the most frequently contributing factors?

5. How would you measure your success as a nurse and as a mother?

6. What are the ways you reward yourself?

7. What topic would you like to discuss with your partner related to your dual commitments?

Index

Page numbers followed by *f* indicate figures; *t* following a page number indicates tabular material; page numbers in *italics* indicate exercises.